WML & WMLScript:
A Beginner's Guide

WML & WMLScript:
A Beginner's Guide

Kris Jamsa

Osborne/**McGraw-Hill**

New York Chicago San Francisco
Lisbon London Madrid Mexico City
Milan New Delhi San Juan
Seoul Singapore Sydney Toronto

Osborne/**McGraw-Hill**
2600 Tenth Street
Berkeley, California 94710
U.S.A.

To arrange bulk purchase discounts for sales promotions, premiums, or fund-raisers, please contact Osborne/McGraw-Hill at the above address. For information on translations or book distributors outside the U.S.A., please see the International Contact Information page immediately following the index of this book.

WML & WMLScript: A Beginner's Guide

1234567890 FGR FGR 01987654321

ISBN 0-07-219294-1

Publisher   Brandon A. Nordin
Vice President & Associate Publisher   Scott Rogers
Acquisitions Editor   Jim Schachterle
Project Editor   Jody McKenzie
Acquisitions Coordinator   Tim Madrid
Technical Editor   Phil Schmauder
Copy Editor   Andy Carroll
Proofreader   Susie Elkind
Indexer   Karin Arrigoni
Computer Designers   George Toma Charbak, Lauren McCarthy, Kelly Stanton-Scott
Illustrators   Michael Mueller, Alex Putney, Beth E. Young
Series Design   Gary Corrigan
Cover Design   Greg Scott
Cover Illustration   Kevin Curry

This book was composed with Corel VENTURA™ Publisher.

To Debbie,
For making each sunrise and sunset special.

About the Author

Kris Jamsa, Ph.D., MBA, is the author of more than 90 computer books, with cumulative sales of several million copies. Jamsa holds a Bachelor of Science degree in computer science from the United States Air Force Academy, a Masters degree in computer science from the University of Nevada, Las Vegas, a Ph.D. in computer science with an emphasis in operating systems from Arizona State University, and a Masters of Business Administration from San Diego State University.

In 1992, Jamsa and his wife, Debbie, founded Jamsa Press, a computer-book publishing company. After expanding the company's presence to 70 countries and 28 languages, Jamsa sold Jamsa Press to a larger publishing house. Today, Jamsa is the founder of WirelessLookup.com, a company that puts people and businesses on the Wireless Web. Jamsa is also very active in analyzing emerging technologies.

Jamsa lives on a ranch in Houston, Texas, with his wife, their three dogs, and five horses. When he is not in front of his PC, Kris is normally riding and jumping his horse Robin Hood.

Contents at a Glance

Contents

Acknowledgements

It has been almost 10 years since I teamed with Osborne/McGraw-Hill on a book project. I want to thank everyone at Osborne for making me feel welcome and for your tireless support and effort on this project. After the manuscript leaves the author's PC, editors, illustrators, and the production team work their magic to create "the book." Please take time to acknowledge the Osborne team (listed at the front of this book) whose efforts greatly improved the quality of this book. It was a pleasure to work with each of them.

Introduction

Although the Wireless Web is still very much in its infancy, a vast majority of television commercials focus on ways users will exploit their Web-enabled phones to become more productive at work, to perform time-consuming tasks while they are on the go, and even how users will purchase items ranging from fast food to airline tickets using their phones. Several groups estimate that by the end of 2001, more than 10 million users within the United States will be connected to the Wireless Web. They further predict that the number of Web-enabled phones worldwide will grow to 48 million users by 2002 and to 204 million by 2005. In addition, the analysts estimate that sales of Web-enabled phones will grow more than ninefold by 2005 to $7.8 billion. Recent surveys have shown that 52 percent of users explained that they will use Web-enabled phones for a mix of e-mail, personal data, and business information; 24 percent will use it for e-mail and personal data; and 13 percent will use it for e-mail only. As a programmer, you now have the opportunity to align yourself with the Wireless industry, whose need for applications is about to explode.

Who Should Read this Book

It has been less than ten years since the World Wide Web made its debut. When the Web and HTML first came on the scene, many programmers were slow to recognize their need to learn and use HTML, believing HTML was not a programming language, but rather, it was a tool for designers. Today, however, things have changed. Programmers now make extensive use of HTML to host Web applications and active server pages. HTML has evolved from a design markup language into a fundamental Web development tool.

The Wireless Web, which is still very much in its infancy, will closely mirror the evolution of the World Wide Web in many ways. Likewise, the use and integration of WML (the Wireless Markup Language) will increase on a path similar to that of HTML. Initially, the early adopters who create Wireless sites will create fairly simplistic sites, using basic WML tags. Then, just as sites on the World Wide Web expanded their capabilities using scripting languages such as JavaScript, Wireless Web sites will increase their functionality using WMLScript. After that, Wireless sites will start to support mobile-commerce (m-commerce), just as e-commerce drove the explosive growth of the World Wide Web.

In the near future, most applications will require a Wireless component:

- Sales personnel will monitor inventory levels and the status of orders through Web-enabled phones

- Managers will monitor productivity levels and milestones by connecting Web-enabled phones to corporate intranets

- Project team members will exchange information via e-mail, short messages, and instant text messages using Web-enabled phones

- Customers will order lunch for pickup or delivery using a fast-food chain's Wireless Web site

- Business travelers will schedule airlines and hotels, and track their itinerary using a Web-enabled phone

- Customers will look up information about and directions to companies via the company's Wireless Web site

- Company locators will move to the Wireless Web where they can be easily kept current

- And much more

To develop and support Wireless applications, programmers must have the ability to create WML applications. This book's modules present WML and WMLScript in detail. Each module provides many sample applications you can easily and quickly customize to implement Wireless solutions that meet your needs.

What You Need to Create Wireless Applications

To create WML applications, this book is all you need. You do not need to buy any software in order to build Wireless applications. Further, if you do not yet have a Wireless phone, that is not a problem. In Module 1, you will learn how to download and install phone simulator software that, as shown in Figure 1-1, runs on your PC. Using the phone simulator software, you can run all the applications this book presents, and you can "surf" the Wireless Web right from your PC.

Downloading this Book's Applications

This book presents more than 100 WML and WMLScript applications. To save you time, we have placed the source code for each application on the Osborne/McGraw-Hill Web site at www.osborne.com. Before you start a module, visit the Osborne Web site and download the module's source code.

What this Book Covers

This book contains ten modules and three appendices. The modules provide step-by-step instructions for creating Wireless applications using WML. In Module 1 you will learn how to download phone simulator software, which you can use to run this book's programs and surf the Wireless Web right from your PC. Then, in Module 2, you will start creating your own Wireless applications. The modules that follow will teach you how to use specific features of WML and WMLScript to expand the capabilities of your Wireless applications.

At the end of this book, you will find three appendices. The first is an answer guide, giving you correct answers to the Mastery Check questions that are at the end of each module. The second provides a WML reference that will quickly give you the format and options for each of the WML tags. The third provides a list of sites on the Wireless Web you should visit for more information on developing and hosting Wireless applications.

Here is a little more information about each of the modules and appendices:

- **Module 1, "Getting Started on the Wireless Web"** This module gets you up and running on the Wireless Web. To start, you will download phone-simulator software you can use to surf the Wireless Web from your PC. If you have a Web-enabled phone, this module will show you how to use your phone to connect to sites on the Wireless Web. Finally, the module will present sites on the Wireless Web that can help you quickly build your own Wireless Web site, without having to write any programming code.

- **Module 2, "Creating Your First WML Application"** In this module, you will use a text editor to create your first Wireless applications using WML tags. You will learn how to structure a WML application and how to run your application using phone-simulator software. You will also learn how to host your application on the Wireless Web.

- **Module 3, "Formatting Output"** Like HTML, WML provides many tags you can use to format text. In Module 3, you will use these tags to align paragraphs, to create bold and italic text, and to control line wrapping. In addition, you will learn how to use tables to organize data and how to display simple black-and-white images, called Wireless bitmaps (or WBMPs) within a Wireless application.

- **Module 4, "Working with Multiple Cards and Variables"** As the capabilities of your Wireless applications increase, you will need to store information, such as a username, phone number, or credit card number, as the application executes. In Module 4, you will learn how to use variables within WML to store information. In addition, you will learn how to better organize your WML statements by grouping related statements within individual cards.

- **Module 5, "Performing User Input Operations"** In this module, you will learn how to prompt the user for information, such as a name or phone number. Then you will learn how to create WML applications that respond the user's input.

- **Module 6, "Building Real-World WML Applications"** In Module 6, you will put the WML tags you learned about in the previous modules to use, building real-world Wireless applications. To start, you will create your own Wireless Web site that provides visitors with your phone number, address, and current news. Then, you will expand the Web site to include information about your entire family. Next, you will create a company-wide locator that users can visit to find phone number and office-locator information for the company's employees. Finally, you will build a WML site that implements a news feed whose contents you can change to provide users with news about your company, your products, or news, sports, and entertainment information.

- **Module 7, "Automating WML Applications Using WMLScript"** Like HTML, WML does provide limited tags for building logic (decision making) into an application. To automate a WML application, you use the WMLScript scripting language (much as HTML sites use JavaScript). In Module 7, you will learn how to use WMLScript to perform arithmetic operations, to make decisions, and to repeat specific statements within your application.

- **Module 8, "Using the WMLScript Libraries"** To help you perform common operations, such as using a dialog box to prompt the user for information, or calculating the result of an arithmetic operation, WMLScript provides a collection of library functions your scripts can use to perform specific tasks. In Module 8, you will examine each of the WMLScript functions and see examples of how to use each within your code.

● **Module 9, "Building Real-World WMLScript Applications"**   In Module 9, you will put WMLScript to use by building real-world applications. To start, you will learn how to use WMLScript to force the user to enter a password before he or she can access a site. Then, you will learn how to debug applications using the WMLScript Console library functions. Finally, you will use WMLScript to implement a Wireless Tic-Tac-Toe game.

● **Module 10, "Advanced Concepts"**   To store and retrieve information, WML applications, like HTML sites, often interact with a server that is running Perl scripts or Active Server Pages (ASP). In this module, you will learn how to store and retrieve information from a server that is using Perl or ASP.

● **Appendix A, "Answers to Mastery Checks"**   Each module contains questions at the end (called Mastery Checks) that check to make sure you have absorbed the basics. Appendix A provides the answers to these questions.

● **Appendix B, "WML Language Reference"**   In this appendix, you will find a reference listing each of the WML tags and their attributes.

● **Appendix C, "Wireless References on the World Wide Web"**   This appendix provides the addresses of sites on the World Wide Web that you should visit to find more information on WML, WMLScript, and hosting Wireless Web sites.

How to Read this Book

This book's modules build on the information the previous module presents. If you are just starting with WML, you should read each module in order. If you are familiar with WML and you want to get started with WMLScript or interacting with servers, you can turn to the module that best meets your needs.

Each module explains key topics using many example applications. You should take time to experiment with each application this book presents. In addition, each module provides a project that illustrates, step-by-step, the creation of an application. Again, you should take time to implement each project. Finally, before you move on to the next module, take time to review the mastery questions that appear at the end of a module. The questions cover the key information you should know about the module's topics.

Special Features

Throughout each module are *Hints* and *Notes*, as well as *detailed code listings*. You can download the working code from the Osborne/McGraw-Hill Web site, as previously discussed. There are *1-Minute Drills* that check to make sure you are retaining what you have read (and that help you focus your attention on the more important points). There are *Ask the Expert* question-and-answer sections that give in-depth explanations about the current subject. Included with the book and on the Web site are *Projects* that take what you have learned and put it into a working application. At the end of each module are *Mastery Checks* to give you another opportunity for review (the answers to the questions appear in Appendix A). Overall, the objective is to get you up to speed quickly, without a lot of obtuse, abstract, and dry reference to formal coding practices.

So, let's get started. You won't believe how easy and fun it is to create Wireless applications using WML. Good luck!

Module 1

Getting Started on the Wireless Web

The Goals of This Module

- Introduce you to the Wireless Web and types of Wireless sites that exist today
- Download and install one or more phone simulators—special programs you can run on your PC that let you access sites on the Wireless Web and display the WML applications you create throughout this book
- Introduce you to Wireless Access Protocol (WAP)
- Create your first Wireless site

For years, computer users have made extensive use of the World Wide Web to find information, send and receive electronic mail, buy and sell stocks, use e-commerce to shop, and more. To "surf" the World Wide Web, users use a browser, such as Internet Explorer or Netscape Navigator, to view the contents of specific Web sites. The Wireless Web extends content much like you find on the traditional World Wide Web to Web-enabled cellular phones and other handheld devices. This module will introduce you to the Wireless Web. Throughout this module you will find, with the exception that you are viewing sites on your cellular phone, that the Wireless Web is very similar to the traditional World Wide Web. To view sites on the Wireless Web, you use a special program called a microbrowser, which resides within a Web-enabled phone. Like sites on the traditional World Wide Web, sites on the Wireless Web have unique addresses, which look very much like traditional Web addresses. If you do not yet have a Web-enabled phone, this module will show you how to download a phone simulator, a program you can run on your PC, that lets you view Wireless Web sites.

What You Need to Access the Wireless Web

To "surf" the Wireless Web, you need a device that contains a microbrowser —special software that is capable of displaying a Wireless Web site. If you have a new cellular phone, your phone quite likely contains a built-in microbrowser. In other words, it is "Web enabled." If you are shopping for a new phone, you will find that almost all newer phones are Web enabled.

With a Web-enabled phone in hand, you must normally contact your cellular-phone provider to have them turn on (enable) your phone's access to the Wireless Web. Normally, there is no charge to enable the Wireless Web for your account. However, when you use your phone to surf the Wireless Web, your phone company will charge your account on a per-minute basis, just as if you were placing a voice call using your phone.

If you do not yet have a Web-enabled phone, you can download phone-simulator software to your PC. As shown in Figure 1-1, the phone simulator software behaves as a Web-enabled phone. Thus, using your PC's connection

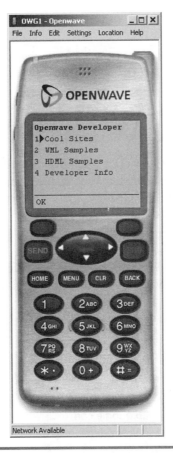

Figure 1-1 Using phone-simulator software to access the Wireless Web using your PC

to the Internet and the phone simulator, you can traverse the Wireless Web. Later in this module, you will learn how to download and install various phone simulators. As you create your own WML applications, you should test each application using each of the simulators. As your applications become more complex, you will find that different simulators implement various Wireless Markup Language (WML) tags differently. Because users may access your Wireless applications using different phones, you should get into the habit of testing your applications with the various simulators.

1-Minute Drill

- What is a Web-enabled phone?
- What is a microbrowser?

Previewing the Wireless Web

Although the Wireless Web is still very much in its infancy, you can find a variety of useful sites on the Wireless Web today. This section examines several sites you should visit and bookmark.

Wireless Search Engines

Just as you use search engines, such as Yahoo, Google, and Excite, to locate information on the World Wide Web, you will also find various Wireless search engines, as shown in Figure 1-2.

Table 1-1 lists several search engines on the Wireless Web.

Search Engine	Address
2thumbsWAP.com	http://2thumbswap.com/wap/
Google	http://wap.google.com
Gixom	http://webfront.de/i.wml
m-find	http://m-find.com
Mfinder	http://mfinder.cellmania.com
Wapall	http://www.wapall.com
WapUSeek	http://www.wapuseek.com

Table 1-1 Search Engines on the Wireless Web

- A Web-enabled phone is a cellular phone that contains built-in software—a microbrowser—you can use to view sites on the Wireless Web.
- A *microbrowser* is a program built into a Web-enabled phone that you can use to view a Wireless Web site.

```
WELCOME TO              Welcome. Please
WAPALL™                 select an option.
Your wireless        ▶[[Login]]
internet Directory     [[FREE Registration]
and Search Engine      ]

ENTER      Copyright    Link
```

```
Welcome to the
m-find.com
Wireless Intelligent
Search Engine
NEW!!, now faster,
more pages and better

OK
```

Figure 1-2   Search engines on the Wireless Web

Wireless News and Information Sites

Using a Web-enabled phone, you are only a few clicks away from Wireless sites
that provide news and information, as shown in Figure 1-3.

Table 1-2 lists several news and information sites on the Wireless Web.

Site	Address
The Guardian	http://www.guardian.co.uk/wml/
NewsAide.com	http://www.newsaide.com/wap/index.wml
Honolulu Star Bulletin	http://holo.starbulletin.com/
Ananova	http://wap.ananova.com/
Excite UK	http://www.excite.co.uk/wap/news/

Table 1-2   News and Information Sites on the Wireless Web

| **Figure 1-3** | News and information sites on the Wireless Web |

Wireless Sports Information Sites

If you are sitting in the stands watching one sporting event, you can use a Web-enabled phone to stay up to date with other games and events via sports information sites on the Wireless Web, as shown in Figure 1-4.

Table 1-3 lists several sports-related sites on the Wireless Web.

Site	Address
WAPaRESULT	http://www.waparesult.com/index.wml
Home of Formula One	http://wap.homeofformulaone.com/
NASCAR Fan Site	http://tagtag.com/sites/n/a/s/nascar/0.php3?tagtagrequest=1
Sports.com	http://mobile.sports.com/
Home of Tennis	http://wap.homeoftennis.com/

| **Table 1-3** | Sports Sites on the Wireless Web |

Figure 1-4   Sports sites on the Wireless Web

Wireless Financial Sites

The financial industry was one of the first to readily adopt the Wireless Web. Using a Web-enabled cellular phone, you can check stock prices, receive alerts regarding your investments, or even make trades, as shown in Figure 1-5.

Table 1-4 lists several finance-related sites on the Wireless Web.

Site	Address
Stock Smart	http://agsub.stocksmart.com/ss.wml
Currency Converter	http://www.oanda.com/converter/classic?user=wap11
Charles Schwab	http://pocketbroker.schwab.com
CSFBdirect	http://phone.csfbdirect.com
TD Waterhouse	http://www.wtdw.com

Table 1-4   Financial Sites on the Wireless Web

Figure 1-5 Financial sites on the Wireless Web

Wireless Mobile Commerce (M-Commerce) Sites

If you need flowers, airline tickets, or a book on wireless protocols, you can order them at mobile-commerce (m-commerce) sites on the Wireless Web, as shown in Figure 1-6.

Table 1-5 lists several sites on the Wireless Web that support m-commerce.

Site	Address
Planetwide Mall	http://wapgoshop.com
PriceGrabber	http://www.atpgw.com
StoreScanner	http://www.StoreScanner.com
Edmonds.com	http://wap.edmunds.com
Webswappers	http://wap.webswappers.com

Table 1-5 Ways to Spend Money on the Wireless Web

| **Figure 1-6** | M-commerce sites on the Wireless Web |

Surfing the Wireless Web

As it turns out, surfing the Wireless Web using your Web-enabled phone, or a phone simulator, is not that much different than traversing the traditional World Wide Web using a browser such as Microsoft Internet Explorer or Netscape Navigator. To surf the Wireless Web, you will use a browser, which users refer to as a microbrowser, to display a site's contents and to move from one site to another.

Hint

To save you from having to type on the phone's numeric keypad, most Web-enabled cellular phones let you bookmark the sites you use on a regular basis. After you bookmark a site, you can normally quickly select the site from a menu that appears within your browser.

To visit a Wireless site, you specify the site's address within the microbrowser. If you are using a phone simulator, you can simply type the address (URL) of the site you desire, using your keyboard. If you are using a Web-enabled cellular phone, you will use your phone's keypad to enter the address.

Hint

Depending on the Web-enabled phone you are using, the steps you must perform to bookmark your commonly used sites will differ. Some of the phone services that let you view your cellular-phone information on your computer using the World Wide Web, also let you type in bookmarks as you customize your account settings. For more information on setting bookmarks for sites on the Wireless Web, contact your cellular provider or visit your provider's Web site.

Typing on a Phone's Numeric Keypad

To type using your phone's numeric keypad, you will press the number key that corresponds to the letter you desire. For example, for the letter A, you would press the 2 key one time. Likewise, for the letter D you would press the 3 key one time. For the letter B, which is the second letter listed for the 2 key, you would press the 2 key twice. For the letter C, which is the third letter listed for the 2 key, you would press the 2 key three times.

As you press the keys, your phone will toggle through the corresponding letters. If you happen to press a key too many times, simply continue to press the key until you get back to the letter you desire. To type two successive letters, such as AA, you would press the 2 key one time, pause until the phone advances the cursor to the next letter position, and then press the key a second time for the next letter.

1-Minute Drill

● How would you type the letters K and M using a cellular phone's numeric keypad?

● To type the letter K, press the 5 key twice in quick succession. To type the letter M, press the 6 key once.

Accessing the Wireless Web via a Web-Enabled Phone

To access the Wireless Web using your cellular phone, you will normally select a menu option on your phone that corresponds to the Wireless Web. Most Web-enabled cellular phones will then display a menu of links to news feeds, search engines, and other sites. In addition, many phones provide a "Go to" option you can select, which then lets you type in the URL for the Web site you desire. After you type in the address using your phone's keypad, the microbrowser will display the corresponding site.

Hint

As more companies move to the Wireless Web, many will use the same URL for their traditional and Wireless Web sites. For example, using the URL http://www.WirelessLookup.com, you can view the WirelessLookup.com Web site using a traditional browser, such as Internet Explorer, or a microbrowser within a Web-enabled phone.

Traversing Wireless Links

As you view a site from a microbrowser, you may encounter links to other pages on the site, as well as links to other sites. By selecting the link, you can quickly move from one page or one site to another. For example, the left image in Figure 1-7 illustrates the links within the Go2 site at http://www.Go2.com.

Figure 1-7   Using a link to move from one Wireless site to another

If, for example, you highlight the Restaurants link and press the phone's accept button, the browser will load and display a page from which you can select the type of food you desire, as shown in the right image in Figure 1-7.

Downloading a Phone Simulator

To simplify your WML development and to better test your applications, you should download phone-simulator software that you can use to view Wireless sites and to run the WML applications you create. Across the World Wide Web, you can download phone simulator software for various types of phones. In general, you will likely pick one simulator that you use on a regular basis. However, before you place your applications on the Wireless Web, you should use each simulator to test your applications. As you will learn, each phone simulator behaves slightly differently for various WML statements. By testing your applications within each simulator, you will reduce the errors users may encounter as they view your Wireless site using a variety of Web-enabled phones.

Downloading the Phone.com
Software Development Kit

The most commonly used microbrowser is that produced by Openwave (the simulator was previously available from Phone.com). Throughout this book, the examples will use the Openwave simulator to display the output of the sample programs. To download the phone simulator, visit the Openwave Web site, at http://www.Openwave.com, shown in Figure 1-8. From within the site, download the software development kit.

After you download the phone simulator software, run the program to install the phone simulator on your system. Then, to run the simulator, select Start | Programs | UP.SDK. Windows, in turn, will display a submenu of options. Within the submenu, select the UP.Simulator option to display the

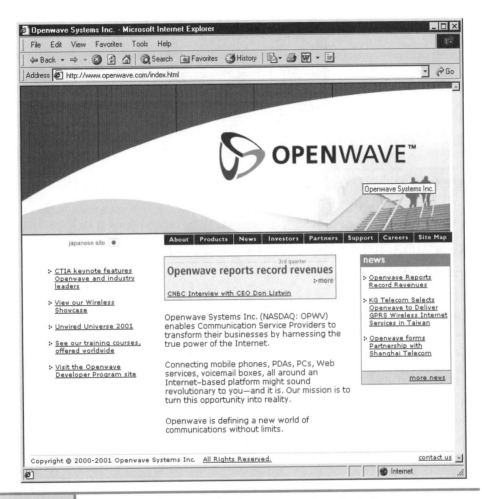

Figure 1-8   The Openwave Web site, where you can download the
Phone.com simulator

Openwave simulator, as shown in Figure 1-9. Using this simulator, you can
type in the addresses of the Wireless sites this lesson presents, as well as the
filenames of the WML applications you create throughout this book.

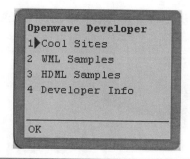

Figure 1-9 Using the Openwave phone simulator to view Wireless sites or WML applications

Downloading the Nokia Software Development Kit

Within the cellular-phone industry, Nokia is one of the most widely known cellular-phone manufacturers. Like Phone.com, Nokia provides a software development kit you can use to run WML-based applications on your PC. Figure 1-10, for example, shows an application running with the Nokia phone simulator.

To download the Nokia software development kit, visit http://www.Nokia.com and register as a developer. Then, you can download the Nokia WAP Toolkit. After you download the Toolkit, use the WinZip utility to unzip the file, and then perform the software installation. After the installation is completed, you can start the simulator from the Start | Programs submenu.

Downloading the Ericsson Software Development Kit

Like Nokia, Ericsson, which is also a well-known cellular-phone manufacturer, provides a software development kit you can use to create and test WML

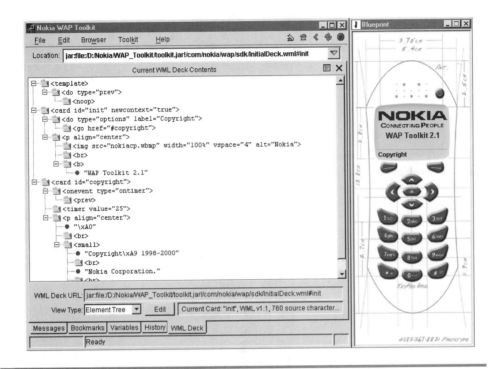

Figure 1-10   Using the Nokia phone simulator

applications. To download the Ericsson software development kit, visit http://www.ericsson.com, join the developer's zone, and then download the software. Figure 1-11 shows the Ericsson phone simulator.

Note

For more information on the Wireless Access Protocol, you should download the protocol's specification from the WAP Forum Web site at http://www.WAPForum.com.

Figure 1-11 Using the Ericsson phone simulator to run a WML application

Ask the Expert

Question: What is WAP?

Answer: WAP stands for Wireless Access Protocol. In general, WAP, like any set of protocols, provides a standard set of rules that programs must follow. In the case of WAP, the rules specify how programs will communicate across the Wireless Web. One rule, for example, might specify how much information one program can transfer to another at one time. Another might specify how the program should organize the information it sends. For example, to send a large amount of information, the program may break the program into smaller pieces of information, called packets. Within WAP, programmers will find rules that tell them how to format data within each packet. By following such rules, a computer that receives the incoming packets can easily reassemble the smaller pieces into the original larger piece of information.

Within the Wireless Web, WAP is very much like TCP/IP (the Transmission Control Protocol/Internet Protocol), which governs the rules programs follow to send and receive information across the Internet and World Wide Web. Think of WAP as a set of layers, each of which performs a specific function. The bottom layer, for example, is responsible for data transmission (which usually occurs via satellite links or over fiber-optic cables). At the topmost layer sits the WML applications you will create. Because WML sits on top of WAP, the applications you create do not have to worry about such issues as packets, data transmission errors, or communication speeds, just as HTML Web site developers do not have to worry about such issues on the Internet. Instead, the software that makes up the various layers of WAP perform these functions behind the scenes. Thus, when you create WML applications, you normally do not have to worry about WAP. Instead, you can focus on your WML statements, which sit above, yet take advantage of, WAP.

Question: Are there protocols other than WAP?

Answer: Yes. Within the United States and Europe, the Wireless Access Protocol is the most widely used protocol for Wireless applications. In contrast, in Japan, the most widely used protocol is I-MODE, whose use is driven by NTT DoCoMo. Today, nearly 20 million Wireless users in Japan access I-MODE sites.

To create a WAP-based site, developers normally use languages such as WML. To create an I-MODE site, developers use cHTML (compact HTML), a subset of HTML, which Web developers use to build sites on the World Wide Web.

Technically I-MODE sits on top of NTT DoCoMo's mobile voice system. While the voice system is circuit-switched, which means you dial your calls, I-MODE is packet-switched, which means that I-MODE is essentially always on. When a user selects an I-MODE item on the phone's menu, the microbrowser within the phone can immediately download the corresponding data, without having to first dial in to the Wireless Web. In addition, because I-MODE is packet-switched, I-MODE users pay for the data they transfer, as opposed to paying a flat connection time. Today, NTT DoCoMo is aggressively positioning I-MODE for use within Europe. In the future, you should expect to find I-MODE–based phones that support cHTML and WML.

Understanding WML—the Wireless Markup Language

To create a site on the traditional World Wide Web, developers use HTML (the Hypertext Markup Language). In contrast, to build a site on the Wireless Web, developers often use WML (the Wireless Markup Language). Like HTML, WML provides several different tags you can use to format data. For example, to format a paragraph of text, you would use the WML start and end paragraph tags <p> and </p>, as shown here:

```
<p>WML is the Wireless Markup Language</p>
```

Within a paragraph, you might use the start and end bold text tags <b> and </b> or the start and end italics tags <i> and </i> to highlight text, as shown here:

```
<p><b>WML</b> is the <i>Wireless Markup Language</i></p>
```

Throughout this book, you will learn how to use the various WML tags. To create a WML application, you create a file, to which you assign the .wml extension. Within the file, you will place WML tags that format your text, as well as WML tags that direct the microbrowser to perform specific operations, such as getting input from the user or branching to another application or Wireless site.

Note

Throughout this book, you will examine WML in detail. Before you start, you may want to download the WML specification from the WAP Forum Web site at http://www.WAPForum.com.

1

Ask the Expert

Question: What is WMLScript and how does it differ from WML?

Answer: To create high-end sites on the traditional World Wide Web, developers often use either the JavaScript or VBScript programming languages. Using these languages, the developer can extend the site's capabilities beyond those provided by HTML. In a similar way, Wireless Web site developers often use WMLScript to extend a site's functionality. Using WMLScript, you can add conditional processing to your applications to let the application make decisions—perform if-then processing. In addition, using WMLScript, your applications can perform iterative processing, employing loops to repeat a set of operations a specific number of times or until a specific condition is met. WMLScript is a very powerful programming language. You will learn how to use WMLScript in Module 7.

Note

In Module 7, you will learn how to use WMLScript to perform conditional and iterative processing within a WML application. In addition, you will learn how to create WMLScript functions that perform specific tasks. Before you begin, you may want to download the WMLScript specification from the WAP Forum Web site at http://www.WAPForum.com.

Where to Place Your Wireless Site

Throughout this book's modules, you will create a myriad of WML applications. Making a WML application available on the Wireless Web is much the same as making an HTML application available on the traditional World Wide Web. To start, you must place the application's files on a server that is connected to the World Wide Web.

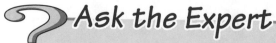

Ask the Expert

Question: How does a Wireless site really differ from a traditional Web site?

Answer: In general, the primary difference between a Wireless Web site and a traditional site on the World Wide Web is the language the developer uses to create the site. Normally, to create a Wireless site, the developer will use a language such as WML. In contrast, to create a traditional site on the World Wide Web, the developer will use HTML.

Just as you place the files for a traditional Web site on a server that is connected to the Internet, the same is true for a Wireless site—you place your WML files on a server connected to the Internet. In fact, it is quite likely that your server will eventually serve both HTML and WML applications.

If you already have a traditional Web server, you simply need to create a folder on the server within which you can place your WML files. If you do not have a Web server, you can use a simple server program, such as the Windows Personal Web Server, to make your applications available to other users.

If you want your Wireless application to be available to users 24 hours a day, 7 days a week (24/7), you can create an account at a commercial site, such as http://www.WirelessLookup.com, which will house your applications for a small fee.

Creating Your First Wireless Site

On the World Wide Web, you will find several sites that will provide templates you can use to quickly create your own Wireless site. Table 1-6 lists several such template sources. Before you start creating your own WML applications, you may want to visit one of these sites to create your own Wireless account, which you can then display using a phone simulator or a Web-enabled cellular phone. Figure 1-12, for example, shows the WirelessLookup.com Web site, which you can use to create a free personal or business site on the Wireless Web. After you create your site, you can view its content using a Web-enabled phone, a phone simulator, or a handheld device such as one that runs the Palm OS, as shown in Figure 1-13.

Site	Address
WirelessLookup.com	http://www.WirelessLookup.com
WAPdrive	http://www.wapdrive.com
Beaker	http://www.beaker.net
Wappy	http://www.wappy.to
Webforwireless	http://www.webforwireless.com

Table 1-6   Web Sites You Can Use to Create a Site on the Wireless Web

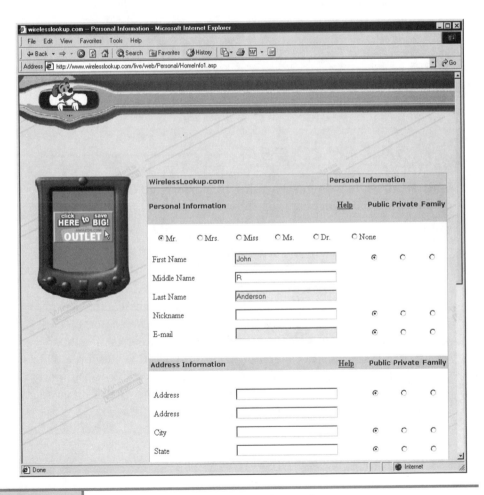

Figure 1-12   Creating a Wireless site at WirelessLookup.com

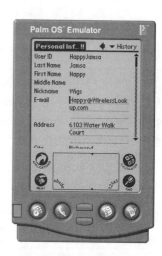

Figure 1-13 Displaying a Wireless Web site

Ask the Expert

Question: What languages, other than WML, do developers use to create Wireless Web sites?

Answer: To create Wireless Web pages, developers use such languages as WML, HDML (Handheld Device Markup Language), XML (Extensible Markup Language), cHTML, Basic XHTML (Extensible Hypertext Markup Language), and XSL (Extensible Stylesheet Language). Different micro-browsers support different languages. Within the United States, most microbrowsers support WML and HDML. In Japan, most support cHTML.

In the future, as the processing and storage capabilities of cellular phones increase, you will encounter microbrowsers that support a wide range of languages. Today, unfortunately, to provide universal support for an application, developers must often replicate their programs using several different programming languages.

1

Question: How do applications written for a Palm OS device differ from WML applications?

Answer: To create applications for the Palm OS, developers normally use the C and C++ programming languages to create programs with a set of tools (application programming interfaces—APIs) that are specific to the Palm. Programs written for the Palm OS will not execute on a cellular phone. Recently, Palm developers have started using a subset of HTML to create "Web clippings," which a browser built into the Palm can display. In the future, you should expect the Palm's browser to support languages such as WML.

Project 1-1: Surfing the Wireless Web

Across the Wireless Web there are a myriad of sites, each of which offers different information and capabilities. To find many of these sites, you can use common search engines, such as Yahoo or Google on the traditional World Wide Web. In this project, you will use various sources to locate Wireless sites.

Step-by-Step

1. If you have not already done so, download a phone simulator that you can use to view Wireless sites from your PC.

2. If you have not already done so, connect to the Internet and run your phone simulator program.

3. Using your traditional Web browser, such as Internet Explorer, connect to the following search engines and search for "WML Wireless Sites Wireless Portals":

    http://www.yahoo.com   http://www.excite.com

    http://www.google.com   http://www.lycos.com

4. Using your phone simulator, try visiting the addresses of the WML sites the search engine displays.

5. Using your phone simulator, visit the following Wireless search engines and search for topics such as News, Sports, Business, Finance, and WML:

    http://wap.google.com   http://webfront.de/i.wml

    http://m-find.com   http://www.wapuseek.com

✔ Mastery Check

1. What is a Web-enabled cellular phone?

   _____

   _____

2. How do you specify a site on the Wireless Web?

   _____

   _____

3. What is a phone simulator?

   _____

   _____

4. Why should you use more than one phone simulator?

   _____

   _____

5. How does WML differ from WAP?

   _____

   _____

6. What is m-commerce?

   _____

   _____

7. What is a fast and easy way to create a Wireless site?

   _____

   _____

8. How do you host a Wireless site?

   _____

   _____

Module 2

Creating Your First WML Application

The Goals of This Module

- Use a text editor to create and later edit a WML source file
- Organize your WML applications with folders on your disk
- Create your first WML application and display the application's results within the phone simulator
- Understand syntax errors and how to eliminate the errors from your source file
- Build an automated phone book that a Web-enabled phone can use to automatically dial numbers
- Understand how the microbrowser treats whitespace (blanks, tabs, and carriage returns) within a WML file

In Module 1, you learned how to run WML-based applications using a Web-enabled cellular phone or a Windows-based phone simulator. The programs you ran in Module 1 were created by another programmer using WML, who made the programs available to others via the Wireless Web. In this module, you will build and run your own WML applications.

To start, this module will teach you how to use a text editor, such as the Windows Notepad accessory to create a file that contains the WML tags for a simple application that displays the message "Hello, Wireless World!" Later, you will build a WML application that displays a list of phone numbers. When you run the application within a Web-enabled phone, you can direct your phone to automatically call a number that appears in the list. Finally, you will learn how to place the WML applications you create on the Wireless Web for others to access.

Selecting a Text Editor

To create a WML application, you will use a text editor, such as the Windows Notepad accessory, to create a file that contains your WML statements. Do not use a word processor, such as Microsoft Word, to create your WML files. As you know, word processors let you format text by aligning paragraphs, bolding and underlining words and phrases, and so on. To perform such formatting, the word processor embeds hidden characters within the document. One character combination, for example, might turn on bolding, while a second set of characters instructs the word processor to turn bolding off. Although such hidden characters are meaningful to the word processor, they will confuse the microbrowser, which will generate errors. A standard text editor, such as Notepad, does not embed such characters within a file.

Using the text editor, you will enter the WML statements that define your application. To start, this book will provide the WML statements you will use. Eventually, however, you will provide your own WML statements.

After you type in the WML statements, you will use the text editor to save your statements to a file. When you name the file, use the .wml extension, as in MyApplication.wml. The .wml extension tells you, other programmers, and a microbrowser that the file contains WML statements. Figure 2-1 shows WML entries within the Windows Notepad. To start the Windows Notepad accessory, select Start | Programs | Accessories | Notepad.

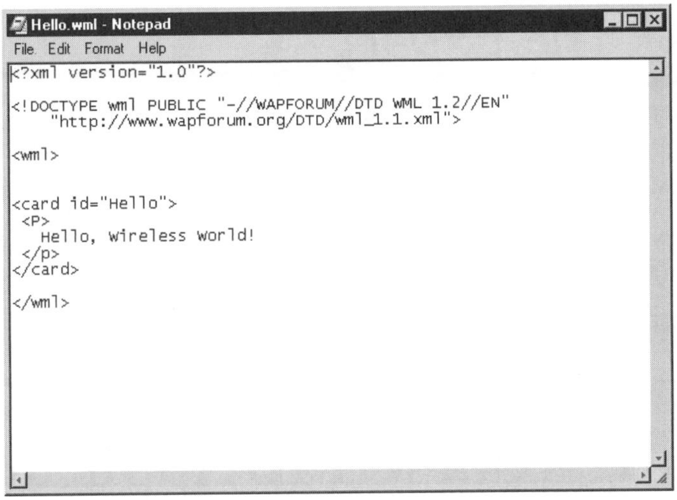

2

```
Hello.wml - Notepad                                    _ □ ×
File  Edit  Format  Help
<?xml version="1.0"?>

<!DOCTYPE wml PUBLIC "-//WAPFORUM//DTD WML 1.2//EN"
     "http://www.wapforum.org/DTD/wml_1.1.xml">

<wml>

<card id="Hello">
 <P>
   Hello, wireless world!
 </p>
</card>

</wml>
```

Figure 2-1   Using the Windows Notepad to create a WML application

Hint

Assign a meaningful name to your file that describes the application in the file. If you are creating a WML-based application that displays the time in cities around the world, you might name your application WorldClock.wml. Likewise, if you are creating an application that lets users purchase movie tickets via their Web-enabled phones, you might name your application MovieTickets.wml.

1-Minute Drill

● Why should you not use a word processor to create WML applications?

● Word processors may insert hidden characters within the WML source file, which you cannot see, but that the microbrowser will not understand. To create a WML source file, you should use a text editor, such as the Windows Notepad accessory.

Ask the Expert

Question: Is there a restriction on the number of characters I can use in a WML filename?

Answer: As a rule, you should assign a name to your WML files that accurately describes the processing the application performs. However, you should keep in mind that a user may eventually have to type in the filename using the small keypad on a cellular phone. If you make your filenames very long, you may frustrate your users.

Organizing Your WML Applications

Throughout this book, you will create a large number of WML applications. To help you better organize your applications, create a folder on your disk called WMLAps, within which you can create other folders specific to your applications. To create the WMLAps folder on your disk, perform these steps:

1. Select Start | Run. Windows will display the Run dialog box.

2. Within the Run dialog box, type **Explorer C:** and press ENTER. Windows will open the Explorer window, displaying the folders that reside on your hard drive.

3. Within the Explorer window, select File | New | Folder. The Explorer will create a new folder within the folder window, highlighting the folder name area that appears beneath the new folder icon.

4. Within the folder name area, type **WMLAps** and press ENTER.

Hint

If you create your WML applications using the Notepad text editor, you can use Notepad to create a folder for your application before you create your application file. To create a folder within Notepad, select File | Save As, and Notepad will display the Save As dialog box. Within the dialog box, navigate to the folder within which you want to create the new folder. Then, click the Create New Folder button.

2

Within the WMLAps folder, you should create individual folders for each WML application. When you create your folders, assign a meaningful name to each folder to help you locate your applications quickly in the future. For simplicity, you may want to save each application this book presents in a folder whose name corresponds to the current lesson. For example, WMLAps\Module2 or WMLAps\Module3.

Hint

As you examine the applications this book presents, you should take time to experiment with each one. After you make changes to an application, save your new WML statements to a file on your disk using a meaningful name that describes the processing your new application performs, such as FlashingHello.wml or GetUsername.wml.

Building Your First WML Application: Hello, Wireless World!

In this section, you will create your first WML application, Hello.wml, which simply displays the message "Hello, Wireless World!", as shown in Figure 2-2.

| **Figure 2-2** | Displaying the output of the Hello.wml application |

To create the Hello.wml application, start your text editor and type in the following WML statements:

```
<?xml version="1.0"?>

<!DOCTYPE wml PUBLIC "-//WAPFORUM//DTD WML 1.2//EN"
    "http://www.wapforum.org/DTD/wml_1.1.xml">
<wml>

<card id="Hello">
 <p>
   Hello, Wireless World!
 </p>
</card>

</wml>
```

For now, do not worry about each statement's purpose. Instead, use your text editor to save the application to a file named Hello.wml in the folder WMLAps\Module2.

To run the Hello.wml application using the Openwave simulator, start the simulator from Start | Programs. Depending on the version of the simulator you have downloaded, the menu option that starts the simulator may differ. To start version 4.1 of the simulator, for example, you will select the Programs menu UP.SDK 4.1 option and then choose UP.Simulator. Once you have the simulator running, type the complete pathname of your Hello.wml application within the simulator's Go field, preceding the pathname with file://. For example, if your application resides in the WMLAps directory on drive C, you would type file://c:/WMLAps/Hello.wml.

If you typed the statements exactly as they appeared, and your application's file resides in the directory you specified, the phone simulator will display the "Hello, Wireless World!" message, as previously shown in Figure 2-2. If, however, the simulator cannot find the application file on your disk, the simulator will display an error message, similar to that shown in Figure 2-3.

Note

In Module 1, you learned how to install and run the Openwave simulator. If you have not already installed and used the simulator to view sites on the Wireless Web, turn back to Module 1 now and review the steps the module presents.

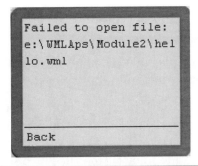

2

Figure 2-3   The phone simulator cannot locate your application file.

When you create the WML applications presented in this book, you must be very careful to ensure that you type your statements using the exact uppercase and lowercase letters shown in the statements. WML is a case-dependent language, which means WML considers an uppercase letter as different from its lowercase counterpart.

Also, within your application statements, make sure you include the correct number of opening and closing brackets. Should you mistype one or more statements, the phone simulator will display a syntax-error message, as shown in Figure 2-4.

Figure 2-4   Syntax errors prevent the simulator from running your WML application.

Ask the Expert

Question: Can I display a WML application within a traditional browser, such as Microsoft's Internet Explorer?

Answer: Yes and No. First, Internet Explorer will not execute a WML application. However, you can use Internet Explorer to validate your WML source code, meaning that Internet Explorer will examine your source code to ensure that you have an ending tag to match each starting tag and that your application's tags follow the WML document type definition (the document that specifies the format of the WML language). To display the WML source file within Internet Explorer, simply enter the URL as file:// followed by the path to the file, such as file://c:/WMLAps/Hello.wml. If you have typed the WML statements correctly, Internet Explorer will display the file's contents, as shown in Figure 2-5.

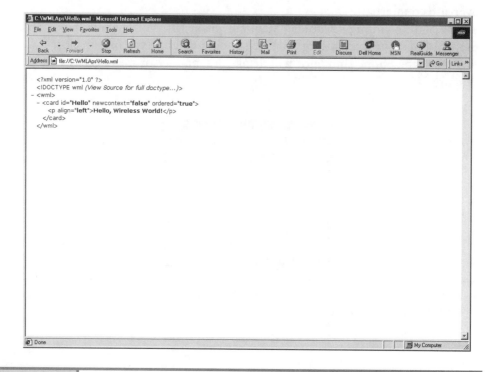

Figure 2-5 Displaying WML source code using Internet Explorer

⊣Note

When you type a WML application, you must pay close attention to the characters you type. WML considers uppercase and lowercase letters to be different, which means WML will not treat the tag <WML> the same as the correct tag <wml>. Should you mistype a tag, either by using an uppercase letter or by forgetting a slash within an ending tag, the microbrowser will not run your program. Instead, most microbrowsers will display a message telling you that the WML application contains syntax errors or invalid data. When such errors occur, you must edit your WML source code, find the error, and correct it. If you are testing your applications using a phone simulator, you can often use the output the simulator displays in its console window to help track down syntax errors.

When a syntax error occurs, you must edit your file to find and correct the cause of the error. Then, reload your application again. Reloading your application is a two-step process when using the Openwave simulator:

1. Select Edit | Clear Cache.

2. Type the application's name within the simulator's Go field (if the name is not currently displayed), or simply place the cursor after the name within the field and press ENTER.

⌐Hint

To improve its performance, the phone simulator loads the WML application's statements into a special cache memory. If you experience a syntax error within a card, you must edit the WML source file to correct the error. If you make a change to an application's statements, you must reload the application into the simulator. However, before you load the card, you should direct the simulator to clear the contents of its cache memory so you can be sure you will run the new version. If you are using the Openwave simulator, you can clear the cache memory by selecting Edit | Clear Cache.

 ## 1-Minute Drill

● How does WML treat uppercase and lowercase letters?

● How do you distinguish a starting tag from an ending tag?

● WML considers uppercase and lowercase letters as different. When you type WML tags, such as <wml> or <card>, you should use lowercase letters.
● An ending tag will have a slash, such as </wml> or </card>.

Using the Phone Simulator's Console Window

To help you locate errors within your applications, most phone simulators provide an MS-DOS–based console window, to which it writes status messages as your application runs, which may help you troubleshoot errors. For example, Figure 2-6 illustrates the messages the console window displays when the simulator cannot find a file. By viewing the console message, you can troubleshoot the problem. In this case, you may have misnamed a file, or perhaps the file resides in a different folder.

Likewise, Figure 2-7 shows the error message the simulator writes to the console window when it encounters a syntax error. By examining the console message, you can quickly locate the cause of the syntax error within your application.

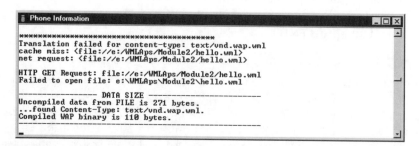

| **Figure 2-6** | A console window message for a file not found |

```
▓ Phone Information                                            _ □ ×
------------------ DATA SIZE ------------------
Uncompiled data from FILE is 218 bytes.
...found Content-Type: text/vnd.wap.wml.

====================== WML Errors ======================
WML translation failed.
(10) : error: Invalid element 'P' in content of 'card'. Expected onevent | timer
| do | p
(10) : error: Couldn't find element declaration for 'P' in content model
(12) : error: Close tag 'p' does not match start tag 'P'

====================== End Errors ======================
```

Figure 2-7   A console window message for a syntax error

Taking a Closer Look at Hello, Wireless World!

Each of the WML applications you create will begin with a header entry, similar to the following, that provides the microbrowser with information about your document's format:

```
<?xml version="1.0"?>

<!DOCTYPE wml PUBLIC "-//WAPFORUM//DTD WML 1.2//EN"
    "http://www.wapforum.org/DTD/wml_1.1.xml">
```

Programmers refer to this header as the *document type definition*. In short, the header provides the browser with a URL (Web address) of a document that defines the WML language. If you do not provide the header at the start of your WML files, the browser will not process your WML entries. In Module 10, you will examine the WML document type definition in detail. For now, simply keep in mind that you must start each of your WML applications with a header entry similar to that just shown.

Ask the Expert

Question: How does WML relate to XML?

Answer: As you have learned, WML is short for Wireless Markup Language. XML stands for Extensible Markup Language. Within Web-based applications, developers use XML to describe data. For example, a site that lets users download video clips might use XML statements to provide the downloading program with information about the video clip, such as its size, format (WAV or MPEG), the number of frames per second, and so on. Likewise, Web-based software that performs banking operations might use XML to describe a transaction, by specifying information such as the bank account number, the transaction type (withdrawal or deposit), the bank account type (checking or savings), and so on. XML lets developers specify an object's attributes. WML is a subset of XML. Using WML, you define an application's attributes, such as the cards into which you group related statements, its paragraphs, the text within paragraphs, and how the microbrowser should format the text.

When you create a WML application, you must place your WML statements between `<wml>` and `</wml>` tags. Your application file will contain only one set of these tags.

Each WML application that you create will consist of one or more *cards*. Normally, a card will contain statements that direct the microbrowser to perform specific processing. One card, for example, might display information about yourself. A second card might display information about your spouse, and so on. Your WML application will often consist of a series of cards, which developers refer to as a *WML card deck* or *deck*, and each card in the deck must have a unique name. Within a WML deck, you specify a card's name using the ID attribute. The following statements, for example, create a card named MyInfo:

```
<card id="MyInfo">
 <p>Name: Amanda Brinkman</p>
 <p>Phone: 281-555-1212</p>
 <p>Address: 123 Main St</p>
 <p>City: Houston</p>
 <p>State: Texas</p>
</card>
```

---Hint---

Within a WML application, you group related statements within cards. As you create cards, you should assign a meaningful name to each card that corresponds to the processing the card performs, much as you would assign a meaningful name to a file. By assigning meaningful card names, you will make it easier for others who read or must change your code to understand the processing each card performs.

To use a card within a WML application, you place the card statements within a file that contains the document type definition header and the `<wml>` and `</wml>` tags. For example, the following application, MyInfo.wml, displays information about the application's developer:

```
<?xml version="1.0"?>

<!DOCTYPE wml PUBLIC "-//WAPFORUM//DTD WML 1.2//EN"
    "http://www.wapforum.org/DTD/wml_1.1.xml">

<wml>

<card id="MyInfo">
 <p>Name: Amanda Brinkman</p>
 <p>Phone: 281-555-1212</p>
 <p>Address: 123 Main St</p>
 <p>City: Houston</p>
 <p>State: Texas</p>
</card>
</wml>
```

When you load the MyInfo.wml application into the phone simulator, the simulator will display the output shown in Figure 2-8.

```
Name: Amanda Brinkman
Phone: 281-555-1212
Address: 123 Main St
City: Houston
State: Texas
_____
Back
```

Figure 2-8   Displaying the output of the MyInfo.wml application

In this case, the card name and application name happen to be the same; however, the card's name does not have to match the filename. As your WML applications become more complex, your applications will eventually consist of multiple cards. When the microbrowser loads a WML file, the browser begins your application's execution with the first card it encounters.

Hint

Unless you tell the microbrowser to do otherwise, the microbrowser will start your program's execution with the first card it encounters in the WML file. To ensure that the browser loads the correct card, make sure that you place the first card you want the application to execute first in the file. You can also specify a starting card name with the URL you provide the browser (such as http://www.WL.com/SomeApplication.wml#Card2).

As mentioned earlier, WML is case dependent, and thus considers uppercase and lowercase letters as different. Take time now to experiment with the MyInfo.wml application by changing the lowercase <wml> entry to <WML>. Then, save your changes and reload the application. Because the uppercase <WML> is invalid, the phone simulator will display a syntax-error message. Remember to reload an application after you make changes; you normally must clear the simulator's cache memory and then load the application a second time using the Go field.

Ask the Expert

Question: In other programming languages, programmers often indent a program's statements to show the relationship between statements, such as which statements correspond to a loop. How should I indent WML statements?

Answer: When you create a WML source file using your text editor, you may want to indent tags within the file to show how tags relate, such as which text corresponds to a card, to a paragraph within a card, and so on. Likewise, you may want to place one or more blank lines within the file to help related items stand out at a glance to a programmer who is viewing your code. For example, the following statements implement two cards:

```
should the term "card" be used? JM<wml>
<card id="MyInfo">
<p>Name: Amanda Brinkman</p>
<p>Phone: 281-555-1212</p>
<p>Address: 123 Main St</p>
<p>City: Houston</p>
<p>State: Texas</p>
</card>
<card id="MomsInfo">
<p>Name: Jude Brinkman</p>
<p>Phone: 832-555-1212</p>
<p>Address: 123 Main St</p>
<p>City: Houston</p>
<p>State: Texas</p>
</card>
</wml>
```

By indenting the statements that appear within the cards and adding blank lines, you make it much easier for another programmer to tell at a glance which statements relate to each card:

```
<wml>

<card id="MyInfo">
  <p>Name: Amanda Brinkman</p>
  <p>Phone: 281-555-1212</p>
  <p>Address: 123 Main St</p>
  <p>City: Houston</p>
  <p>State: Texas</p>
</card>

<card id="MomsInfo">
  <p>Name: Jude Brinkman</p>
  <p>Phone: 832-555-1212</p>
  <p>Address: 123 Main St</p>
  <p>City: Houston</p>
  <p>State: Texas</p>
</card>

</wml>
```

When the microbrowser executes the card's contents, the microbrowser will ignore the indentation, displaying the card's contents correctly.

Within a WML file, you must place the text you want the browser to display within opening and closing paragraph tags: **<p>** and **</p>**. In the previous example, the application surrounded each entry with paragraph tags. In Module 3, you will learn how to use the line-break tag, **
**, to break a line within a paragraph. The following statements use one paragraph and several line-break tags:

```
<card id="MyInfo">
 <p>
  Name: Amanda Brinkman<br/>
  Phone: 281-555-1212<br/>
  Address: 123 Main St<br/>
  City: Houston<br/>
  State: Texas
 </p>
</card>
```

1-Minute Drill

● When do you need to use the <br/> tag?

● How do you assign a name to a WML card?

● What is the purpose of the <card> tag title attribute?

The following WML application, Einstein.wml, uses sets of paragraph tags. The first set displays a quote, and the second set displays the name Albert Einstein:

```
<?xml version="1.0"?>

<!DOCTYPE wml PUBLIC "-//WAPFORUM//DTD WML 1.2//EN"
    "http://www.wapforum.org/DTD/wml_1.1.xml">

<wml>

<card id="Einstein">
 <p>Great spirits have always encountered violent opposition from mediocre minds.
</p>
 <p>Albert Einstein</p>
</card>

</wml>
```

● The <br/> tag directs the microbrowser to wrap text to the start of the next line.
● To assign a name to a card within a WML file, you use the <card> tag id attribute. The following tag creates a card named "demo": <card id="demo">.
● Many microbrowsers ignore the title attribute. Some microbrowsers, however, will display the title on the screen in some way, so that the user has a way to identify the current card.

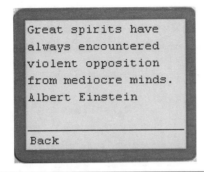

Great spirits have always encountered violent opposition from mediocre minds. Albert Einstein

Back

Figure 2-9 Using paragraph tags to format a quote from Albert Einstein

When you load the Einstein.wml application into the phone simulator, the simulator will display the output shown in Figure 2-9.

In Module 3, you will learn ways to format (align, bold, or underline) text that appears within paragraph tags. The following WML statements, QuoteEinstein.wml, use the special characters (**"**) to place a double quote (") character at the start and end of the quote. In addition, the statements use the tags **<i>** and **</i>** to turn italics on and off around Einstein's name:

```
<?xml version="1.0"?>

<!DOCTYPE wml PUBLIC "-//WAPFORUM//DTD WML 1.2//EN"
    "http://www.wapforum.org/DTD/wml_1.1.xml">

<wml>

<card id="QuoteEinstein">
  <p>
    &quot;Great spirits have always encountered violent opposition from mediocre minds.&quot;
  </p>

  <p>
    <br/>
      <i>Albert Einstein</i>
  </p>
</card>

</wml>
```

When you load the QuoteEinstein.wml application into the phone simulator, the simulator will display the output shown in Figure 2-10.

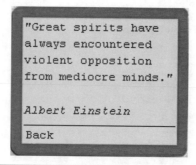

Figure 2-10 Creating double-quote characters and using italics

The following application, List5.wml, uses WML statements to display the names of five cities:

```
<?xml version="1.0"?>

<!DOCTYPE wml PUBLIC "-//WAPFORUM//DTD WML 1.2//EN"
    "http://www.wapforum.org/DTD/wml_1.1.xml">

<wml>

<card id="Cites">
 <p>Atlanta</p>
 <p>Boston</p>
 <p>Chicago</p>
 <p>Houston</p>
 <p>New York</p>
</card>

</wml>
```

As you can see, the application places paragraph tags at the start and end of each city name. When you load this application in the phone simulator, the simulator will display the output shown in Figure 2-11.

When you display a list of names within a microbrowser that requires more lines than the browser's screen can display, the browser may add a scroll bar that you can use to scroll through the items. For example, the following WML

| **Figure 2-11** | Displaying a list of city names |

application, NBATeams.wml, displays the names of the teams in the National
Basketball Association:

```
<?xml version="1.0"?>

<!DOCTYPE wml PUBLIC "-//WAPFORUM//DTD WML 1.2//EN"
    "http://www.wapforum.org/DTD/wml_1.1.xml">

<wml>

<card id="NBA">
 <p>Atlanta Hawks</p>
 <p>Boston Celtics</p>
 <p>Charlotte Hornets</p>
 <p>Chicago Bulls</p>
 <p>Cleveland Cavaliers</p>
 <p>Dallas Mavericks</p>
 <p>Denver Nuggets</p>
 <p>Detroit Pistons</p>
 <p>Golden State Warriors</p>
 <p>Houston Rockets</p>
 <p>Indiana Pacers</p>
 <p>Los Angeles Clippers</p>
 <p>Los Angeles Lakers</p>
 <p>Miami Heat</p>
 <p>Milwaukee Bucks</p>
```

```
<p>Minnesota Timberwolves</p>
<p>New Jersey Nets</p>
<p>New York Knickerbockers</p>
<p>Orlando Magic</p>
<p>Philadelphia 76ers</p>
<p>Phoenix Suns</p>
<p>Portland Trail Blazers</p>
<p>Sacramento Kings</p>
<p>San Antonio Spurs</p>
<p>Seattle SuperSonics</p>
<p>Toronto Raptors</p>
<p>Utah Jazz</p>
<p>Vancouver Grizzlies</p>
<p>Washington Wizards</p>
</card>

</wml>
```

When you load the NBATeams.wml application into the phone simulator, the simulator will display output similar to that shown in Figure 2-12. Using your keyboard arrow keys, you can scroll through the list of teams.

Figure 2-12   Scrolling through output within a phone's display screen

1-Minute Drill

● How does the <b> tag differ from the <br/> tag?

Building an Automated Phone Book

In the previous applications, you used the paragraph tags <p> and </p> to
create lists of information. Similarly, the following application, PhoneBook.wml,
uses paragraph tags to create a list of names and phone numbers:

```
<?xml version="1.0"?>

<!DOCTYPE wml PUBLIC "-//WAPFORUM//DTD WML 1.2//EN"
    "http://www.wapforum.org/DTD/wml_1.1.xml">

<wml>

<card id="PhoneBook">
 <p>
    Work: 800-555-1212<br/>
    Home: 281-555-1212<br/>
    Judy work: 888-555-1212<br/>
    Judy cell: 281-555-1212</p>
</card>

</wml>
```

When you load the PhoneBook.wml application into the phone simulator,
the simulator will display the names and numbers as shown in Figure 2-13.

● The <b> tag marks the start of text that you want to bold. To mark the end of the text to bold, you use the
</b> tag. In contrast, the <br/> tag has nothing to do with bold text. Rather, the <br/> tag directs the
microbrowser to wrap text to the start of the next line.

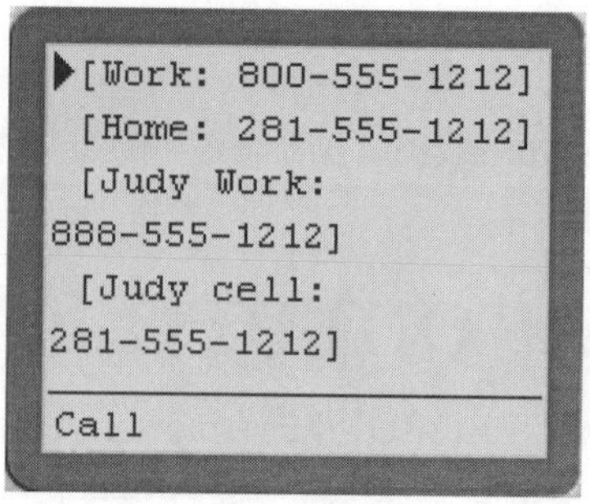

```
  ▶[Work: 800-555-1212]
   [Home: 281-555-1212]
   [Judy Work:
  888-555-1212]
    [Judy cell:
  281-555-1212]

  Call
```

Figure 2-13 | Using a WML application to display a phone directory

Although the list of phone numbers the previous application displays is useful when you need to look up someone's number, a better application would let you select and automatically dial a number. To create such an application, you must use an **<a>** tag, which Module 4 discusses in detail, to link to code that resides in a special library within a Web-enabled phone, called the Wireless Telephony Application Interface (WTAI). The following WML application, AutoCall.wml, changes the previous application slightly so that it automatically dials the number you select.

To direct the microbrowser to place the call, the application places each phone number within the **<a>** tag similar to the following:

```
<a href="wtai://wp/mc;18002723623" title="Call">Judy cell: 281-555-1212</a>
```

Within the **<a>** tag, the **href** attribute directs the microbrowser to use a special function that resides within the WTAI library to place the call to the specified number. The **title** attribute specifies the text the microbrowser will display above the Accept button when you highlight the link. The text that appears between the **<a>** and **</a>** tags is the text the microbrowser will display for the link.

For now, do not worry about how the **<a>** tag actually works—you will examine the tag in detail later in this book. For now, you may simply want to experiment with the application by replacing the numbers shown with phone numbers of importance to you. The following statements implement the AutoCall.wml application:

```
<?xml version="1.0"?>

<!DOCTYPE wml PUBLIC "-//WAPFORUM//DTD WML 1.2//EN"
```

2

```
                    "http://www.wapforum.org/DTD/wml_1.1.xml">

<wml>

<card id="PhoneBook">
 <p>
    <a href="wtai://wp/mc;18005551212" title="Call">Work: 800-555-1212</a>
    <a href="wtai://wp/mc;18885551212" title="Call">Home: 888-555-1212</a>
    <a href="wtai://wp/mc;18885551212" title="Call">
        Judy work: 888-555-1212</a>
    <a href="wtai://wp/mc;2815551212" title="Call">
        Judy Home: 281-555-1212</a>
  </p>
</card>

</wml>
```

When you run the application on a Web-enabled cell phone, the phone's microbrowser will recognize the phone numbers within each entry. If you use your phone's arrow keys to highlight an entry, the microbrowser will let you place an immediate call to the number by selecting the Call option. To place a phone call using the application, you would simply load the application into your phone's microbrowser, and then select the number you desire.

Admittedly, most phones have built-in phone books. However, many families today have multiple cell phones. Rather than struggle to keep each phone's phone book current, you can create one application that contains the numbers you desire. Then, when you need a number, you simply load the application across the Wireless Web.

The following application, FamilyPhoneBook.wml, extends the application to support a phone book for various family members:

```
<?xml version="1.0"?>

<!DOCTYPE wml PUBLIC "-//WAPFORUM//DTD WML 1.2//EN"
    "http://www.wapforum.org/DTD/wml_1.1.xml">

<wml>

<card id="FamilybookBook" title="Listings">
  <p align="center">Johnson Family</p>
  <p align="center">Phone Book</p>

  <p>
    <br/>
      <a href="#Dad">Dad's Numbers</a>
      <a href="#Mom">Mom's Numbers</a>
      <a href="#Kids">Kid's Numbers</a>
```

```
    </p>
  </card>

  <card id="Dad" title="Dad's Numbers">
    <p align="center">
       Dad's Numbers<br/>
    </p>

    <p>
      <a href="wtai://wp/mc;2815551212" title="Call">Home: 281-555-1212</a>
      Fax: 281-555-1212
      <a href="wtai://wp/mc;2815551212" title="Call">
         Cellular: 281-555-1212</a>
      <a href="wtai://wp/mc;18005551212" title="Call">
         Work: 800-555-1212</a>
      E-mail: BillJohnson@aol.com

      <do type="prev" label="Back"><prev/></do>
    </p>
  </card>

  <card id="Mom" title="Mom's Numbers">
    <p align="center">
       Mom's Numbers<br/>
    </p>

    <p>
      <a href="wtai://wp/mc;2815551212" title="Call">
         School: 281-555-1212</a>
      <a href="wtai://wp/mc;18885551212" title="Call">
         Cellular: 888-555-1212</a>
      <a href="wtai://wp/mc;2815551212" title="Call">
         Home: 281-555-1212</a>
      <a href="wtai://wp/mc;2815551212" title="Call">Work: 281-555-1212</a>
      <a href="wtai://wp/mc;18005551212" title="Call">
         Grandma: 800-555-1212</a>
      E-mail: JaneJohnson@aol.com

      <do type="prev" label="Back"><prev/></do>
    </p>
  </card>

  <card id="Kids" title="Kid's Numbers">
    <p align="center">
       Kid's Numbers<br/>
    </p>

    <p>
      <a href="wtai://wp/mc;2815551212" title="Call">
         Karate: 281-555-1212</a>
      <a href="wtai://wp/mc;7135551212" title="Call">
```

```
      Jim: 713-555-1212</a>
   <a href="wtai://wp/mc;18885551212" title="Call">
      Al: 888-555-1212</a>
   <a href="wtai://wp/mc;18005551212" title="Call">
      Doctor: 800-555-1212</a>

   <do type="prev" label="Back"><prev/></do>
  </p>
</card>

</wml>
```

When you load the application, it will display a menu that lets you select Mom's, Dad's, or Kids' phone book. After you select a phone book, the application will display the corresponding listings, as shown in Figure 2-14.

For now, do not be concerned with the statements that implement the application. You will examine the application's processing in detail later in this book.

Figure 2-14   Using a WML-based family phone book

WML and Arithmetic Operations

When you create WML-based applications, there are many times when the application must perform arithmetic operations. For example, the application may need to add two or more numbers, or multiply one value by another, such as when calculating the sales tax on a purchase. WML, however, does not provide a way for you to perform such operations. For example, the following application, Forty.wml, uses two techniques to display a programmer's age:

```
<?xml version="1.0"?>

<!DOCTYPE wml PUBLIC "-//WAPFORUM//DTD WML 1.2//EN"
    "http://www.wapforum.org/DTD/wml_1.1.xml">

<wml>

<card id="Forty" title="Author's Age">

  <p>
    The author is 20+20 <br/>
    His age is 40
  </p>
</card>

</wml>
```

When you load the application into the phone simulator, the simulator will display the output shown in Figure 2-15.

Figure 2-15 WML does not perform arithmetic operations.

2

As you can see, the application does not display the sum of the arithmetic operation 20+20. Instead, the application treats the operation as text. To perform arithmetic operations within a WML application, you must use WMLScript, which Module 7 describes in detail.

Understanding Whitespace

When a microbrowser displays a WML application, most microbrowsers will convert successive whitespace characters (space, tab, carriage returns, and new lines) into a single space. For example, the following WML application, BadList.wml, does not place the days of the week on individual lines, although it looks that way in the application:

```
<?xml version="1.0"?>

<!DOCTYPE wml PUBLIC "-//WAPFORUM//DTD WML 1.2//EN"
    "http://www.wapforum.org/DTD/wml_1.1.xml">

<wml>

<card id="BadList">
  <p>
     Sunday
     Monday
     Tuesday
     Wednesday
     Thursday
     Friday
     Saturday
  </p>
</card>

</wml>
```

When you load the BadList.wml application into the phone simulator, the simulator will convert the carriage-return characters that follow each day into a space, as shown in Figure 2-16.

```
Sunday Monday Tuesday
Wednesday Thursday
Friday Saturday



─────────────────────
Back
```

Figure 2-16 The microbrowser will convert carriage returns into a single space character.

In this case, to display the days of the week on individual lines, you must place the line-break tag **
** after each entry, as shown here:

```
<?xml version="1.0"?>

<!DOCTYPE wml PUBLIC "-//WAPFORUM//DTD WML 1.2//EN"
    "http://www.wapforum.org/DTD/wml_1.1.xml">

<wml>

<card id="BetterList">
  <p>
    Sunday<br/>
    Monday<br/>
    Tuesday<br/>
    Wednesday<br/>
    Thursday<br/>
    Friday<br/>
    Saturday<br/>
  </p>
</card>

</wml>
```

Note also that the WML browser converts the leading spaces that precede each day into a single space. Thus, the microbrowser will treat the WML statements

```
<p>
one         two three
 four          five              six

                                    seven

</p>
```

the same as this statement:

```
<p>one two three four five six seven</p>
```

As such, to better organize their statements, many WML programmers will use leading spaces to indent related code. In this way, they can quickly see which statements correspond to a particular card or element within that card.

1-Minute Drill

● What is whitespace?

● How do most microbrowsers handle whitespace that appears in a WML application?

● Whitespace is characters such as a blank, tab, carriage return, or linefeed that separate other characters.
● Most microbrowsers will ignore leading and trailing whitespace characters. Some microbrowsers will replace successive whitespace characters with a single whitespace character.

Correcting Logic Errors

Earlier in this module, you learned that if your WML application contains syntax errors, such as a misspelled tag, the microbrowser will not compile your application for execution. In such cases, you must edit your WML source code, correct the error, and then reload the application into the microbrowser.

As your WML applications become more complex, there will also be times when your program compiles, but it does not work the way you intended, due to programming errors (which programmers refer to as *bugs* or *logic errors*). In such cases, you must again edit your source code, locate and correct the cause of the error, and then reload your application into the microbrowser.

Using the Personal Web Server to Launch Your Wireless Application

After you create and test a WML application, you will likely want to make your application available to others across the Wireless Web. As discussed in Module 1, to place an application on the Wireless Web, you must simply host the application on a site that is connected to the Internet. If you work at an office that has a Web server, you could simply move your application to a folder that the Web server can access.

If you do not currently have a Web server, but you are running Windows 98, you can use the Personal Web Server application to host your Wireless applications. To install the Personal Web Server on your system, perform these steps:

1. Insert your Windows 98 CD-ROM into the CD-ROM drive.

2. Select Start | Run. Windows will display the Run dialog box.

3. Within the Run dialog box's Open field, type **x:\add-ons\pws\setup.exe**, replacing the drive letter *x* with your CD-ROM drive. Windows, in turn, will install the Personal Web Server on your system.

To make your WML applications available to the server, you must move the applications into a folder that resides within the inetpub\wwwroot directory on your hard drive. Next, you will need to customize your system to associate the .wml extension with the MIME type text/vnd.wap.wml and the .wmls extension with text/vnd.wap.wmlscript. To create the associations, perform these steps:

1. Within Explorer, click the My Computer icon.

2. Select View | Folder Options to display the Folder Options dialog box.

3. Within the Folder Options dialog box, click the File Types tab.

4. Within the File Types sheet, click the New Type button to display the Add New File Type dialog box.

5. Within the Add New File Type dialog box, type in the association and click OK.

To run the application using your phone or phone simulator, you must type in the URL that contains your system's IP address and the path to the application, such as http://111.123.230.122/WMLaps/Hello.wml.

Ask the Expert

Question: If I use the Personal Web Server for my WML applications, I will need to specify my local IP address within the URL to access the application. How can I determine my local IP address?

Answer: To determine your IP address, run the IPCONFIG command within an MS-DOS window:

```
C:\> IPCONFIG  <Enter>
Windows 98 IP Configuration

0 Ethernet adapter :

        IP Address. . . . . . . . . : 199.174.5.34
        Subnet Mask . . . . . . . . : 255.255.255.0
        Default Gateway . . . . . . : 199.174.5.34
```

GroceryList.wml

Project 2-1: Creating a Virtual Grocery List

This WML application, GroceryList.wml, will display on your Web-enabled phone the following items that you need to pick up at the grocery store. If you get to store and you can't remember the items you need, you can display the list on your phone. Further, if one of your family members has access to your computer and can edit the WML application, they can add items as you shop:

- Milk (half gallon)
- Eggs (large)
- Chicken
- Cheese Pizza
- Beer

Step-By-Step

1. Open a text editor, such as the Windows Notepad accessory.

2. All WML applications begin with the same header information. Within the text editor, type the following header:

```
<?xml version="1.0"?>

<!DOCTYPE wml PUBLIC "-//WAPFORUM//DTD WML 1.2//EN"
    "http://www.wapforum.org/DTD/wml_1.1.xml">
```

3. All WML applications start with the <wml> tag. Within the editor, type the tag as shown here:

```
<wml>
```

4. When you create a WML application, you organize related WML tags within a card that has a unique name within the deck. In this case, use the following <card> tag to create a card named "Groceries":

```
<card id="Groceries">
```

5. To specify the list of groceries, place each item within the opening and closing paragraph tags (<p> and </p>). After each item in the list, place the line-break tag <br/>, as shown here:

```
<p>
   Milk (half gallon)<br/>
   Eggs (large)<br/>
   Chicken<br/>
   Cheese Pizza<br/>
   Beer<br/>
</p>
```

6. Use the </card> tag to end the card and the </wml> tag to end the WML application. Your application should appear as follows:

```
<?xml version="1.0"?>

<!DOCTYPE wml PUBLIC "-//WAPFORUM//DTD WML 1.2//EN"
    "http://www.wapforum.org/DTD/wml_1.1.xml">

<wml>

<card id="Groceries">
 <p>
   Milk (half gallon)<br/>
   Eggs (large)<br/>
   Chicken<br/>
   Cheese Pizza<br/>
   Beer<br/>
 </p>
</card>

</wml>
```

☑ Mastery Check

1. What do the letters WML stand for?

_____

_____

2. How does WML differ from XML?

_____

_____

3. Create a WML application named KeyNumbers.wml that displays the
following information:

Name: Amanda
Cell: 281-555-1212
Work: 800-555-1212
Fax: 888-555-1212
E-mail: Amanda@Wireless.com

4. How would you change the application you created in Question 3 so that
the application will automatically dial the cell and work phone numbers?

_____

_____

5. List two ways you can use the phone simulator's console window.

_____

_____

6. How can you perform arithmetic operations within WML?

_____

_____

2

☑ *Mastery Check*

7. Create a WML application named BoldItalic.wml that displays the following output:

Amanda Smith
211 Main Street
Houston, Texas 77469

8. What is unique about the WML line-break tag?

_____

_____

9. How do you place an application on the Wireless Web?

_____

_____

Module 3

Formatting Output

The Goals of This Module

- Learn how to use the align attribute within a paragraph tag to center text, or right or left justify it
- Understand how to use the paragraph tag's mode attribute to enable or disable the microbrowser's automatic text wrap
- Use the WML text formatting tags, such as **\<b\>** and **\<i\>**, to highlight text
- Use the WML **\<img\>** tag to display a Wireless bitmap image
- Use the **\<img\>** tag's localsrc attribute to display images built into a phone's ROM (local source) image store
- Organize related output using tables
- Use the WML text-formatting tags to highlight information within a table

In Module 2, you learned how to use paragraph tags to display output within a WML application. Depending on the information your application displays, there will be times when you will want WML to center paragraph text, or right or left justify it. Likewise, there may be times when you will want to bold, blink, or highlight key text in some way. This module examines WML text formatting in detail.

To start with, this module examines the steps you must perform to align text within a paragraph—using left, right, or center justification. Next, you will learn how to control line wrapping within an application and how to highlight text using attributes such as bolding and italics. Then, you will learn how to display images, called Wireless bitmaps (WBMPs), within an application and how to take advantage of images that are built into the phone itself. Finally, this module examines ways you can organize an application's output using tables.

Aligning Paragraph Text

Within a paragraph, you can center text, or right or left justify it. To specify the text alignment you want the microbrowser to perform, you use the align attribute within the opening paragraph tag, as shown here:

```
<p  align=center>
<p  align=right>
<p  align=left>
```

The following WML application, CenterEinstein.wml, uses `align=center` attribute to center a quote by Albert Einstein:

```
<?xml version="1.0"?>

<!DOCTYPE wml PUBLIC "-//WAPFORUM//DTD WML 1.2//EN"
    "http://www.wapforum.org/DTD/wml_1.1.xml">

<wml>

<card id="CenterEinstein">
  <p align="center">
    Great spirits have always encountered violent opposition from mediocre minds.<br/><br/>
    Albert Einstein
  </p>
</card>

</wml>
```

When you load the CenterEinstein.wml application into the phone simulator, the simulator will display the output shown in Figure 3-1.

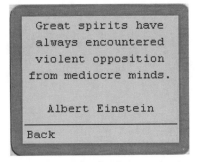

Great spirits have
always encountered
violent opposition
from mediocre minds.

Albert Einstein

Back

3

| **Figure 3-1** | Displaying centered paragraph text |

When you use the align attribute to specify a paragraph's alignment, the alignment setting remains in effect only for the current paragraph. If you create a second paragraph, you must use an align attribute within that paragraph as well, or WML will use its default alignment (left justification).

Depending on the information your application displays, there may be times when you want to right justify text. For example, the following application, Prices.wml, uses the **align=right** attribute to justify a list of prices:

```
<?xml version="1.0"?>

<!DOCTYPE wml PUBLIC "-//WAPFORUM//DTD WML 1.2//EN"
    "http://www.wapforum.org/DTD/wml_1.1.xml">

<wml>

<card id="Prices">
  <p align="right">
    Books   $$19.99<br/>
    CD-ROM $$25.99<br/>
    Pizza   $$9.99<br/>
    Beer    $$29.99<br/>
  </p>
</card>

</wml>
```

When you load the Prices.wml application into the phone simulator, the simulator will display the output shown in Figure 3-2.

```
                    Books $19.99
                   CD-ROM $25.99
                     Pizza $9.99
                      Beer $29.99



        Back
```

Figure 3-2 Displaying right-justified text

Note that in Prices.wml, the code uses two dollar-sign characters ($$) to display a single dollar sign in the program's output. As you will learn in Module 4, WML uses the dollar character to retrieve the value stored within a variable. To output a dollar-sign character, you must use two dollar signs, as shown.

Hint

To align numbers on a decimal point, such as a set of prices, programmers sometimes right justify a paragraph's text. To align other types of data, such as two rows of text values, you should place the data within a table, as discussed later in this module, starting with the "Organizing Data in Tables" section.

1-Minute Drill

● Create WML statements to center the letters A, B, and C on three separate lines.

● When you use the align attribute in a paragraph tag, will the alignment you select remain in effect for subsequent paragraphs?

● The following tags will center the letters A, B, and C on three separate lines:
`<p align="center">A</p><p align="center">B</p><p align="center">C</p>`
Or you can use:
`<p align="center">A<br/>B<br/>C<br/></p>`

● No. When you use an align attribute within a paragraph tag, the alignment you specify is only in effect for that paragraph.

Controlling Line Wrapping

By default, a microbrowser will automatically wrap text to the next line when the text reaches the margin. Depending on your application's output, there may be times when you will want to control line wrapping. Using the paragraph tag's mode attribute, you can turn line wrapping on and off:

```
<p   mode=wrap>
<p   mode=nowrap>
```

When you turn line wrapping off, the microbrowser will not wrap text to the next line. Instead, the microbrowser will either add a horizontal scroll bar you can use to scroll the text into view, or the browser will flash different sections of the text into view. The following WML application, NoWrap.wml, uses the **mode=nowrap** attribute to turn off wrapping for the Einstein quote:

```
<?xml version="1.0"?>

<!DOCTYPE wml PUBLIC "-//WAPFORUM//DTD WML 1.2//EN"
    "http://www.wapforum.org/DTD/wml_1.1.xml">

<wml>

<card id="EinsteinNoWrap">
  <p mode="nowrap">
    Great spirits have always encountered violent opposition from mediocre minds.<br/><br/>
    Albert Einstein
  </p>
</card>

</wml>
```

Again, depending on your microbrowser, the screen may or may not let you view text that appears beyond the margin. If you load the NoWrap.wml application into the phone simulator, the simulator will display the output shown in Figure 3-3.

Hint

Because existing microbrowsers do not display horizontal scroll bars in a consistent manner, you should avoid using the mode=nowrap attribute within your applications.

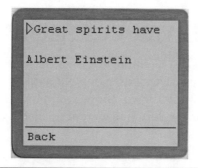

Figure 3-3 Using the mode=nowrap attribute

Using Styles to Format Text

When your WML applications display text on the screen, there will be times when you want to highlight specific text. As shown in Table 3-1, WML supports several tags you can use to select a text style. Unfortunately, not all microbrowsers treat the styles the same way.

To use a style, you simply place the text to be styled between opening and closing style tags. The following WML statement, for example, will highlight the www.WirelessLookup.com site name using bold text:

```
<p>Go wireless at <b>www.WirelessLookup.com</b></p>
```

Tag	Purpose	Example
<b>	Displays bold text	<b>Bold text</b>
<big>	Displays a larger font	<big>Big text</big>
<em>	Displays emphasized text	<em>Emphasized text</em>
<i>	Displays italic text	<i>Italic text</i>
<small>	Displays a smaller font	<small>Smaller text</small>
<strong>	Displays strong text	<strong>Bigger, bolder text</strong>
<u>	Displays underlined text	<u>Underlined text</u>

Table 3-1 WML Tags You Can Use to Select a Text Style

Depending on the microbrowser that is displaying the text, the actual display of the text style may differ. For example, one microbrowser may display text that you emphasize using the **<strong>** tag differently from another.

The following WML application, ShowStyles.wml, illustrates the use of each of the WML text styles:

3

```
<?xml version="1.0"?>

<!DOCTYPE wml PUBLIC "-//WAPFORUM//DTD WML 1.2//EN"
    "http://www.wapforum.org/DTD/wml_1.1.xml">

<wml>

<card id="Styles">
  <p>
    <b>Bold text</b><br/>
    <big>Big text</big><br/>
    <em>Emphasized text</em><br/>
    <i>Italic text</i><br/>
    <small>Small text</small><br/>
    <strong>Strong text</strong><br/>
    <u>Underlined text</u><br/>
  </p>
</card>

</wml>
```

If you load this application into the phone simulator, the simulator will display the output shown in Figure 3-4. Depending on the microbrowser you use to run the application, the way the microbrowser displays the styles may differ.

1-Minute Drill

● Why should you avoid the use of the mode=nowrap attribute within a paragraph tag?

● Create WML statements to display the following words using the corresponding text attributes: **Bold**, *Italic*, ***BoldItalic***.

● The mode=nowrap attribute directs the microbrowser to not automatically wrap text to the next line when the text will not fit completely on the current line. Because microbrowsers do not handle the text that appears beyond the screen's right margin in a consistent way, you should avoid the use of the mode=nowrap attribute.

● The following statement will display the words **Bold**, *Italic*, and ***BoldItalic*** using the corresponding text attributes:

```
<p><b>Bold</b><i>Italic</i><b><i>BoldItalic</i></b></p>
```

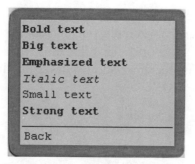

Figure 3-4 Displaying text styles

Displaying Simple Images

Because of the limited processing power of cellular phones, and the slow bandwidth across which WML-based applications can download data to the phone, most WML applications make extensive use of text and very little use of graphics. In fact, some microbrowsers do not yet support graphics. On the Wireless Web, you will normally find graphics used only for site logos, for which the developer can use a small image.

To display graphics within a WML application, you will use a low-resolution black-and-white image format, called a Wireless bitmap (or WBMP) file. In the following section, you will learn how to create and use WBMP files.

Creating a WBMP File

As mentioned, a WBMP file is a low-resolution black-and-white image, well suited for display on a small cellular-phone screen. There are several sites on the Web that offer tools you can use to create WBMP files. Table 3-2 lists several such sites.

Site	Web Address
Teraflops Online WBMP Converter	http://www.teraflops.com/wbmp/
WapTiger WBMP Converter	http://www.waptiger.de/download.html
WBMPcreator	http://www.wbmpcreator.com/
Wbmp Butterfly	http://inin-wap.avalon.hr/zdravko/wbmpfly.htm
WAPDraw	http://www.phnet.fi/public/jiikoo/

3

Table 3-2   Sites on the World Wide Web That Provide Tools for WBMP Files

Figure 3-5, for example, illustrates the Wbmp Butterfly utility, which you can use to convert a bitmap (BMP) file into a WBMP image.

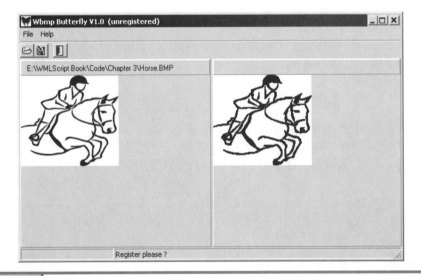

Figure 3-5   Using Wbmp Butterfly to convert a BMP file into a WBMP image for use on the Wireless Web

Placing a WBMP Image in a WML Application

As in HTML, you can place an image into a WML application by using an `<img>` tag. The following `<img>` tag, for example, loads an image named beagle.wbmp into an application:

```
<img src="beagle.wbmp" alt="Beagle Image" />
```

Within the `<img>` tag, you must use the alt attribute to specify text that the microbrowser will display if it cannot display the WBMP image. In the previous example, if the microbrowser cannot display the beagle.wbmp image, it will instead display the text "Beagle Image". As a rule, you should place meaningful text within an alt attribute. The following WML application, Beagle.wml, uses the `<img>` tag to display the Beagle image:

```
<?xml version="1.0"?>

<!DOCTYPE wml PUBLIC "-//WAPFORUM//DTD WML 1.2//EN"
    "http://www.wapforum.org/DTD/wml_1.1.xml">

<wml>

<card id="Beagle">
  <p>
     <img src="beagle.wbmp" alt="Beagle Image" />
  </p>
</card>

</wml>
```

If you load the Beagle.wml application into the phone simulator, the simulator will display the output shown in Figure 3-6.

When you use a WBMP image in a WML application, the microbrowser actually compiles the image into the application's binary code. Depending on the image size, there may be times when a microbrowser cannot store the image within the application. Even though you are working with a WBMP image, the

| **Figure 3-6** | Displaying a WBMP image |

image may be too large for your browser. Likewise, if your application uses multiple images, you may need to place the images into their own card.

The following application, HorseLogo.wml, displays a WBMP image of a horse as a logo above a company's name and contact information.

```
<?xml version="1.0"?>

<!DOCTYPE wml PUBLIC "-//WAPFORUM//DTD WML 1.2//EN"
    "http://www.wapforum.org/DTD/wml_1.1.xml">

<wml>

<card id="HorseLogo">
  <p>
    <img src="Horse.wbmp" alt="Welcome" />
    <br/>Welcome to Amanda's<br/>
    Horse Training<br/>
    800-555-1212<br/><br/>
    123 Horse Lane<br/>
    Houston, Texas 77469
  </p>
</card>

</wml>
```

When you load the HorseLogo.wml application into the phone simulator, the simulator will display the output shown in Figure 3-7.

Figure 3-7 Displaying a WBMP image as a logo within a WML application

1-Minute Drill

● What is a WBMP?

● How can you create a WBMP?

● Specify the `<img>` tag to display the WBMP file MyLogo.wbmp.

Hint

Because most cellular phones transmit data at slow speeds (often 9,600 bps), you should limit your use of WBMP images, which may, despite their low resolution, take considerable time to download. Instead, whenever possible, take advantage of local-source images that are built into the phone, as discussed shortly.

● A WBMP is a file that contains a low-resolution graphics image well suited for display on a cellular-phone screen or other handheld device.

● You can find several software programs on the Web, such as Wbmp Butterfly, that you can use to convert a traditional BMP (bitmap) image into a WBMP file.

● The following `<img>` tag displays the WBMP file MyLogo.wbmp:

```
<img src="MyLogo.wmp" alt="Company Logo">
```

Ask the Expert

Question: I want to create my own WBMP graphics for display on my site. How can I best do this?

Answer: You will find several tools on the Web that let you convert existing bitmap images into WBMP graphics. Some of these programs may let you draw your own WBMP images. Or, you can use a drawing package, such as Photoshop or the Windows Paintbrush accessory, to create a BMP file that you can then convert using one of the tools listed in Table 3-2.

Using Your Phone's Built-In Images

As you just learned, using the `<img>` tag, a WML application can display images that reside in WBMP files. In addition to displaying WBMP images, though, the `<img>` tag also lets applications display images that reside in a phone's read-only memory (ROM). Most Wireless phones support a standard set of built-in images that programmers refer to as the phone's *local-source images*. Using the `<img>` tag's localsrc attribute, you can specify a name that corresponds to the image you desire. Figure 3-8 illustrates local-source images the phone simulator supports.

To display a smiley-face image, for example, your application would use the following `<img>` tag:

```
<img localsrc="smileyface" src="file.wbmp" alt="Happy face">
```

When you use the localsrc attribute, you must also specify the src and alt attributes. The src attribute specifies the name of a WBMP image the microbrowser will display if the phone does not support the specified local-source image. Even if you do not have an image to display, you must specify the src attribute and a value. If the microbrowser cannot locate the WBMP image you specify (if, for example, the image does not exist), the microbrowser will display the text you specify using the alt attribute.

exclamation1	!	baseball		downtri3		leaf	
exclamation2	!	clock		usa		hound	
question1	?	moon2		note3		battery	
question2	?	bell		clipboard		scroll	
lefttri1		pushpin		cup		thumbtack	
righttri1		smallface		camera1		lockkey	
lefttri2		heart		rain		dollar	
righttri2		martini		football		lefthand	
littlesquare1		bud		book1		righthand	
littlesquare2		trademark		stopsign		tablet	
isymbol		multiply		trafficlight		paperclip	
wineglass		document1		book2		present	
speaker		hourglass1		book3		tag	
dollarsign	$	hourglass2		book4		meal1	
moon1		floppy1		document2		books	
bolt		snowflake		scissors		truck	
medsquare1		cross1		day		pencil	
medsquare2		cross2		ticket		uplogo	
littlediamond1		rightarrow1		cloud		envelope2	
littlediamond2		leftarrow1		envelope1		wrench	
bigsquare1		mug		check		outbox	
bigsquare2		divide		videocam		inbox	
littlecircle1		calendar		camcorder		phone2	
littlecircle2		smileyface		house		factory	
wristwatch		star2		flower		ruler1	
plus	+	rightarrow2		knife		ruler2	
minus		leftarrow2		vidtape		graph2	
star1		gem		glasses		meal2	
uparrow1		checkmark1		roundarrow1		phone3	
downarrow1		dog		roundarrow2		plug	
circleslash		star3		magnifyglass		family	
downtri1		sparkle		key		link	
uptri1		lightbulb		note1		package	
downtri2		bird		note2		fax	FAX
uptri2		folder1		boltnut		partcloudy	
bigdiamond1		head1		shoe		plane	
bigdiamond2		copyright		car		boat	
biggestsquare1		registered		floppy2		dice	
biggestsquare2		briefcase		chart		newspaper	
bigcircle1		folder2		graph1		train	
bigcircle2		phone1		mailbox		blankfull	
uparrow2		voiceballoon		flashlight		blankhalf	
downarrow2		creditcard		rolocard		blankquarter	
sun		uptri3		check2			

Figure 3-8 Images Supported by the Phone Simulator's Local Source

The following WML application, Faces.wml, uses local-source images to display two faces:

```
<?xml version="1.0"?>

<!DOCTYPE wml PUBLIC "-//WAPFORUM//DTD WML 1.2//EN"
    "http://www.wapforum.org/DTD/wml_1.1.xml">

<wml>

<card id="LocalSrc">
  <p>
     <img localsrc="smileyface" src="bad.wbmp" alt="Happy face" /><br/>
     <img localsrc="smallface" src="bad.wbmp" alt="Small face" />
  </p>
</card>

</wml>
```

As you can see, the **<img>** tag references the WBMP file bad.wbmp, which should not exist on your system. If the microbrowser does not support one of the local-source images, the microbrowser will first try to display the bad.wbmp image. Because the image does not exist, the microbrowser would then display the text provided by the alt attribute.

When you load the Faces.wml application into the phone simulator, the simulator will display the output shown in Figure 3-9.

Figure 3-9   Displaying local-source images

The following WML application, WeatherReport.wml, uses several local-source images to display information about the current weather:

```
<?xml version="1.0"?>

<!DOCTYPE wml PUBLIC "-//WAPFORUM//DTD WML 1.2//EN"
    "http://www.wapforum.org/DTD/wml_1.1.xml">

<wml>

<card id="Weather">
  <p>Mon <img localsrc="snowflake" src="bad.wbmp" alt="Snow" />
    Snow 32</p>
  <p>Tue <img localsrc="cloud" src="bad.wbmp" alt="Cloudy" />
    Cloudy 40</p>
  <p>Wed <img localsrc="partcloudy" src="bad.wbmp"
    alt="Cloudy" />Cloudy 41</p>
  <p>Thu <img localsrc="rain" src="bad.wbmp" alt="Rain" />
    Rain 39</p>
  <p>Fri <img localsrc="sun" src="bad.wbmp" alt="Sunny" />
    Sunny 45</p>
</card>

</wml>
```

If you load the WeatherReport.wml application into the phone simulator, the simulator will display the output shown in Figure 3-10.

| **Figure 3-10** | Displaying local-source weather images |

Hint

Earlier you learned that when the microbrowser cannot find the WBMP image you specify in an <img> tag, the microbrowser will display the text you specify in the alt attribute. Several of the previous examples that used local-source images specified the name of an invalid bitmap file, which the browser will not find. In this way, the application will either display the local-source image or the alt attribute text. Rather than specifying an invalid image name in this way, which may confuse other programmers who are reading the source code, many WML developers use an empty string to specify the WBMP file, such as src="".

Finally, the following WML application, TravelItinerary.wml, uses several local-source images to display information about a user's upcoming trip:

```
<?xml version="1.0"?>

<!DOCTYPE wml PUBLIC "-//WAPFORUM//DTD WML 1.2//EN"
    "http://www.wapforum.org/DTD/wml_1.1.xml">


<wml>

<card id="Trip">
  <p><b>Monday</b><br/>
     <img localsrc="plane" src="bad.wbmp" alt="Flight" />
        United 332 1:15<br/>
     <img localsrc="car" src="bad.wbmp" alt="Limo" />
        Limo 212-555-1212<br/>
     <img localsrc="martini" src="bad.wbmp" alt="Meeting" />
        Drinks Bill Smith<br/>
     <img localsrc="meal1" src="bad.wbmp" alt="Meeting" />
        Alfredos 800-555-1212<br/>
  </p>
  <p><b>Tuesday</b><br/>
     <img localsrc="dollar" src="bad.wbmp" alt="Sales Call" />
        8:15 Smith Tower<br/>
     <img localsrc="train" src="bad.wbmp" alt="Train" />
        Boston 4:30 <br/>
     <img localsrc="house" src="bad.wbmp" alt="Hotel" />
        Hotel Jones 555-1212<br/>
  </p>
  <p><b>Wednesday</b><br/>
```

```
        <img localsrc="plane" src="bad.wbmp" alt="Flight" />
          United 33 7:15<br/>
        <img localsrc="family" src="bad.wbmp" alt="Home" />
          Family Dinner<br/>
    </p>

  </card>

  </wml>
```

When you load the TravelItinerary.wml application into the phone simulator, the simulator will display the output shown in Figure 3-11.

Hint

When you display local-source images within a WML application, you can use the align attribute to align the images with an imaginary line that runs through the center of the line's text, or above or below that line, by using the middle, top, or bottom values. For example, to assign an image above the line, you would use `<img localsrc="imagename" align="top" src="image.wbmp" alt="message">`.

1-Minute Drill

● What is a local-source image?

● How do you display a local-source image within a WML application?

● A local-source image is an image that resides within the phone's ROM memory.
● To display a local-source image, you use the <img> tag's localsrc attribute.

Figure 3-11   Displaying a variety of local-source images

Ask the Expert

Question: Do all phones use the same local-source images?

Answer: Not necessarily. Just as all microbrowsers do not treat WML tags in the same way, cellular phones do not have to use the same local-source images. That said, most newer phones will support the local-source images shown here, and you should feel confident to use the images within your applications.

Organizing Data in Tables

As you display information within a WML application, there may be times when you will find it convenient to group related information within a table. Like HTML, WML provides support for tables. However, different microbrowsers do not treat tables consistently, and some microbrowsers do not support tables at all.

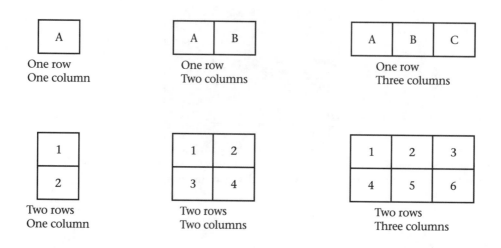

Figure 3-12 Tables consist of rows and columns

A table consists of one or more horizontal rows, which, in turn, consist of one or more vertical columns. Figure 3-12 illustrates several different tables.

To create a table using WML, you use the **<table>** and **</table>** tags. Within these tags, you specify a table's rows using the **<tr>** and **</tr>** tags. Within each row, you define one or more columns using the table data tags, **<td>** and **</td>**. The following entries create a table with three rows:

```
<table columns="1">
<tr><td>First row</td></tr>
<tr><td>Second row</td></tr>
<tr><td>Third row</td></tr>
</table>
```

Within the **<table>** tag, you must specify the number of columns the table will contain by using the columns attribute, as shown in the preceding example. The following WML application, FiveRows.wml, creates a table that contains five rows. Each row, in turn, contains one data element:

3

```
<?xml version="1.0"?>

<!DOCTYPE wml PUBLIC "-//WAPFORUM//DTD WML 1.2//EN"
    "http://www.wapforum.org/DTD/wml_1.1.xml">

<wml>

<card id="FiveRows">
  <p>
    <table columns="1">
      <tr><td>Row one</td></tr>
      <tr><td>Row two</td></tr>
      <tr><td>Row three</td></tr>
      <tr><td>Row four</td></tr>
      <tr><td>Row five</td></tr>
    </table>
  </p>
</card>

</wml>
```

When you load this application into the phone simulator, the simulator will display the output shown in Figure 3-13.

Figure 3-13 | Displaying a simple table

The next WML application, NamePhone.wml, stores ten names and phone numbers within a table:

```
<?xml version="1.0"?>

<!DOCTYPE wml PUBLIC "-//WAPFORUM//DTD WML 1.2//EN"
    "http://www.wapforum.org/DTD/wml_1.1.xml">

<wml>

<card id="NamePhone">
  <p>
    <table columns="2">
      <tr><td>Andy</td><td>800-555-1212</td></tr>
      <tr><td>Bill</td><td>888-555-1212</td></tr>
      <tr><td>Charles</td><td>900-555-1212</td></tr>
      <tr><td>Jim</td><td>212-555-1212</td></tr>
      <tr><td>Pete</td><td>281-555-1212</td></tr>
      <tr><td>Roger</td><td>800-555-1212</td></tr>
      <tr><td>Stacy</td><td>832-555-1212</td></tr>
      <tr><td>Steve</td><td>623-555-1212</td></tr>
      <tr><td>Wiley</td><td>619-555-1212</td></tr>
      <tr><td>Zeke</td><td>702-555-1212</td></tr>
    </table>
  </p>
</card>

</wml>
```

When you load the application into the phone simulator, the simulator will display the output shown in Figure 3-14.

1-Minute Drill

● Use a table within a WML application to display the following product information:

```
Product      Units
Books        500
CDs          300
DVDs         400
```

```
<table columns="2">
<tr><td>Product</td><td>Units</td></tr>
<tr><td>Books</td><td>500</td></tr>
<tr><td>CDs</td><td>300</td></tr>
<tr><td>DVDs</td><td>400</td></tr>
</table>
```

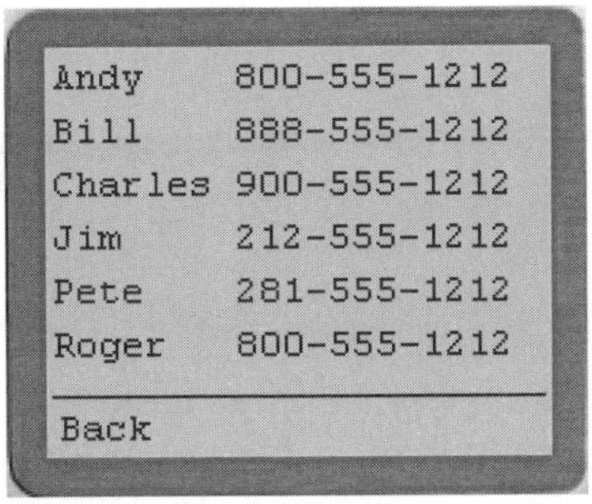

Figure 3-14 Displaying a multicolumn table

Formatting Table Data

When you store information within a table, there may be times when you will want to format the data in some way, such as using bold or italic text. To format text within a table, you simply place the corresponding style tags within the table. For example, the following application, BoldNames.wml, modifies the previous application to display names using bold text:

```
<?xml version="1.0"?>

<!DOCTYPE wml PUBLIC "-//WAPFORUM//DTD WML 1.2//EN"
    "http://www.wapforum.org/DTD/wml_1.1.xml">

<wml>

<card id="NamePhone">
  <p>
    <table columns="2">
      <tr><td><b>Andy</b></td><td>800-555-1212</td></tr>
      <tr><td><b>Bill</b></td><td>888-555-1212</td></tr>
      <tr><td><b>Charles</b></td><td>900-555-1212</td></tr>
      <tr><td><b>Jim</b></td><td>212-555-1212</td></tr>
      <tr><td><b>Pete</b></td><td>281-555-1212</td></tr>
      <tr><td><b>Roger</b></td><td>800-555-1212</td></tr>
      <tr><td><b>Stacy</b></td><td>832-555-1212</td></tr>
      <tr><td><b>Steve</b></td><td>623-555-1212</td></tr>
      <tr><td><b>Wiley</b></td><td>619-555-1212</td></tr>
      <tr><td><b>Zeke</b></td><td>702-555-1212</td></tr>
```

```
   </table>
  </p>
</card>

</wml>
```

When you load the application into the phone simulator, the simulator will
display the output shown in Figure 3-15. Keep in mind that this application
will only display the phone numbers, it will not automatically dial the numbers.
To automatically dial numbers, you must use the Wireless Telephony Application
Interface (WTAI), as briefly discussed in Module 2.

Depending on your needs, there may be times when you will want to
highlight an entire table, or specific rows within a table. For example, the
following application, BoldTable.wml, bolds the entire contents of a table by
placing the **** and **** tags around the **<table>** and **</table>** tags:

```
<?xml version="1.0"?>

<!DOCTYPE wml PUBLIC "-//WAPFORUM//DTD WML 1.2//EN"
    "http://www.wapforum.org/DTD/wml_1.1.xml">

<wml>

<card id="BoldTable">
  <p>
   <b>
    <table columns="2">
      <tr><td>Month</td><td>Sales</td></tr>
      <tr><td>September</td><td>5,444</td></tr>
      <tr><td>October</td><td>5,582</td></tr>
      <tr><td>November</td><td>6,433</td></tr>
      <tr><td>December</td><td>6,332</td></tr>
    </table>
   </b>
  </p>
</card>

</wml>
```

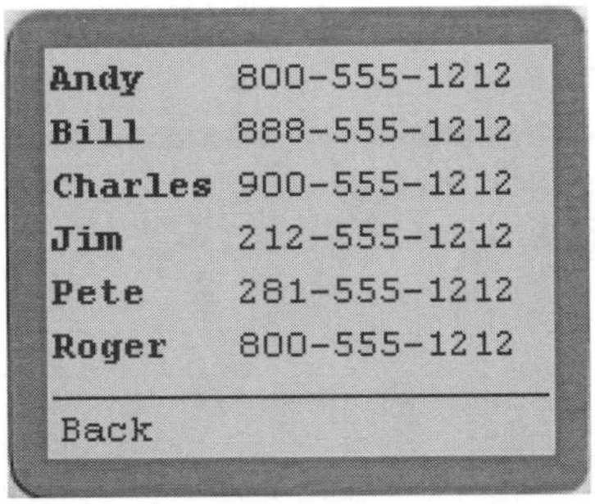

Figure 3-15 Displaying table data using a bold font

When you load the application into the phone simulator, the simulator will display the output shown in Figure 3-16.

Similarly, the WML application InStock.wml uses the **** and **** tags to bold the table rows that correspond to in-stock items:

```
<?xml version="1.0"?>

<!DOCTYPE wml PUBLIC "-//WAPFORUM//DTD WML 1.2//EN"
    "http://www.wapforum.org/DTD/wml_1.1.xml">

<wml>

<card id="InStock">
  <p>
    <table columns="2">
      <tr><td>Part</td><td>Number</td></tr>
      <tr><td><b>Keyboard</b></td><td><b>K441</b></td></tr>
      <tr><td>Mouse</td><td>Mo11</td></tr>
      <tr><td><b>Video Camera</b></td><td><b>V44b</b></td></tr>
      <tr><td>Monitor</td><td>M44a</td></tr>
    </table>
  </p>
</card>

</wml>
```

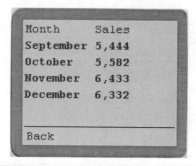

Figure 3-16 Bolding an entire table

When you load the application into the phone simulator, the simulator will display the output shown in Figure 3-17.

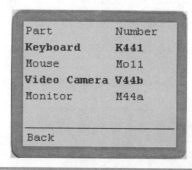

Figure 3-17 Displaying specific rows of a table using a bold font

Finally, the following WML application, LocalSource.wml, uses a table to display the names and graphics that correspond to several of the phone's local-source images:

```
<?xml version="1.0"?>

<!DOCTYPE wml PUBLIC "-//WAPFORUM//DTD WML 1.2//EN"
    "http://www.wapforum.org/DTD/wml_1.1.xml">

<wml>

<card id="LocalSrc">
  <p>
    <table columns="2">
      <tr><td>exclamation1</td><td>
        <imglocalsrc="exclamation1" src="bad.wbmp"
          alt="Missing" /></td></tr>
      <tr><td>exclamation2</td><td>
        <img localsrc="exclamation2" src="bad.wbmp"
          alt="Missing" /></td></tr>
      <tr><td>question1</td><td>
        <img localsrc="question1" src="bad.wbmp"
          alt="Missing" /></td></tr>
      <tr><td>question2</td><td>
        <img localsrc="question2" src="bad.wbmp"
          alt="Missing" /></td></tr>
      <tr><td>lefttri1</td><td>
        <img localsrc="lefttri1" src="bad.wbmp"
          alt="Missing" /></td></tr>
      <tr><td>righttri1</td><td>
        <img localsrc="righttri1" src="bad.wbmp"
```

3

```
          alt="Missing" /></td></tr>
<tr><td>lefttri2</td><td>
  <img localsrc="lefttri2" src="bad.wbmp"
    alt="Missing" /></td></tr>
<tr><td>righttri2</td><td>
  <img localsrc="righttri2" src="bad.wbmp"
    alt="Missing" /></td></tr>
<tr><td>littlesquare1</td><td>
  <img localsrc="littlesquare1" src="bad.wbmp"
    alt="Missing" /></td></tr>
<tr><td>littlesquare2</td><td>
  <img localsrc="littlesquare2" src="bad.wbmp"
    alt="Missing" /></td></tr>
<tr><td>isymbol</td><td>
  <img localsrc="isymbol" src="bad.wbmp"
    alt="Missing" /></td></tr>
<tr><td>wineglass</td><td>
  <img localsrc="wineglass" src="bad.wbmp"
    alt="Missing" /></td></tr>
<tr><td>speaker</td><td>
  <img localsrc="speaker" src="bad.wbmp"
    alt="Missing" /></td></tr>
<tr><td>dollarsign</td><td>
  <img localsrc="dollarsign" src="bad.wbmp"
    alt="Missing" /></td></tr>
<tr><td>moon1</td><td>
  <img localsrc="moon1" src="bad.wbmp"
      alt="Missing" /></td></tr>
<tr><td>bolt</td><td>
  <img localsrc="bolt" src="bad.wbmp"
      alt="Missing" /></td></tr>
<tr><td>medsquare1</td><td>
  <img localsrc="medsquare1" src="bad.wbmp"
      alt="Missing" /></td></tr>
<tr><td>medsquare2</td><td>
```

3

```
        <img localsrc="medsquare2" src="bad.wbmp"
           alt="Missing" /></td></tr>
<tr><td>littlediamond1</td><td>
    <img localsrc="littlediamond1" src="bad.wbmp"
       alt="Missing" /></td></tr>
<tr><td>littlediamond2</td><td>
    <img localsrc="littlediamond2" src="bad.wbmp"
       alt="Missing" /></td></tr>
<tr><td>bigsquare1</td><td>
    <img localsrc="bigsquare1" src="bad.wbmp"
       alt="Missing" /></td></tr>
<tr><td>bigsquare2</td><td>
    <img localsrc="bigsquare2" src="bad.wbmp"
       alt="Missing" /></td></tr>
<tr><td>littlecircle1</td><td>
    <img localsrc="littlecircle1" src="bad.wbmp"
       alt="Missing" /></td></tr>
<tr><td>littlecircle2</td><td>
    <img localsrc="littlecircle2" src="bad.wbmp"
       alt="Missing" /></td></tr>
<tr><td>wristwatch</td><td>
    <img localsrc="wristwatch" src="bad.wbmp"
       alt="Missing" /></td></tr>
<tr><td>plus</td><td>
    <img localsrc="plus" src="bad.wbmp"
       alt="Missing" /></td></tr>
<tr><td>minus</td><td>
    <img localsrc="minus" src="bad.wbmp"
       alt="Missing" /></td></tr>
<tr><td>star1</td><td>
    <img localsrc="star1" src="bad.wbmp"
       alt="Missing" /></td></tr>
<tr><td>uparrow1</td><td>
    <img localsrc="uparrow1" src="bad.wbmp"
       alt="Missing" /></td></tr>
```

```
    <tr><td>downarrow1</td><td>
      <img localsrc="downarrow1" src="bad.wbmp"
        alt="Missing" /></td></tr>
    <tr><td>circleslash</td><td>
      <img localsrc="circleslash" src="bad.wbmp"
        alt="Missing" /></td></tr>
    <tr><td>downtri1</td><td>
      <img localsrc="downtri1" src="bad.wbmp"
        alt="Missing" /></td></tr>
    <tr><td>uptri1</td><td>
      <img localsrc="uptri1" src="bad.wbmp"
        alt="Missing" /></td></tr>
    <tr><td>downtri2</td><td>
      <img localsrc="downtri2" src="bad.wbmp"
        alt="Missing" /></td></tr>
    <tr><td>uptri2</td><td>
      <img localsrc="uptri2" src="bad.wbmp"
        alt="Missing" /></td></tr>
  </table>
 </p>
</card>

</wml>
```

By expanding the LocalSource.wml application, you can create an application you can use to look up the name of a specific local-source image. When you load the application into the phone simulator, the simulator will display the output shown in Figure 3-18.

Figure 3-18   Displaying local-source images

Recipe.wml

Project 3-1: Creating a Virtual Cookbook

This WML application, Recipe.wml, will use a table to display the following recipe on a Web-enabled phone. By moving your favorite recipes on to the Wireless Web, you can view a recipe when you are at the grocery store shopping or you can quickly provide the recipe to your friends and family.

2	Eggs

Cups	Item
1	Shortening
3/4	Sugar
3/4	Brown Sugar
2	Choc. chips
2 1/4	Flour

Teaspoons	Item
2	Vanilla
1	Salt
1	Baking soda

Bake 8 to 10 minutes at 350 degrees F.

Step-By-Step

1. Using a text editor, create the file Recipe.wml. Type the following header information into the file, along with the tags to create a paragraph within a card named "Recipe":

```
<?xml version="1.0"?>

<!DOCTYPE wml PUBLIC "-//WAPFORUM//DTD WML 1.2//EN"
    "http://www.wapforum.org/DTD/wml_1.1.xml">

<wml>

<card id="Cookies">
 <p>
```

2. Use the following `<table>` tag to create a table with two columns:

```
<table columns="2">
```

3. Within the table, each row will consist of two data entries. Use the following WML tags to create the table (note the use of the bold tag, `<b>`, to highlight table headings):

```
<tr><td>2</td><td>Eggs</td></tr>
<tr><td><b>Cups</b></td><td><b>Item</b></td></tr>
<tr><td>1</td><td>Shortening</td></tr>
<tr><td>3/4</td><td>Sugar</td></tr>
<tr><td>3/4</td><td>Brown Sugar</td></tr>
<tr><td>2</td><td>Choc. chips</td></tr>
<tr><td>2 1/4</td><td>Flour</td></tr>
<tr><td><b>Teaspoons</b></td><td><b>Item</b></td></tr>
<tr><td>2</td><td>Vanilla</td></tr>
<tr><td>1</td><td>Salt</td></tr>
<tr><td>1</td><td>Baking soda</td></tr>
</table>
```

4. Type in the baking instructions, and then use the `</p>`, `</card>`, and `</wml>` tags to close the current paragraph, card, and the application. Your application should contain the following statements:

```
<?xml version="1.0"?>

<!DOCTYPE wml PUBLIC "-//WAPFORUM//DTD WML 1.2//EN"
    "http://www.wapforum.org/DTD/wml_1.1.xml">

<wml>

<card id="Cookies">
 <p>
   <table columns="2">
     <tr><td>2</td><td>Eggs</td></tr>
     <tr><td><b>Cups</b></td><td><b>Item</b></td></tr>
     <tr><td>1</td><td>Shortening</td></tr>
     <tr><td>3/4</td><td>Sugar</td></tr>
     <tr><td>3/4</td><td>Brown Sugar</td></tr>
     <tr><td>2</td><td>Choc. chips</td></tr>
     <tr><td>2 1/4</td><td>Flour</td></tr>
```

```
   <tr><td><b>Teaspoons</b></td><td><b>Item</b></td></tr>
   <tr><td>2</td><td>Vanilla</td></tr>
   <tr><td>1</td><td>Salt</td></tr>
   <tr><td>1</td><td>Baking soda</td></tr>
 </table>

 <br/>
 Bake 8 to 10 minutes at 350 degrees F
</p>
</card>

</wml>
```

Taking Advantage of Special Characters

When you display text within a WML application, there are several characters whose values have special meaning to WML that you cannot use. For example, the left and right angle brackets (<, >) signify the start and end of a tag. Likewise, the double quote character (") marks the start or end of a string. When you need to display such characters within your text, you must use the symbols shown in Table 3-3.

Character	Symbol	Example
&	&amp;	\Kris & Phil\
'	&apos;	\<i>It's his\</i>
>	&gt;	\<p>44 > 33\</p>
<	&lt;	\<p>33 < 44\</p>
Non-breaking space		\<p>Houston, Texas 77469\</p>
"	&quot;	\<p>"Hello, Wireless"\</p>
Soft hyphen	&shy;	\<p>Windows operating­system tools\</p>

Table 3-3   Special Symbols for WML-Based Text Output

The following WML application, ShowSymbols.wml, illustrates the use of the special-character symbols:

```
<?xml version="1.0"?>

<!DOCTYPE wml PUBLIC "-//WAPFORUM//DTD WML 1.2//EN"
    "http://www.wapforum.org/DTD/wml_1.1.xml">

<wml>

<card id="Symbols">
  <p>
    Programmers: Kris &amp; Phil<br/>
    Code: &quot;ShowSymbols&quot;<br/>
    Two  Spaces<br/>
    14.33 &lt; 33.44<br/>
  </p>
</card>

</wml>
```

When you load the ShowSymbols.wml application into the phone simulator, the simulator will display the output shown in Figure 3-19.

Depending on your application's output, there may be times when you must display other special symbols. In such cases, you can use the character's Unicode value. For example, to display the letter W, you would use W.

Figure 3-19   Displaying special character symbols

3

The following application, Unicode.wml, displays the message "Hello, Wireless" using Unicode values:

```
<?xml version="1.0"?>

<!DOCTYPE wml PUBLIC "-//WAPFORUM//DTD WML 1.2//EN"
    "http://www.wapforum.org/DTD/wml_1.1.xml">

<wml>

<card id="Unicode">
  <p>
    &#72;&#101;&#108;&#108;&#111;&#44;&#32;&#87;&#105;
    &#114;&#101;&#108;&#101;&#115;&#115;
  </p>

</card>

</wml>
```

When you load the Unicode.wml application into the phone simulator, the simulator will display the output shown in Figure 3-20.

| **Figure 3-20** | Displaying Unicode characters |

☑ *Mastery Check*

1. How would you use WML to center the company's name above their contact information:

   > Osborne/McGraw-Hill
   > 2600 Tenth Street
   > Berkeley, CA 94710
   > www.Osborne.com

2. If text does not fit on the current line of output, and you have used the `mode=nowrap` attribute, how will the microbrowser display the text?

3. Use WML to display the following text with the attributes shown:

   > **Osborne/McGraw-Hill**
   > 2600 Tenth Street
   > Berkeley, CA 94710
   > *www.Osborne.com*

4. How many colors do WBMP images support?

   _____

   _____

5. What happens when a phone does not support the local-source image you specify with an `<img>` tag?

   _____

   _____

6. Give two reasons why large WBMP images are a problem.

   _____

   _____

☑ *Mastery Check*

7. Create a WML table to display the following output:

Name	Office	Phone
Smith	3A	444-1221
Jones	2B	555-1111
Adams	3D	666-1112
Burns	2C	554-3331

8. Modify the WML you used to create the table in Question 7 to present the column headings in bold, as shown here:

Name	**Office**	**Phone**
Smith	3A	444-1221
Jones	2B	555-1111
Adams	3D	666-1112
Burns	2C	554-3331

9. How would you use WML to display the text "Our Price's"?

_____

_____

10. Write a WML statement to display the output: 4 * 5 < 21.

3

Module 4

Working with Multiple Cards and Variables

The Goals of This Module

- Create a WML application that uses two or more cards

- Use the **<go>** tag to direct the microbrowser to load and execute a specific card

- Use the **<do>** tag to specify the action the application will perform when a user presses the accept button

- Use the **<prev/>** tag to direct the microbrowser to reload the previous card

- Use the **<a>** tag to create a link to a card

- Use the **<setvar>** tag to assign a value to a variable

In Module 3, you learned how to use WML tags to format an application's output. You also learned how to organize information within tables and to display Wireless bitmap (WBMP) images. Thus far, the applications you have examined have consisted of one card. Programmers often refer to a WML application as a card deck, which implies that an application can consist of multiple cards. In this module, you will learn how to create multiple cards within a WML application and how to move from one card to another. You will also learn how to link from one card deck to another. In addition, this module will teach you how to use variables to store information as your application executes. You might use a variable to store a user's name, telephone number, or even the name of a card deck the user would like to view.

To start, you will learn to create WML applications that use two or more cards, and you will use the **<go>** and **<prev/>** tags to move between cards, much like you would move between links on a traditional Web page. Next, you will learn how to branch to a specific card that resides within a different WML deck. Then, you will learn how to use the **<setvar>** tag to assign values to variables and how to later access the variable's value. Finally, you will learn how to use the comment tag **<!--text-->** to place notes in your source code that explain to other programmers the processing that your application performs.

Using Two or More Cards

As your WML applications become more complex, you will often use individual cards to perform specific tasks. For example, one card may display a menu of options. Then, based on a user's menu selection, the application may load a second card that performs the user's desired task.

As the term *card deck* implies, a WML application can consist of more than one card. To create multiple cards within a WML application, you simply place multiple **<card>** and **</card>** tags within the WML file:

```
<card id="FirstCard">
</card>

<card id="SecondCard">
</card>
```

Each card within a WML card deck must have a unique name. When your application starts, the microbrowser will load and execute the contents of the first card it encounters. You can use several different WML tags to move from one card to the next. For example, the following **<go>** tag directs the microbrowser to load and execute the contents of a card named Two:

```
<go  href="#Two" />
```

Using the href attribute, you specify the name of the card or deck you want the microbrowser to load. If the card you desire resides in the current deck, you simply place a pound sign (#) in front of the card name. Names that identify only cards within a deck are called *fragments*, as opposed to names that specify decks. In the previous **<go>** tag, for example, the **#Two** is a fragment that corresponds to card Two within the current deck.

The following WML application, GoCardTwo.wml, uses the **<go>** tag to move from one card to another:

```
<?xml version="1.0"?>

<!DOCTYPE wml PUBLIC "-//WAPFORUM//DTD WML 1.2//EN"
    "http://www.wapforum.org/DTD/wml_1.1.xml">

<wml>

<card id="One" title="Card One">
  <p>
    In card One
    <do type="accept" label="Go to Two">
      <go href="#Two"/>
    </do>
  </p>
</card>

<card id="Two" title="Card Two">
  <p>
    In card Two
    <do type="accept" label="Go to One">
      <go href="#One"/>
    </do>
  </p>
```

4

```
</card>

</wml>
```

In this case, when the application begins, the microbrowser will load and execute the contents of card One, the first card it encounters. Card One will display a message that lets you know the microbrowser is executing the card's contents. The card will then display the "Go to Two" prompt on the phone's screen, as shown in Figure 4-1.

When the user presses the accept button that appears immediately beneath the prompt (or, if you are using the phone simulator, you click your mouse on the button), the microbrowser will load and execute the contents of card Two, which in turn displays a message and a prompt to return to card One, as shown in Figure 4-2.

If you examine cards One and Two in the previous application, you will find that each card uses the <do> tag. In general, the <do> tag tells the microbrowser what code to execute when a specific event occurs. In this case, the <do> tag tells the microbrowser what card to load when the user presses the accept button.

You will examine aspects of the <do> tag throughout this book, and we'll look next at the <do type="accept" label="accept_button_text"> tag shown in the previous application.

Figure 4-1   Displaying the prompt in the lower-left corner of the phone's screen

| Figure 4-2 | Using the <go> tag to branch to a second card |

4

Hint

When you name your cards, keep in mind that WML treats uppercase and lowercase letters as distinct. If you name a card AddressInfo, for example, you must later use the same uppercase and lowercase letters to branch to the card using an href attribute.

1-Minute Drill

● What is the purpose of the <go> tag?

● What is the purpose of the <do> tag?

Ask the Expert

Question: Is there a limit to the number of cards my application can use?

Answer: Yes and no. Although most browsers will not restrict the number of cards your application can use, you should keep in mind that the more cards your application contains, the more difficult your code may become for others to understand. If possible, you should

● The WML <go> tag directs the microbrowser to load the card (or deck) that the tag's href attribute specifies.
● The WML <do> tag directs the microbrowser to perform a specific operation, such as loading a new card when the user presses the accept button or reloading a previous card when the user presses the back button.

group related cards within their own decks. Then, using a **<go>** tag, for example, your application can move from deck to deck as necessary.

Question: Is there a limit on the amount of information I can put in a card?

Answer: Yes. Most microbrowsers have a limit on the size of a card. For many, that size is between 1KB and 2KB. That means you may have to break up large pieces of information into multiple cards. Further, if you include a WBMP image in a card, you decrease by the image's size the amount of text you can place in the card. Remember also that the microbrowser must download cards over slow Wireless connections— the larger the card, the longer the download time. Although current browsers are quite restrictive on the size of cards, limiting a card's size makes a degree of sense.

Understanding the <do type="accept" label="text"> Tag

As briefly discussed in earlier modules, programmers refer to the special button on the cellular phone that the user presses to select an option as the *accept button*. Within your applications, you will use the **<do>** tag to specify the operation a card should perform when the user presses the accept button. The format of the **<do>** tag you will use is as follows:

```
<do type="accept" label="text">
   <other tag>
</do>
```

Within the **<do>** tag, the **type="accept"** attribute setting tells the microbrowser that you are specifying the operation the card should perform when the user presses the accept button. The label attribute, in turn, lets you specify the text you want the browser to display on the phone's screen, above the button. The following tag, for example, directs the browser to display the word "Continue" above the button:

```
<do type="accept" label="Continue">
  <other tag>
</do>
```

The following WML application, Stooges.wml, uses four cards to display hello messages from each of the three stooges (Larry, Curly, and Moe):

```
<?xml version="1.0"?>

<!DOCTYPE wml PUBLIC "-//WAPFORUM//DTD WML 1.2//EN"
    "http://www.wapforum.org/DTD/wml_1.1.xml">

<wml>

<card id="Welcome" title="Welcome">
  <p align="center">
    Welcome<br/><br/>
    Nyuck, nuk, nuk<br/>
  </p>

  <do type="accept" label="Go to Larry">
    <go href="#Larry" />
  </do>

</card>


<card id="Larry" title="Larry">
  <p>
    Hello dere!<br/><br/>
    Larry
  </p>

  <do type="accept" label="Go to Curly">
    <go href="#Curly" />
  </do>
</card>


<card id="Curly" title="Curly">
  <p>
    Hello, hello<br/><br/>
```

4

```
    Curly
  </p>

  <do type="accept" label="Go to Moe">
    <go href="#Moe" />
  </do>
</card>


<card id="Moe" title="Moe">
  <p>
    Hello, hello, hello<br/><br/>
    Moe
  </p>

  <do type="accept" label="Go to Start">
    <go href="#Welcome" />
  </do>

</card>

</wml>
```

As you use the microbrowser to move through the cards, the phone simulator will display the screens shown in Figure 4-3.

When the application starts, the microbrowser loads and executes the Welcome card, which displays a welcome message to the user. The application uses the paragraph tag's align attribute to center the welcome text. Then it uses a **<do>** tag to display a prompt above the accept button for the user to continue with the Larry card. When the user presses the accept button, the application will load the Larry card, which displays the hello message from Larry and changes the accept-button prompt to direct the user to display information about Curly. When the user presses the accept button, the application will display Curly's hello message and prompt the user to display Moe's message. Finally, as shown in Figure 4-4, when

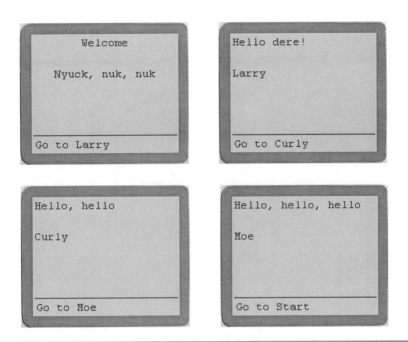

Figure 4-3   Viewing cards within the Stooges.wml application

the user presses the accept button to view Moe's message, the application displays the message and provides an option for the user to return to the card that started the application.

Hint

Depending on the microbrowser you are using, how the microbrowser will display a label above the accept button may differ. As a rule, you should choose short meaningful text for the labels you specify. In fact, to ensure that your labels display on the greatest number of phones, you should restrict your labels to five characters or less.

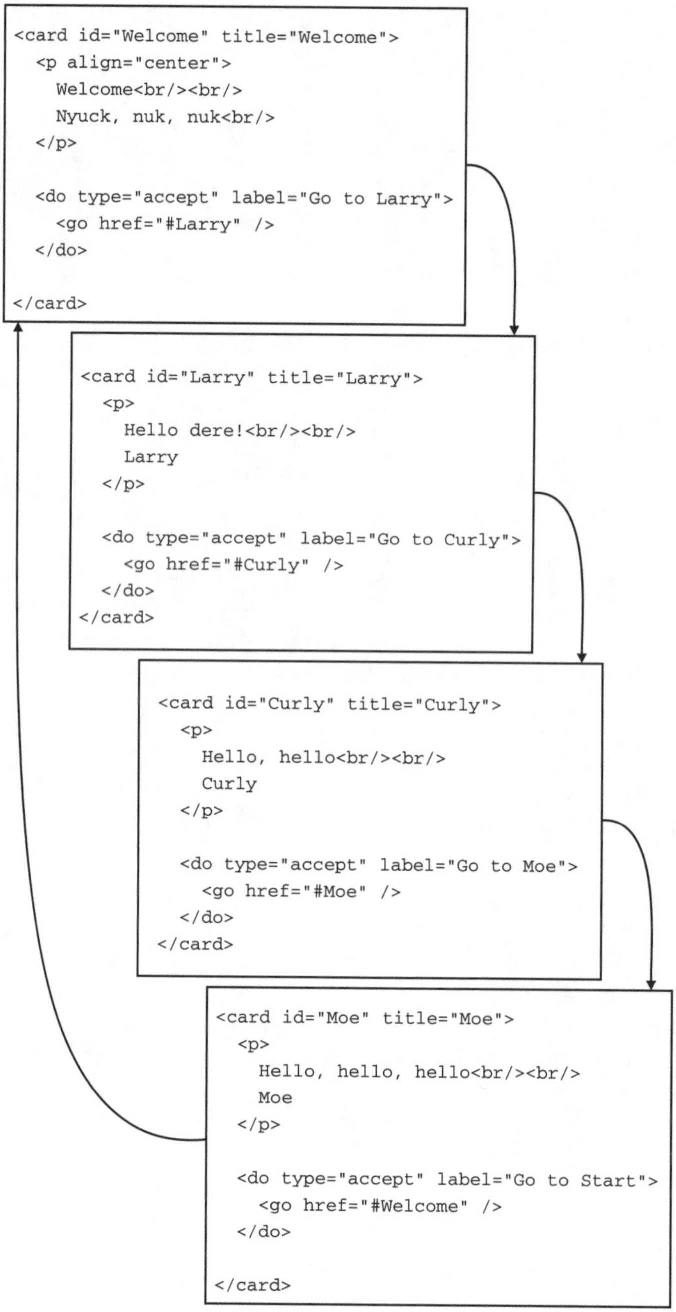

```
<card id="Welcome" title="Welcome">
  <p align="center">
    Welcome<br/><br/>
    Nyuck, nuk, nuk<br/>
  </p>

  <do type="accept" label="Go to Larry">
    <go href="#Larry" />
  </do>

</card>
```

```
<card id="Larry" title="Larry">
  <p>
    Hello dere!<br/><br/>
    Larry
  </p>

  <do type="accept" label="Go to Curly">
    <go href="#Curly" />
  </do>
</card>
```

```
<card id="Curly" title="Curly">
  <p>
    Hello, hello<br/><br/>
    Curly
  </p>

  <do type="accept" label="Go to Moe">
    <go href="#Moe" />
  </do>
</card>
```

```
<card id="Moe" title="Moe">
  <p>
    Hello, hello, hello<br/><br/>
    Moe
  </p>

  <do type="accept" label="Go to Start">
    <go href="#Welcome" />
  </do>

</card>
```

Figure 4-4   Traversing cards within the Stooges.wml application

Displaying a Week's Weather Report

In the previous section, you learned how to use the **<go>** tag to move from one card in a WML deck to the next. The following WML application, WeatherReport.wml, uses seven cards to display a weekly weather report:

```
<?xml version="1.0"?>

<!DOCTYPE wml PUBLIC "-//WAPFORUM//DTD WML 1.2//EN"
    "http://www.wapforum.org/DTD/wml_1.1.xml">

<wml>

<card id="Weather" title="Weather">
  <p align="center">
    Welcome to the<br/><br/>
    Weather Forecast<br/>
  </p>

  <do type="accept" label="View Monday">
    <go href="#Monday" />
  </do>

</card>


<card id="Monday" title="Monday">
  <p>
    <img localsrc="sun" src="" alt="Sunny" /><br/><br/>
    Monday<br/>
    Sunny<br/>
    High: 84<br/>
    Low: 58
  </p>

  <do type="accept" label="View Tuesday">
    <go href="#Tuesday" />
  </do>
</card>


<card id="Tuesday" title="Tuesday">
  <p>
    <img localsrc="sun" src="" alt="Sunny" /><br/><br/>
    Tuesday<br/>
```

```
      Sunny<br/>
      High: 88<br/>
      Low: 62
    </p>

    <do type="accept" label="View Wednesday">
      <go href="#Wednesday" />
    </do>
</card>


<card id="Wednesday" title="Wednesday">
  <p>
    <img localsrc="partcloudy" src="" alt="Cloudy" /><br/><br/>
    Wednesday<br/>
    Partly Cloudy<br/>
    High: 76<br/>
    Low: 52
  </p>

  <do type="accept" label="View Thursday">
    <go href="#Thursday" />
  </do>
</card>


<card id="Thursday" title="Thursday">
  <p>
    <img localsrc="cloud" src="" alt="Cloudy" /><br/><br/>
    Thursday<br/>
    Cloudy<br/>
    High: 69<br/>
    Low: 50
  </p>

  <do type="accept" label="View Friday">
    <go href="#Friday" />
  </do>
</card>


<card id="Friday" title="Friday">
  <p>
```

```
    <img localsrc="rain" src="" alt="Rain" /><br/><br/>
    Friday<br/>
    Rain<br/>
    High: 64<br/>
    Low: 52
  </p>

  <do type="accept" label="View Saturday">
    <go href="#Saturday" />
  </do>
</card>


<card id="Saturday" title="Saturday">
  <p>
    <img localsrc="partcloudy" src="" alt="Cloudy" /><br/><br/>
    Saturday<br/>
    Partly Cloudy<br/>
    High: 72<br/>
    Low: 54
  </p>

  <do type="accept" label="View Sunday">
    <go href="#Sunday" />
  </do>
</card>


<card id="Sunday" title="Sunday">
  <p>
    <img localsrc="sun" src="" alt="Sunny" /><br/><br/>
    Sunday<br/>
    Sunny<br/>
    High: 81<br/>
    Low: 60
  </p>

  <do type="accept" label="Main">
    <go href="#Welcome" />
  </do>
</card>

</wml>
```

When the application starts, the microbrowser will load and execute the contents of the Weather card (which is the card the application encounters first). From the Weather card, the user can branch to the Monday card which displays Monday's weather forecast. Within the Weather card, the application uses a <do> tag to place the prompt View Monday above the accept button. When the user presses the button, the microbrowser will load the Monday card. Using a <go> tag, the Monday card lets the user view the Tuesday card, which lets the user view the Wednesday card, and so on, as shown in Figure 4-5.

If you experiment with the Stooges.wml application and the WeatherReport. wml application, it will not take you long before you recognize the application's shortcomings. First, within each application you will quite likely want the ability to move backward as well as forward through the cards. Second, you

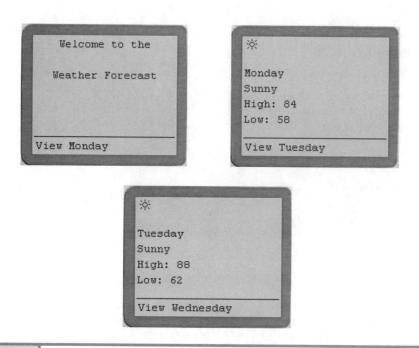

Figure 4-5   Traversing cards within the WeatherReport.wml application

might want the application to display a menu when it first starts, which you can use to select a specific card.

In the following section, you will learn how to move backward to a previous card, much like you would use the Back button within your browser as you surf the World Wide Web.

Moving Back to the Previous Card

Each of the previous applications used the **<go>** tag to move forward from one card to the next. Often, however, a user will want to return to a previous card.

To help users return to the previous card, many phones have a Back button that performs a **<prev/>** operation when pressed. However, to support phones that do not have a Back button, you can place the following **<do>** tag within a card, which uses the **<prev/>** tag to direct the browser to return to the previous card:

```
<do type="options" label="Back">
  <prev/>
</do>
```

When the microbrowser encounters the **<do>** tag, the microbrowser will display the label the tag specifies; in this case, the word "Back", above one of the phone's buttons. If the user presses the corresponding button, the microbrowser will reload the previous card. The following WML application, BackStooges.wml places **<do>** tags within several cards to allow the user to move forward and backward between the cards:

```
<?xml version="1.0"?>

<!DOCTYPE wml PUBLIC "-//WAPFORUM//DTD WML 1.2//EN"
    "http://www.wapforum.org/DTD/wml_1.1.xml">

<wml>

<card id="Welcome" title="Welcome">
  <p align="center">
```

```
      Welcome<br/><br/>
      Nyuck, nuk, nuk<br/>
    </p>

    <do type="accept" label="Go to Larry">
      <go href="#Larry" />
    </do>

</card>


<card id="Larry" title="Larry">
  <p>
    Hello dere!<br/><br/>
    Larry
  </p>

    <do type="accept" label="Go to Curly">
      <go href="#Curly" />
    </do>

    <do type="options" label="Back">
      <prev/>
    </do>

</card>


<card id="Curly" title="Curly">
  <p>
    Hello, hello<br/><br/>
    Curly
  </p>

    <do type="accept" label="Go to Moe">
      <go href="#Moe" />
    </do>

    <do type="options" label="Back">
      <prev/>
    </do>
```

```
</card>

<card id="Moe" title="Moe">
  <p>
    Hello, hello, hello<br/><br/>
    Moe
  </p>

  <do type="accept" label="Go to Start">
    <go href="#Welcome" />
  </do>

  <do type="options" label="Back">
    <prev/>
  </do>

</card>

</wml>
```

When you display the Larry card, for example, the microbrowser will place a prompt over one button that you can press to display the Curly card, and the microbrowser may display a Back prompt over a button you can press to return to the previous card, as shown in Figure 4-6.

| **Figure 4-6** | Using a Back button to return to a previous card |

Ask the Expert

Question: What is the purpose of the **<prev/>** tag?

Answer: The WML <prev/> tag directs the microbrowser to reload the previous card, giving the user the ability to back up one card.

Question: How does the tag **<do type="accept" label="text">** differ from the tag **<do type="prev">**?

Answer: The tag <do type="accept" label="text"> specifies the operation the microbrowser will perform when the user presses the accept button. In contrast, the tag <do type="prev"> specifies the operation the microbrowser will perform when the user presses the back button. Note that many microbrowsers will not let you specify a label within a <do type="prev"> tag.

Question: Does an application always have to return to the previous card when the user presses the back button, or can the application return to a different card?

Answer: Normally, an application will use the <prev /> tag to return to the previous card when the user presses a back button. Depending on the application's processing, however, there may be times when you will want the application to display a different card, such as the program's main card. In such cases, you can use the <go> tag to branch to the card you desire as shown here:

```
<do type="prev">
  <go href="#Cardname" />
</do>
```

Hint

When you use the type="options" attribute within a <do> tag, different microbrowsers may display the label you specify differently, and some microbrowsers may not display a label. If, for example, you want to display a "Yes" and "No" prompt to the user, you can use the tag <do type="accept" label="Yes"> to display the Yes prompt. Then, to display the No label, you can use the type="option" attribute within the tag as shown here: <do type="options" label="No">.

RecipeList.wml

Project 4-1: Putting Your Favorite Recipes on the Wireless Web

This WML application, RecipeList.wml, creates links to recipes that reside within their own card deck. By adding additional cards and links to the deck, you can easily place your favorite recipes on the Wireless Web, making them readily available for whenever you need them.

Step-By-Step

1. Using a text editor, create the file RecipeList.wml. Within the file, type in the following header information:

```
<?xml version="1.0"?>

<!DOCTYPE wml PUBLIC "-//WAPFORUM//DTD WML 1.2//EN"
    "http://www.wapforum.org/DTD/wml_1.1.xml">

<wml>
```

2. Create the card Recipes that uses <a> tags to create links to recipe cards:

```
<card id="Recipes">
 <p align="center">
    My Best Recipes<br/><br/>
```

```
</p>

<p>
  <a href="#ChocolateChip">Chocolate Chip Cookies</a>
  <a href="#RumBalls">Rum Balls</a>
</p>
</card>
```

3. Create a card for the chocolate chip cookie recipe that you created in Module 3. Within the card, use a <do> tag that lets the user return to the previous card:

```
<card id="ChocolateChip">
 <p align="center">
   Chocolate Chip<br/>
   Cookies<br/>
 </p>

 <p>
   <table columns="2">
     <tr><td>2</td><td>Eggs</td></tr>
     <tr><td><b>Cups</b></td><td><b>Item</b></td></tr>
     <tr><td>1</td><td>Shortening</td></tr>
     <tr><td>3/4</td><td>Sugar</td></tr>
     <tr><td>3/4</td><td>Brown Sugar</td></tr>
     <tr><td>2</td><td>Choc. chips</td></tr>
     <tr><td>2 1/4</td><td>Flour</td></tr>
     <tr><td><b>Teaspoons</b></td><td><b>Item</b></td></tr>
     <tr><td>2</td><td>Vanilla</td></tr>
     <tr><td>1</td><td>Salt</td></tr>
     <tr><td>1</td><td>Baking soda</td></tr>
   </table>

   <br/>
   Bake 8 to 10 minutes at 350 degrees F
 </p>

 <do type="options" label="Back">
   <prev/>
 </do>

</card>
```

4. Create a card for a rum ball recipe, which also uses a <do> tag to return to the previous card:

```
<card id="RumBalls">
 <p align="center">
   Rum Balls<br/>
 </p>

 <p>
   <table columns="2">
     <tr><td><b>Cups</b></td><td><b>Item</b></td></tr>
     <tr><td>1/2</td><td>Light rum</td></tr>
     <tr><td>1</td><td>Melted semisweet choc.</td></tr>
     <tr><td>1/4</td><td>Corn syrup</td></tr>
     <tr><td>3</td><td>Crushed vanilla wafers</td></tr>
     <tr><td>1</td><td>Sugar</td></tr>
     <tr><td>2</td><td>Diced coconut</td></tr>
   </table>

   <br/>
   Mix and roll into 1-inch balls, powder with brown sugar
 </p>

 <do type="options" label="Back">
   <prev/>
 </do>

</card>
```

4

5. Use the </wml> tag to mark the end of your deck.

Accessing Cards That Reside Outside of the Current Deck

As your WML applications become more complex, it will not be uncommon for one application to direct the microbrowser to load a second application. To load an "external" application whose cards reside in a different file, you simply change the href attribute. For example, the following application,

LoadDeck.wml, directs the microbrowser to load the contents of the file
SecondDeck.wml:

```
<?xml version="1.0"?>

<!DOCTYPE wml PUBLIC "-//WAPFORUM//DTD WML 1.2//EN"
    "http://www.wapforum.org/DTD/wml_1.1.xml">

<wml>

<card id="LoadDeck" title="LoadDeck">
  <p align="center">
    Welcome<br/><br/>
    to Deck One<br/>
  </p>

  <do type="accept" label="View Deck 2">
    <go href="SecondDeck.wml" />
  </do>

</card>

</wml>
```

As you can see, within the **<go>** tag, the application specifies a complete
pathname to the SecondDeck.wml file:

```
<do type="accept" label="View Deck 2">
  <go href="SecondDeck.wml" />
</do>
```

When you load the LoadDeck.wml application, the phone simulator will
display a message that tells you the LoadDeck.wml application is running, as
shown in Figure 4-7.

When you press the View Deck 2 accept button, the microbrowser will
load the SecondDeck.wml (which must reside in the same directory as the
LoadDeck.wml file), displaying a message as shown in Figure 4-8.

If the microbrowser cannot locate the external deck, the phone simulator
will display an error message similar to that shown in Figure 4-9. In such cases,

Figure 4-7 Viewing the LoadDeck.wml application

make sure the file resides within the directory path you have specified, and that you have spelled the file's name correctly.

The following code illustrates how you can change the SecondDeck.wml application to let the user return to the previous card which, in this case, directs the microbrowser to reload LoadDeck.wml:

```
<?xml version="1.0"?>

<!DOCTYPE wml PUBLIC "-//WAPFORUM//DTD WML 1.2//EN"
"http://www.wapforum.org/DTD/wml_1.1.xml">

<wml>

<card id="SecondDeck" title="SecondDeck">
<p align="center">
Hello from<br/><br/>
the Second deck<br/>
</p>

<do type="accept" label="Return to Deck 1">
<go href="LoadDeck.wml" />
</do>

</card>

</wml>
```

Figure 4-8 Viewing the SecondDeck.wml application

In this case, SecondDeck.wml also uses a **\<go\>** tag to direct the microbrowser to reload the previous application. The application could have also used the following statements, which use a **\<prev/\>** tag to reload the previous card (which in this case would correspond to LoadDeck.wml):

```
<do type="option" label="Back">
  <prev/>
</do>
```

As you will learn later in this module, to branch to a WML deck that resides on another Wireless Web site, simply specify the site's URL and card name within a **\<go\>** tag, as shown here:

```
<go href="http://www.Wireless.com/SomeDeck.wml">
```

Figure 4-9 If the microbrowser cannot locate a deck, it will display a file-not-found error message.

Likewise, to access a specific card within a remote deck, place the card name after a pound sign (#) as shown:

```
<go href="http://www.Wireless.com/SomeDeck.wml#CardName">
```

Using an Anchor to Create a Link

If you have created traditional Web sites using HTML, you have likely created links from one document to another. Within a WML application, you can use the **\<a>** tag to create a link. For example, the following entry creates a link to the search engine at www.WirelessLookup.com:

```
<a  href="www.WirelessLookup.com" >Search Engine</a>
```

In this case, the microbrowser will associate the link www.WirelessLookup. com with the text "Search Engine". Within the screen display, the microbrowser will surround the link with right and left brackets: [Search Engine]. Within the phone (or phone simulator), you use the up and down arrow keys to highlight the line containing the text. Then, to select the highlighted link, press the accept button.

Using the **\<a>** tag, you can create a link to another card or deck by using the href attribute to specify the name of the card you are linking to:

```
<a  href="#cardname">Link text</a>
```

Within the href attribute, the pound sign (#) indicates to the microbrowser the start of the card name. Most microbrowsers will highlight the text you specify for the link in some way. For example, the Openwave browser will group the text between left and right brackets, such as [Link text].

As briefly discussed, you can use the **\<a>** tag to branch to a card that resides within a different deck by specifying the deck name, followed by a pound sign and the card name you want to branch to:

```
<a  href="http://www.somesite.com/deckname#cardname">Link Text</a>
```

The following WML application, AnchorCardTwo.wml, uses the **\<a>** tag to direct the microbrowser to load and execute the contents of card Two. That card, in turn, uses the **\<a>** tag to branch back to card One:

```
<?xml version="1.0"?>
```

```
<!DOCTYPE wml PUBLIC "-//WAPFORUM//DTD WML 1.2//EN"
    "http://www.wapforum.org/DTD/wml_1.1.xml">

<wml>

<card id="One" title="Card One">
  <p>
    <a href="#Two">In card One</a>
  </p>
</card>

<card id="Two" title="Card Two">
  <p>
    <a href="#One">In card Two</a>
  </p>
</card>

</wml>
```

1-Minute Drill

● What is the purpose of the <a> tag?

● How does the WML <a> tag differ from the <go> tag?

The following WML application, SearchEngine.wml, illustrates the use of the <a> tag to create links to various Search Engines across the Wireless Web:

```
<?xml version="1.0"?>

<!DOCTYPE wml PUBLIC "-//WAPFORUM//DTD WML 1.2//EN"
    "http://www.wapforum.org/DTD/wml_1.1.xml">

<wml>

<card id="SearchEngine" title="SearchEngine">
  <p align="center">
    Wireless<br/>
    Search Engines<br/>
```

● The WML <a> tag creates a link the user can use to branch to a specific card, another deck, or to a specific card that resides within another deck.

● The WML <a> tag creates a link to a card. If the user selects the link, the microbrowser will load the corresponding card. The <go> tag, in contrast, directs the microbrowser to immediately branch to the specified card—the <go> tag does not create a link the user can select.

```
   </p>
   <p>
     <a href="http://www.wapWarp.com">WapWarp</a>
     <a href="http://m-find.com">m-find</a>
     <a href="http://www.WirelessLookup.com">WirelessLookup.com</a>
     <a href="http://mfinder.cellmania.com">M-finder</a>
   </p>
</card>

</wml>
```

When you load the SearchEngine.wml application into the phone simulator, the simulator will display the output shown in Figure 4-10. If you highlight a search engine within the list and press the accept button, the application will branch to the corresponding search engine, displaying the site's opening screen.

By editing the Search Engine application, you can create an application that gives you your favorite links from one easy-to-use location.

Creating a Link to a Card Within an External Deck

In the previous examples, you learned how to use the <a> tag to create a link to a card within the current deck and to a remote deck. By specifying a card's name after a pound sign (#) when you specify an external deck within the href attribute, you can create a link to a specific card within that deck. For example,

| **Figure 4-10** | Using the <a> tag to create a link |

assume that you have the WML application CityInfo.wml, which displays information about key cities, as shown here:

```
<?xml version="1.0"?>

<!DOCTYPE wml PUBLIC "-//WAPFORUM//DTD WML 1.2//EN"
    "http://www.wapforum.org/DTD/wml_1.1.xml">

<wml>

<card id="Houston">
  <p align="center">
    Houston<br/>
  </p>
  <p>
    Area code: 281, 713<br/>
    Airport: Bush (IAH), Hobby<br/>
    Basketball: Rockets<br/>
    Football: Texans<br/>
    Baseball: Astros<br/>
    Newspaper: Chronicle
  </p>

  <do type="options" label="Back">
    <prev/>
  </do>

</card>


<card id="NewYork">
  <p align="center">
    New York<br/>
  </p>
  <p>
    Area code: 212<br/>
    Airport: JFK, La Guardia, Newark<br/>
    Basketball: Knicks<br/>
    Football: Jets, Giants<br/>
    Baseball: Mets, Yankees<br/>
    Newspaper: Times
  </p>
```

```
    <do type="options" label="Back">
      <prev/>
    </do>

</card>

<card id="Seattle">
  <p align="center">
    Seattle<br/>
  </p>
  <p>
    Area code: 206<br/>
    Airport: Sea Tac<br/>
    Basketball: Sonics<br/>
    Football: Seahawks<br/>
    Baseball: Mariners<br/>
    Newspaper: Times
  </p>

  <do type="options" label="Back">
    <prev/>
  </do>

</card>

</wml>
```

Now assume that you are creating an application that displays information about a business that resides in Seattle. Rather than creating a card within the CityInfo.wml application, which contains the information about Seattle, you can instead simply place a link to the external card. To link to the Seattle card within the CityInfo.wml application, you can use the **<a>** tag as follows:

```
<a href="CityInfo.wml#Seattle">About Seattle</a>
```

The following WML application, SeattleBiz.wml, displays information about a Seattle company and then uses the **<a>** tag to link to the Seattle card within the CityInfo.wml application:

```
<?xml version="1.0"?>

<!DOCTYPE wml PUBLIC "-//WAPFORUM//DTD WML 1.2//EN"
```

```
      "http://www.wapforum.org/DTD/wml_1.1.xml">

<wml>

<card id="SeattleBusiness">
  <p align="center">
    Seattle's Best<br/>
    Software and Coffee<br/>
  </p>
  <p>
    122 Main Street<br/>
    Seattle, WA 98888<br/>
    206-555-1212<br/>
    www.NoBugsAndGrounds.com<br/>

    <a href="CityInfo.wml#Seattle">About Seattle</a>
  </p>
</card>

</wml>
```

If you load the application within the phone simulator, the simulator will display information about the company, as shown in Figure 4-11. If you then select the About Seattle link, the simulator will load and execute the information contained in the external card.

Side Effects When Linking

When you link to a card that resides within another deck, you must consider links that exist on that card, because your user may get lost traversing the other

Figure 4-11   Linking to an external card

deck's cards. For example, the following application, AStooges.wml, uses the
<a> tag to create links to the cards Curly, Larry, and Moe that appear in the deck
BackStooges.wml:

```
<?xml version="1.0"?>

<!DOCTYPE wml PUBLIC "-//WAPFORUM//DTD WML 1.2//EN"
    "http://www.wapforum.org/DTD/wml_1.1.xml">

<wml>

<card id="UseCardFragment ">
  <p align="center">
    Hello Stooges<br/>
  </p>
  <p>
    <a href="backstooges.wml#Larry">Hello from Larry</a>
    <a href="backstooges.wml#Curly">Hello from Curly</a>
    <a href="backstooges.wml#Moe">Hello from Moe</a>
  </p>
</card>

</wml>
```

   When you load the AStooges.wml application into the phone simulator,
the simulator will display the links for Larry, Curly, and Moe, as shown in
Figure 4-12. If you highlight and select a link, the microbrowser will load
and execute the corresponding card. Within each card, a **<prev>** tag lets

Figure 4-12   Links within an external card may let the user travel to cards you did
not intend the user to visit.

you return to the AStooges.wml application. Keep in mind, however, that the cards within the BackStooges.wml application also let you move between that deck's cards. Take time to experiment with the application, moving between cards. If, for example, you view the Moe card, you can select the Return to Start link, which, as you might not expect, takes you to the opening screen of the BackStooges.wml application. When you link to a card within another deck, you need to be aware of such "side effects" that may confuse the user.

Storing Information in Variables

As your WML applications execute, there will be many times when the application must store information, such as a user's name, movie-ticket information, airline arrival and departure times, and so on. To store information as they execute, WML applications place the information into one or more named storage locations called *variables*.

Within an application, each variable must have a unique name. The name you select for a variable should accurately describe the information the variable contains, such as UserName, CurrentDate, MovieTicket, FlightNumber, and so on. Unlike other programming languages that require you to declare a variable (by specifying the variable's name and the type of value the variable will store, such as a number or string of characters) before you can use the variable, in WML you define a variable simply by assigning a value to the variable. To assign a value to a variable, you can use the tags listed in Table 4-1. As you will learn in Module 8, you can also assign values to WML variables using various WMLScript library functions. When you assign a value to a new variable within a WML application, meaning a variable you have not yet used, WML will allocate storage space to store the variable's value. If you instead assign a value to an existing

Tag	Description	Example
<input>	Assigns the value a user types at the keypad to the variable whose name the tag specifies.	<input name="UserId">
<setvar>	Assigns a value to the variable whose name the tag specifies.	<setvar name="PhoneNumber" value="555-1212">

Table 4-1   WML Tags That Assign Values to Variables

variable, WML will essentially toss out the variable's current value, replacing it with the new value.

For example, the following statement uses the **<setvar>** tag to assign a value to the variable called Message:

```
<setvar name="Message" value="Hello Wireless People!" />
```

The **<setvar>** tag uses two attributes. The name attribute specifies the variable to which the tag assigns the value. The value attribute specifies the value the application will assign to the variable. Note that the **<setvar>** tag is a single tag that contains a slash. There is no **</setvar>** tag.

In a similar way, the following **<setvar>** statement assigns a value to a variable named City:

```
<setvar name="City" value="Houston" />
```

1-Minute Drill

● What is a variable?

● How do you create a variable within a WML application?

Ask the Expert

Question: How do you assign a value to a variable within a WML application?

Answer: To assign a value to a variable in WML, you use the **<setvar>** or **<input>** tags.

Question: How do you access the value stored in a WML variable?

Answer: To access the value stored in a WML variable, you simply precede the variable name with a dollar sign ($VariableName).

● A variable is a named storage location within which an application can store information, such as the user's name, address, phone number, or the price of an item the user wants to order.

● To create a variable within a WML application, you simply use the variable's name in a <setvar> or <input> tag.

Naming Your Variables

WML has some requirements for variable names. A variable name begins with a letter or an underscore, such as _UserName. In WML, a variable name cannot begin with a number; however, the name can use numbers after the first character. The following are valid variable names within WML:

- UserName

- _PhoneNumber

- AddressPart2

- Windows2000

- _2ndImage

When you create a variable name, keep in mind that WML is case sensitive. As such, WML considers the following variable names distinct:

- UserName

- USERNAME

- Username

- username

When you name variables within a WML application, choose names that meaningfully describe the information the variables contain. For example, the following **<setvar>** tag assigns a value to a variable named x:

```
<setvar name="x" value="555-1212" />
```

Based on the information in the **<setvar>** tag, you can assume that the application is assigning a phone number to the variable x. Consider, instead, how using a more meaningful name makes the processing easier to understand:

```
<setvar name="OfficePhoneNumber" value="555-1212" />
```

Because the variable name OfficePhoneNumber is more meaningful than x, the code becomes easier to understand.

If you examine the following statements, which display several variables' values, you should find the two statements that use meaningful variable names much easier to understand than the two statements that do not:

```
<p>
  $P<br/>
  $PhoneNumber<br/>
  $A<br/>
  $Address
</p>
```

1-Minute Drill

● Why is the variable name 4Items invalid?

WML Variables Store Character Strings

Unlike other programming languages that let you store specific types of values within variables, such as integer numbers (0, 1, 2, 3, …) and floating-point numbers (3.14159), WML variables only store character-string values. For example, the following **<setvar>** tag assigns the value 19.99 to the variable named Price:

```
<setvar  name="Price"  value="19.99" />
```

As you can see, the **<setvar>** tag places the value 19.99 within double quotes, which makes the value a character string (as opposed to a floating-point value). If you try to eliminate the quotes around the value within the **<setvar>** tag, the WML browser will generate an error.

Using the Value a Variable Contains

You now know how to assign a value to a variable, but you will eventually want to use the value that the variable contains. To access a variable's value, simply

---

● WML variable names cannot begin with a number. They must start with a letter or underscore character.

precede the variable's name with a dollar sign ($VariableName). For example, the following statements will display the value stored in the variable named Message:

```
<p>
  $Message
</p>
```

Using <setvar> to Assign a Value to a Variable

When you use the **<setvar>** tag to assign a value to a variable, you must place the tag within a **<go>**, **<prev>**, or **<refresh>** tag. You cannot, for example, simply place a **<setvar>** tag within a paragraph. Should you try to do so, the microbrowser will generate a syntax error and will not execute your application.

The following WML application, HelloVariable.wml, uses the **<setvar>** tag to assign a value to the Message variable. In this case, the **<setvar>** tag appears within a **<go>** tag, which branches control to a card named ShowVariable. Within the ShowVariable card, the code displays the value the variable contains using $Message:

```
<?xml version="1.0"?>

<!DOCTYPE wml PUBLIC "-//WAPFORUM//DTD WML 1.2//EN"
    "http://www.wapforum.org/DTD/wml_1.1.xml">

<wml>

<card id="HelloVariable">
  <p>
    About to create the variable.
  </p>

  <do type="accept" label="View Variable">
    <go href="#ShowVariable">
      <setvar name="Message" value="Hello, Wireless People!" />
    </go>
  </do>
```

```
</card>

<card id="ShowVariable">
  <p>
    $Message
  </p>

  <do type="options" label="Back">
    <prev/>
  </do>
</card>

</wml>
```

When you load the HelloVariable.wml application into the phone simulator, the simulator will display the output shown in Figure 4-13.

Changing a Variable's Value

Variables are so named because an application can change (vary) their values as the application executes. The following WML application, RestaurantInfo.wml, displays a menu from which a user can select his or her favorite food. Based on the user's menu selection, the application branches to a specific card. Within the card, the application assigns the corresponding food type to the variable Food. In addition, the card will assign a suggested restaurant to the variable Restaurant.

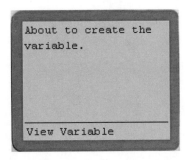

Figure 4-13 | Assigning a value to and displaying the contents of the Message variable

Ask the Expert

Question: Is there a way to restrict an application's knowledge of a variable to just one card?

Answer: No. When you create a variable within a WML application, you essentially create a global variable whose value is accessible and can be changed by any card in the deck, as well as by other decks the application may call. Programmers refer to an application's current variables as the application's *context*. Any card can access information stored in the context. You can, however, use the `newcontext="true"` attribute setting within a card to direct the microbrowser to discard the current context and, hence, to discard the current variables.

Then, the application calls a card named Recommendation that displays each variable's contents:

```
<?xml version="1.0"?>

<!DOCTYPE wml PUBLIC "-//WAPFORUM//DTD WML 1.2//EN"
    "http://www.wapforum.org/DTD/wml_1.1.xml">

<wml>

<card id="RestaurantInfo">
  <p align="center">
    Welcome<br/>
    Restaurant Finder<br/>
  </p>
  <p>
    <a href="#Chinese">Chinese</a>
    <a href="#Indian">Indian</a>
    <a href="#Italian">Italian</a>
    <a href="#Mexican">Mexican</a>
  </p>
</card>

<card id="Chinese">
  <p>
```

```
    Select Chinese?
  </p>

  <do type="accept" label="Yes">
    <go href="#Recommendation">
      <setvar name="Food" value="Chinese" />
      <setvar name="Restaurant" value="Grand Dragon 800-555-1212" />
    </go>
  </do>

  <do type="unknown" label="No">
    <prev/>
  </do>

</card>

<card id="Indian">
  <p>
    Select Indian?
  </p>

  <do type="accept" label="Yes">
    <go href="#Recommendation">
      <setvar name="Food" value="Indian" />
      <setvar name="Restaurant" value="Taj Mahal 888-555-1212" />
    </go>
  </do>

  <do type="unknown" label="No">
    <prev/>
  </do>

</card>

<card id="Italian">
  <p>
    Select Italian?
  </p>

  <do type="accept" label="Yes">
    <go href="#Recommendation">
      <setvar name="Food" value="Italian" />
      <setvar name="Restaurant" value="Vinos 212-555-1212" />
    </go>
```

4

```
      </do>

      <do type="unknown" label="No">
         <prev/>
      </do>

   </card>

   <card id="Mexican">
      <p>
         Select Mexican?
      </p>

      <do type="accept" label="Yes">
         <go href="#Recommendation">
            <setvar name="Food" value="Mexican" />
            <setvar name="Restaurant" value="La Comida 713-555-1212" />
         </go>
      </do>

      <do type="unknown" label="No">
         <prev/>
      </do>

   </card>

   <card id="Recommendation">
      <p>
         For the best $Food, try:<br/><br/>
         $Restaurant
      </p>

      <do type="accept" label="Back">
         <go href="#RestaurantInfo"></go>
      </do>
   </card>

</wml>
```

When you load the RestaurantInfo.wml application into the phone simulator, the simulator will display the menu shown in Figure 4-14.

Assuming the user selects Italian as his or her favorite type of food, the application will then display the message shown in Figure 4-15.

Figure 4-14 Displaying a menu of food types to the user

After the user views the restaurant information, the application will return the user to the main menu. If the user selects a different food type, the application will display information about a different restaurant, by changing each variable's contents.

Understanding the Variable Context

When you use a variable within a WML application, the microbrowser reserves memory to store the variable's value. Programmers refer to the region of memory the microbrowser uses for an application as the application's context. Each time you use a different variable, the microbrowser allocates space for the new variable within the context.

To help you better manage the application's context, WML lets you use the <card> tag's newcontext attribute. When an application sets the attribute's

Figure 4-15 Displaying restaurant information for the user's favorite type of food

value to "true", the microbrowser will discard its current context and create a new context. Many applications will use the newcontext variable in the application's first card. The following statements, for example, will reset the application context when the browser loads the corresponding card:

```
<card id="FirstCard"  newcontext="true">

</card>
```

When a card uses the newcontext attribute, the microbrowser will discard the context each time it loads the card, which will cause the microbrowser to discard existing variables. In Module 5, you will use the `<input>` tag to assign values to variables. At that time, you may want to use the newcontext attribute within cards that prompt the user for input. Otherwise, the cards may display a variable's preexisting value when they prompt the user to enter a new value.

Viewing Variables with the Phone Simulator's Console Window

When you test WML applications that use variables, there will be times when you will want to know a variable's current value. One way to display a variable's value as you test your programs is simply to show the value within a card's output:

```
<p>
  Username contains $Username
</p>
```

If you are using a phone simulator to test your application, you may be able to display information about the application's variables within the simulator's console window. For example, if you are using the Openwave phone simulator, you can display the current variables (which programmers refer to as the current context) by selecting the Info | Vars menu option.

The following WML application, AssignVariables.wml, assigns information about this book to several different variables using the `<setvar>` tag. The application then uses the ShowVars card to display the information. Figure 4-16 illustrates the output the Openwave phone simulator's console window displays if you direct the simulator to display current variable values when the ShowVars card is active.

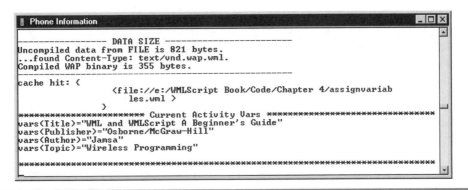

Figure 4-16 Viewing variable information within the phone simulator's console window

Using Comments to Explain Your Application's Processing

As your WML applications become more complex, it will become very important that you place comments within your code that explain the processing the code performs. By placing comments in your code, you make it much easier for another programmer (or yourself, for that matter) to understand an application's processing before he or she tries to make changes to the code. To place a comment within your code, you use a comment tag, the format of which is as follows:

```
<!-- Comment text here -->
```

Comments within your application exist for the benefit of programmers who must read and understand your code. Comments do not impact your application's processing in any way. When the microbrowser encounters a comment within your application, the microbrowser will simply ignore the information the comment contains.

Depending on the information you want to include, a comment can span several lines. For example, the following comment explains the processing that a **<do>** tag performs:

```
<!-- Display the Yes prompt above the accept button. If the
     user presses the button, the application will assign values
```

```
           to the variables Food and Restaurant and will then branch to
           the card named Recommendation that displays information based
           on the user's choices -->
<do type="accept" label="Yes">
  <go href="#Recommendation">
    <setvar name="Food" value="Mexican" />
    <setvar name="Restaurant" value="La Comida 713-555-1212" />
  </go>
</do>
```

As a rule, the more comments you place in your application, the easier your application will be for others to understand. At a minimum, you may want to place comments at the start of each card, like the following, to explain the card's processing:

```
<!--
Card: CardName
Purpose: Display information about a user's restaurant selections.
Written by: Kris Jamsa
Date Written: 9/30/01
Last Change: 11/8/01: Display food type.
Variables used: Food, Restaurant
-->
```

As programmers try to remove errors from their code (debug their code), they often find it convenient to disable sections of code in order to locate the problem. For example, if you are having trouble finding a syntax error, it might be convenient to temporarily remove statements from your application as you hunt down the cause of the error. This is another place where comments can be useful. Often, programmers will use comments to "comment out" or disable a section of code.

For example, assume that you are looking for a syntax error in your application, and you have a card you do not want the microbrowser to compile. By placing a comment around the card, you direct the microbrowser to ignore the card.

To comment out a card in this way, simply place the characters `<!--` at the start of the card and the characters `-->` after the card, as shown here:

```
<!--
<card id="SomeCard">
  <p>
      Home: 555-1212<br/>
      Work: 800-555-1212<br/>
  </p>
</card>
-->
```

4

☑ *Mastery Check*

1. When a WML deck contains two or more cards, which card does the microbrowser load first?

_____

_____

2. What is the purpose of the following **<do>** tag?

```
<do type="accept" label="Go">
  <go href="#PhoneList" />
</do>
```

_____

_____

3. What is the purpose of the **<prev />** tag?

_____

_____

4. Create a WML application named GoThere.wml that uses the **<a>** tag to create links to the following sites:

- http://www.WirelessLookup.com
- http://mobile.sports.com
- http://wap.goshop.com

5. What is a variable?

_____

_____

6. What two WML tags assign values to variables?

_____

_____

☑ Mastery Check

7. How do you display a WML variable's value?

_____

_____

8. Create a WML application that assigns the current day, month, and year to the variables Day, Month, and Year, and then uses the ShowDate card to display the current date.

9. Why should you place comments in your code?

_____

_____

4

Module 5

Performing User Input Operations

The Goals of This Module

- Learn to use the **\<input>** tag to get data from the user

- Understand and use formatting strings within an **\<input>** tag

- Use the **\<select>** tag to display a menu of options

- Use the **\<option>** tag within a **\<select>** statement to specify a menu option

- Understand and handle WML events, such as the onpick event, which occurs when a user chooses a **\<select>** tag option

- Use templates to simplify the amount of code you must place within a card

As your WML applications become more complex, they will need to interact with the user. For example, your application may require that the user provide a username and password before he or she can access a site, or your application may prompt the user to enter items for a to-do list. To get such information from a user, a WML application uses an **<input>** tag to assign the information the user enters to a variable. In this module, you will learn how to use the **<input>** tag within your application. In addition, this module will examine the **<select>** tag, which you can use to display a menu of options. Using the **<input>** and **<select>** tags, your WML applications can easily interact with the user.

Performing Input Operations

As your WML applications become more complex, they will perform input operations (using the **<input>** tag) to get data from the user. Users can type their responses using the phone's numeric keypad. As you will learn in this module, the **<input>** tag supports eight attributes, which Table 5-1 briefly describes.

Attribute	Purpose
accesskey	Specifies a key, typically from 0 through 9, that the user can press to select the corresponding link.
emptyok	If true, the user does not have to enter a value. By default, the user must enter a value for each <input> tag.
format	Specifies an input mask that controls the type and number of characters the user can input.
maxlength	Specifies the maximum number of characters the user can input.
name	Specifies the name of a variable to which WML assigns the user input.
size	Specifies to the microbrowser the number of characters in the input field.
tabindex	Specifies an index the microbrowser may use as a navigation aid so the user can tab between input elements. Most browsers ignore this attribute.
type	Lets you select a password operation for which the application will display asterisks (*) for each character the user types.
value	Specifies a default value.

Table 5-1 Attributes of the <input> Tag

As explained in Module 4, when an application uses an **\<input\>** tag to get information from the user, the **\<input\>** tag will assign the data the user enters to a variable specified using the name attribute in the **\<input\>** tag. In its simplest form, the **\<input\>** tag uses only the name attribute to specify the variable to which the application will assign the user input:

```
<input  name="VariableName">
```

Normally, an application will display a prompt using text within a paragraph, and then use the **\<input\>** tag to assign the user's input to a variable. The following statements, for example, will prompt the user to enter his or her name. Using the **\<input\>** tag, the application will assign the user's input to the variable Username:

```
<p>
  Enter your name:
  <input  name="Username">
</p>
```

The following WML application, HelloInput.wml, uses the previous statements to prompt the user for his or her name. Again, using the **\<input\>** tag, the application assigns the information the user types to the variable Username. Then, the application uses the variable to display a personalized greeting to the user:

```
<?xml version="1.0"?>

<!DOCTYPE wml PUBLIC "-//WAPFORUM//DTD WML 1.2//EN"
    "http://www.wapforum.org/DTD/wml_1.1.xml">

<wml>

<card id="HelloInput">
  <p>
    Enter your name:

    <input name="Username" />

    Hello, $Username
  </p>
</card>

</wml>
```

When you load the HelloInput.wml application into the phone simulator, the simulator will display the prompt for the user to enter his or her name, as shown in Figure 5-1. After the user responds to the prompt, the application will use the information in the Username variable to display a hello message.

Restricting the Number of Characters the User Can Input

By default, when an application prompts the user for input, the user can type in as many characters as he or she desires. Normally, however, your applications will want to restrict the number of characters to an amount that corresponds to the value. For example, an application might limit a user to 20 characters for the user's last name and 50 characters for a Web address.

To restrict the number of characters a user can type, you can use the **<input>** tag's maxlength attribute. The following statement, for example, will restrict the number of characters the user can enter for the user's name to 20:

```
<input name="Username" maxlength="20">
```

The following WML application, GetSite.wml, uses the **<input>** tag to prompt the user for the address of a WML card. Using the maxlength attribute,

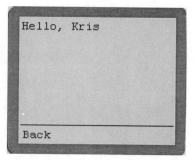

Figure 5-1 Using an <input> tag to get a user's name

the application restricts the address to 30 characters. After the user enters the address, the application tries to load the address using a **\<go\>** tag:

```
<?xml version="1.0"?>

<!DOCTYPE wml PUBLIC "-//WAPFORUM//DTD WML 1.2//EN"
    "http://www.wapforum.org/DTD/wml_1.1.xml">

<wml>

<card id="GetSearchEngine">
  <p>
    <b>Enter Search Engine:</b>

    <input name="Site" value="http://www.WirelessLookup.com"
           maxlength="30"/>
    <do type="accept" label="Go">
       <go href="$(Site:noesc)" />
    </do>

  </p>
</card>

</wml>
```

Using a phone simulator, execute the GetSite.wml application. When the application prompts you for a site address, specify one of the WML applications you have previously created. For example, assuming that your applications reside in a folder named WMLAps on drive C:, you might type `file://c:/WMLAps/MyInfo.wml`. Or, you might try specifying a remote site, such as `http://www.WirelessLookup.com`. If the microbrowser is unable to locate the application you specify, the microbrowser will display an error message similar to that shown in Figure 5-2.

Within GetSite.wml, note the **\<go\>** element that directs the microbrowser to load the site the user enters:

```
<go href="$(Site:noesc)" />
```

Figure 5-2   A microbrowser error message for a file or site not found

The "noesc" characters that follow the variable name in the previous statement direct the microbrowser not to replace any characters the variable may contain. The statement uses the noesc directive because the variable contains a URL, which may contain characters such as a forward slash (/), which separates directory names, as well as hexadecimal values for unique symbols. The noesc directive instructs the microbrowser to process the characters exactly as they appear. In addition to the noesc directive, you can use "escape", which directs the microbrowser to replace non-alphanumeric characters with hexadecimal codes, and "unesc", which directs the microbrowser to replace hexadecimal codes with the corresponding character. Most microbrowsers let you abbreviate the directives using the letters n, e, and u.

The previous application forced the user to precede a site's name with the "http://". Rather than forcing the user to type this information, you can simply precede the variable that contains the site name with the text within the href statement, as shown here:

```
<go href="http://$(Site:noesc)" />
```

Further, you might use the following statement to let the user enter only the site name, such as WirelessLookup, as opposed to a complete name, such as www.WirelessLookup.com:

```
<go href="http://www.$(Variable).com" />
```

In Module 8, you will learn how to use WMLScript to parse a user's input so you can determine which part of the URL the user has specified. Then, your program can precede the user's input with fields such as "http://" as necessary.

Using a Microbrowser-Specific Input Field

Depending on the microbrowser you are using, you may be able to use the `<input>` tag's size attribute to influence how the microbrowser displays the input field within which the user will type data. For example, a microbrowser might display the input field using reverse video, to give the user a visual cue for the number of characters he or she can enter. Unfortunately, most microbrowsers ignore the size attribute. The following WML application, InputSize.wml, uses the size attribute to suggest an input field size of 12 characters:

```
<?xml version="1.0"?>

<!DOCTYPE wml PUBLIC "-//WAPFORUM//DTD WML 1.2//EN"
    "http://www.wapforum.org/DTD/wml_1.1.xml">

<wml>

<card id="SizeDemo">

  <p>
    Field size demo<br/>
    Enter text:

    <input name="Data" size="12" maxlength="12"/>

    You typed: $Data
  </p>
</card>

</wml>
```

Keep in mind that the size attribute only suggests an input field size to the microbrowser. The size attribute does not restrict the number of characters the user can input. To do that, you use the maxlength attribute, discussed previously.

Specifying a Title for the Input Field

Like many WML tags, the `<input>` tag lets you specify a title for an input field that the microbrowser may display in some way on the phone screen. However, the microbrowser may simply ignore the tag. The following statement, directs the microbrowser to display the title "Get Username" when the application prompts the user to enter his or her name:

```
<input name="Username" title="Get Username">
```

Prompting the User for a Password

To improve their security, many applications will prompt the user to enter a password before they grant the user with access to specific data. When a user must type a password, applications normally do not display the letters that the user types. Instead, applications display an asterisk (*) each time the user types a character. That way, should another person view the user's input, that person will not see the user's password.

To prompt the user to enter a password, WML applications use the `<input>` tag's `type="password"` attribute, as shown here:

```
<input name="SecretPassword" type="password">
```

The following WML application, InputPassword.wml, prompts the user to enter a password. After the user types in his or her password, the application uses the Password variable to display the information the user has typed:

```
<?xml version="1.0"?>

<!DOCTYPE wml PUBLIC "-//WAPFORUM//DTD WML 1.2//EN"
    "http://www.wapforum.org/DTD/wml_1.1.xml">

<wml>

<card id="PasswordDemo">

  <p>
    Password:
```

```
    <input name="SecretPassword" type="password" />

    You typed: $SecretPassword
  </p>
</card>

</wml>
```

When you load InputPassword.wml into the phone simulator, the application will prompt you to enter a password. As you type, the application will display an asterisk for each character you input, as shown in Figure 5-3.

If you run this application using the phone simulator, which means you can type your password using a keyboard, you will likely think that the application is similar to many PC-based applications. However, if you try running the application on a Web-enabled cell phone, for which you must type on the phone's numeric keypad, you may find that the application's display of asterisks, as opposed to the letters you type, makes it very difficult for you to tell which letters you have typed.

Because typing on a phone's numeric keypad is difficult under the best situations, most users will find that having asterisks appear on their screen, as opposed to the letters they select, makes an input operation nearly impossible. Because of the phone's small display and the fact that the user can easily move the phone out of the view of others, you normally will not need to use the `<input>` tag's `type="password"` attribute.

Figure 5-3   Displaying asterisks (*) via the <input> tag's type="password" attribute

Providing a Default Input Value

Depending on the information you want the user to provide, there may be times when you can simplify an input operation for the user by providing a default value. To specify a default value, you use the <input> tag's value attribute. For example, the following statement prompts the user to enter his or her favorite food. In this case, the <input> tag uses the value attribute to specify Italian food as the default:

```
<p>
  Enter your favorite<br/>
  food :
  <input  name="Food"  value="Italian" />

</p>
```

When the phone simulator executes these statements, it would display the prompt for the user's favorite food, providing Italian as the default, as shown in Figure 5-4. To select the default value, the user can simply press the accept button. To specify a different food type, the user should first press the CLR key to delete the default value, and then type in the food type they desire.

The following WML application, SearchEngine.wml, prompts the user to enter the Web address of the search engine he or she desires. Within the <input> tag, the application provides WirelessLookup.com as the default.

Figure 5-4   Using the <input> tag's value attribute to specify a default value

After the user enters a search engine, the application uses a **<go>** tag to direct the microbrowser to branch to the corresponding site:

```
<?xml version="1.0"?>

<!DOCTYPE wml PUBLIC "-//WAPFORUM//DTD WML 1.2//EN"
    "http://www.wapforum.org/DTD/wml_1.1.xml">

<wml>

<card id="GetSearchEngine">
  <p>
    <b>Enter Search Engine:</b>

    <input name="Site" value="http://www.WirelessLookup.com" />

    <do type="accept" label="Go">
       <go href="$(Site:noesc)" />
    </do>

  </p>
</card>

</wml>
```

5

Ask the Expert

Question: I would like to add online help support to my applications. How can I create a help link within WML?

Answer: Creating a help link within a WML application is actually quite easy. To start, you create a standard card that contains your help text::

```
<card  id="OnlineHelp">
  <p>
    Enter your first name followed by a space and then your last name.<br/>
    Then, press the accept button to continue.
  </p>
```

Next, place a **<do>** tag in the card that needs a link to the online help:

```
<do  type="options"  label="Help">
  <go  href="#OnlineHelp" />
</do>
```

Depending on your application's complexity, you may provide online help links within each card. You can place links to additional help topics within your online help text.

Controlling Input Format

When a WML application performs an input operation using an **<input>** tag, WML assigns the data the user enters to a variable. As you learned in Module 4, WML variables only store character strings, as opposed to integer or floating-point numbers.

Many applications, however, will prompt the user to enter a numeric value, such as a three-digit area code. Likewise, many applications may require formatted data, such as a date in the form mm-dd-yy. In such cases, the application can use the **<input>** tag's format attribute to specify a "mask" that forces the user to enter data in a specific format.

Within the format attribute, you specify one or more of the formatting characters described in Table 5-2.

Format Specifier	Purpose
A	Forces uppercase input. Allows punctuation symbols.
a	Forces lowercase input. Allows punctuation symbols.
M	Allows any symbol, number, or uppercase character (the microbrowser may change the character to lowercase).
m	Allows any symbol, number, or lowercase character (the microbrowser may change the character to uppercase).
N	Forces numeric (0–9) input.
X	Allows any symbol, number, or uppercase character.
x	Allows any symbol, number, or lowercase character.

Table 5-2 Formatting Characters for Use with the <input> Tag's Format Attribute

Hint

In Module 8, you will learn how to use WMLScript functions to process the contents of a string. Using WMLScript, you can easily convert a string to uppercase or lowercase. You may, therefore, eliminate the burden on the user of entering text using a specific case, and, instead, use WMLScript to put the data in the format that your application requires.

The following WML application, ThreeUpper.wml, uses the `<input>` tag with the "A" formatting character to restrict the user to entering exactly three uppercase letters. (Note, however, that the "A" formatting character allows the user to enter symbols. Should the user type a lowercase letter, the microbrowser will automatically convert the character to uppercase.)

5

```
<?xml version="1.0"?>

<!DOCTYPE wml PUBLIC "-//WAPFORUM//DTD WML 1.2//EN"
    "http://www.wapforum.org/DTD/wml_1.1.xml">

<wml>

<card id="ThreeUpper">
  <p>
    <b>Enter 3 Uppercase Letters:</b>

    <input name="Letters" format="AAA" />

    You entered $Letters
  </p>
</card>

</wml>
```

Take time to experiment with this application, trying to enter numbers and other characters.

The following WML application, TwoLower.wml, uses the "aa" formatting characters to restrict the user to entering exactly two lowercase letters. (Note, however, that the "a" formatting character allows the user to enter symbols.

Should the user type an uppercase letter, the microbrowser will automatically convert the character to lowercase.)

```
<?xml version="1.0"?>

<!DOCTYPE wml PUBLIC "-//WAPFORUM//DTD WML 1.2//EN"
    "http://www.wapforum.org/DTD/wml_1.1.xml">

<wml>

<card id="TwoLower">
  <p>
    <b>Enter 2 Lowercase Letters:</b>

    <input name="Letters" format="aa" />

    You entered $Letters
  </p>
</card>

</wml>
```

Controlling Empty Strings

Depending on the information an application needs the user to provide, there may be times when it is okay for the user to not specify a value. By default, however, when an application performs an input operation, the microbrowser will not let the user continue until a value is specified.

For cases when the application does not require that the user provide input for a value, you can assign the value "true" to the `<input>` tag's emptyok attribute. For example, the following WML application, EmptyOK.wml, uses the emptyok attribute to let the user not enter his or her age:

```
<?xml version="1.0"?>

<!DOCTYPE wml PUBLIC "-//WAPFORUM//DTD WML 1.2//EN"
    "http://www.wapforum.org/DTD/wml_1.1.xml">

<wml>

<card id="EmptyOK">
```

```
<p>
  <b>Enter Your Name:</b>

  <input name="Username" format="M14m"/>

  <b>Enter Your Age:</b>

  <input name="Age" format="NN" emptyok="true" />

  You entered $Username, $Age
</p>
</card>

</wml>
```

5

As you can see, the application first prompts the user to enter his or her name. Because the first <**input**> tag does not specify the emptyok attribute, the user must provide input. Note that the <**input**> tag uses the format "M14m" to force the user to start the name with an uppercase letter. The second <**input**> tag, in contrast, uses the emptyok attribute to direct the microbrowser to let the application continue if the user chooses not to enter a value. In Module 7, you will learn how to use WMLScript functions to examine the information the user enters. An application might, for example, display one list of movies to users under the age of 17 and a second list to adult viewers.

1-Minute Drill

● How do you specify a default value for an input operation?

● What is the purpose of the <**input**> tag's emptyok attribute?

● To specify a default value for an input operation, you use the <**input**> tag's value attribute. The following tag, for example, specifies the default age of 21:

```
<input name="Age" value=21 />
```

● When set to "true", the <**input**> tag's emptyok attribute tells the microbrowser that it is okay if the user does not provide input for the value. By default, the microbrowser will not continue the application's execution until the user provides input.

Structuring Input Format

Depending on an application's purpose, there will be times when you must structure the input to a specific format. For example, the application may need to prompt the user to enter a phone number in the form NNN-NNN-NNNN. Table 5-3 describes several different format specifiers.

To prompt the user to enter a three-digit area code, followed by a seven-digit phone number, you can direct the microbrowser to display the dash character (-) between values by placing a backslash character in front of the dash, as shown here:

```
<input name="Phone" format="NNN\-NNN\-NNNN" />
```

The following WML application, GetPhone.WML, uses the preceding format to prompt the user for a phone number:

```
<?xml version="1.0"?>

<!DOCTYPE wml PUBLIC "-//WAPFORUM//DTD WML 1.2//EN"
    "http://www.wapforum.org/DTD/wml_1.1.xml">

<wml>

<card id="GetPhoneNumber">
  <p>
    <b>Enter Your Phone #:</b>

    <input name="Phone" format="NNN\-NNN\-NNNN" />

    You entered $Phone
  </p>
</card>

</wml>
```

When you load the application into the phone simulator, the simulator will process your first three digits (the area code) and then display a dash. Then, after you enter the next three characters, the simulator will display a second dash. As shown in Figure 5-5, the **<input>** tag will assign characters you specify after the backslash to the variable, along with the user input.

Format	Result
3N	Allows up to three numeric characters
NNN	Requires exactly three numeric characters
AANN	Requires exactly two uppercase letters followed by two numeric characters
NNN\-NNN\-NNNN	Requires numbers in the format of a three-digit area code followed by a seven-digit phone number
NN\-NN-\NN	Requires a user to enter numbers in the form month, day, year (MM-DD-YY)

Table 5-3   Examples of <input> Tag Format Specifiers

5

Depending on your preferences, you may want to make the area code stand out within the phone number by grouping the three area-code digits within parentheses, as shown here:

```
<input name="Phone" format="\(NNN\)\-NNN\-NNNN" />
```

Repeating a Formatting Code a Specific Number of Times

As your applications perform input operations, there will be times when you want the user to enter from one to five characters. In such a case, you can use a format specifier such as "5X". Likewise, to let the user enter from one to three

Figure 5-5   Adding dashes to a phone number

numbers, you would use "3N". It is important that you understand the difference between "3N" and "NNN". The format specifier "3N" lets the user enter from one to three numbers. In contrast, the format specifier "NNN" specifies that the user must enter exactly three numbers. The following WML application, NNN.wml illustrates the use of the "NNN" and "3N" format specifiers:

```
<?xml version="1.0"?>

<!DOCTYPE wml PUBLIC "-//WAPFORUM//DTD WML 1.2//EN"
    "http://www.wapforum.org/DTD/wml_1.1.xml">

<wml>

<card id="NNN">
  <p>
    <b>Testing NNN:</b>
    <input name="First" format="NNN" />

    <b>Testing 3N:</b>
    <input name="Second" format="3N" />

    You entered $First, $Second
  </p>
</card>

</wml>
```

Within the application, the first **<input>** tag requires the user to enter exactly three numbers. The second **<input>** tag, in contrast, lets the user enter from one to three numbers.

1-Minute Drill

- How can you limit the number of characters a user can input?
- What is the purpose of the asterisk (*) in the format specification "*A"?

- To limit the number of characters a user can input, use the <input> tag's maxlength attribute.
- The asterisk within an <input> tag's format specification tells the microbrowser that the user can enter any number of characters. The specifier "*A" tells the microbrowser that the user can enter any number of uppercase characters.

Using the \<select\> Tag to Create a Menu of Choices

Although cell phone–based applications can be very convenient, many users will find typing with the phone's keypad a very frustrating experience. Further, as you just learned, in order to perform specific processing based on a user's input, you must use WMLScript. As an alternative to forcing the user to type options using the keypad, your application can use a **\<select\>** tag to create a menu of options from which the user can select their choice. Using the **\<select\>** tag, you specify the name of a variable to which WML assigns a value that corresponds to the user's selection.

To specify the choices that appear within the **\<select\>** tag, you use one or more **\<option\>** tags. Within each **\<option\>** tag, you use the value attribute to specify the value that WML will assign to the **\<select\>** tag's variable when the user selects a specific choice:

```
<option  value="ValueAssigned">Option Menu Text</option>
```

The following WML application, GetDay.wml, uses a **\<select\>** tag to let the user select the current day of the week. After the user selects a day, WML assigns the user's selection to the variable Day:

```
<?xml version="1.0"?>

<!DOCTYPE wml PUBLIC "-//WAPFORUM//DTD WML 1.2//EN"
    "http://www.wapforum.org/DTD/wml_1.1.xml">

<wml>

<card id="DayOfWeek">
  <p>
    <select name="Day">
      <option value="Sunday">Sunday</option>
      <option value="Monday">Monday</option>
      <option value="Sunday">Tuesday</option>
```

```
      <option value="Wednesday">Wednesday</option>
      <option value="Thursday">Thursday</option>
      <option value="Friday">Friday</option>
      <option value="Saturday">Saturday</option>
    </select>
    You selected $Day
  </p>
</card>
</wml>
```

When you load the GetDay.wml application into the phone simulator, the simulator will first display the menu options, as shown in Figure 5-6. Then, based on the user's selection, the application displays the day that corresponds to the user's choice.

The following WML application, Meetings.wml, uses a **<select>** tag to let the user choose a day from Monday through Friday. Based on the user's

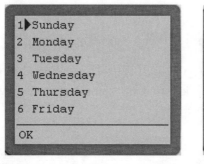
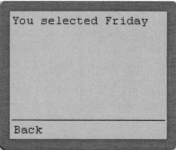

Figure 5-6   Using a <select> tag to create a menu of options

selection, the application loads a card that displays the user's appointments for that day:

```
<?xml version="1.0"?>

<!DOCTYPE wml PUBLIC "-//WAPFORUM//DTD WML 1.2//EN"
    "http://www.wapforum.org/DTD/wml_1.1.xml">

<wml>

<card id="Meetings">
  <p>
    <select name="Day">
      <option value="#Monday">Monday</option>
      <option value="#Tuesday">Tuesday</option>
      <option value="#Wednesday">Wednesday</option>
      <option value="#Thursday">Thursday</option>
      <option value="#Friday">Friday</option>
    </select>
    <do type="accept">
      <go href="$(Day:noesc)" />
    </do>
  </p>
</card>

<card id="Monday">
  <p>
    8:30 Board Breakfast<br/>
   12:30 Conference (Jim)<br/>
    4:15 Sales meeting
  </p>
</card>
```

5

```
<card id="Tuesday">
  <p>
    9:30 Flight to NY<br/>
    7:30 Dinner (Alfredos)
  </p>
</card>

<card id="Wednesday">
  <p>
    8:30 Radio show<br/>
    1:00 Lunch (Carlise)
  </p>
</card>

<card id="Thursday">
  <p>
    6:30 Flight to LA<br/>
    4:30 Interview (Times)
  </p>
</card>

<card id="Friday">
  <p>
    8:30 Flight Home<br/>
    7:30 Movie
  </p>
</card>

</wml>
```

When you load the Meetings.wml application into the phone simulator, the simulator will display a menu with options for Monday through Friday, as shown in Figure 5-7. After you select an option, the application will use a **<go>** tag to load a card that displays that day's appointments.

Assigning an Index Value that Corresponds to a User's Selection

In the previous section, you used the name attribute within a **<select>** tag to assign the **<option>** tag value to a variable that corresponds to a user's selection. By using the **<select>** tag's iname attribute, you can specify a variable to

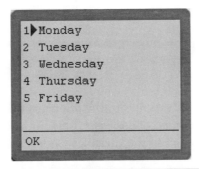

Figure 5-7	Using a <select> tag to display meetings for a specific day

which WML will assign a numeric value, from 1 to n, which corresponds to the user's selection:

```
<select name="Choice" iname="NumericChoice">
```

For example, if the user selects the first option, WML will assign thevariable the value 1. If the user selects the second or third option, WML will assign the variable the value 2 or 3, respectively. The following WML application, iname.wml illustrates the use of the iname attribute:

```
<?xml version="1.0"?>

<!DOCTYPE wml PUBLIC "-//WAPFORUM//DTD WML 1.2//EN"
    "http://www.wapforum.org/DTD/wml_1.1.xml">

<wml>

<card id="inameDemo">
  <p>
    <select name="Choice" iname="NumericChoice">
      <option value="#First">First</option>
      <option value="#Second">Second</option>
      <option value="#Third">Third</option>
      <option value="#Fourth">Fourth</option>
      <option value="#Fifth">Fifth</option>
    </select>
```

```
   You chose $Choice, Option $NumericChoice
  </p>
</card>

</wml>
```

When you load the application into the phone simulator, the simulator will first display a menu of options. Then, based on your selection, the simulator will show the values assigned to the variables Choice and NumericChoice, as shown in Figure 5-8.

Hint

Depending on your application's requirements, there may be times when you want to specify a specific option in a `<select>` tag as the default. To specify a default value, you can use the `<select>` tag's value attribute, to which you assign the value of the option you desire, or you can use the ivalue attribute, to which you assign the index value of the option you desire. Unfortunately, microbrowsers do not treat `<select>` tag default values consistently.

Letting the User Choose Multiple <select> Tag Options

The previous examples have used the **<select>** element to let the user choose one option from a menu list. There may be times, however, when you may want users to select one or more options. In such cases, you can use the **<select>** tag's multiple attribute. When you set the multiple attribute to "true", the

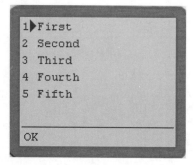
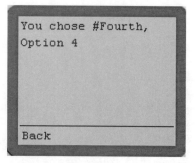

Figure 5-8   Getting a numeric index value for the option chosen in a
`<select>` statement

microbrowser will let the user select multiple options. When the multiple attribute is "false", the default, the user can select only one option. When the user selects two or more options, the microbrowser will assign each option's value to the **<select>** tag variable, separated by a semicolon.

The following WML application, GetLunch.wml, uses the multiple attribute within a **<select>** tag to let the user choose multiple options:

```
<?xml version="1.0"?>

<!DOCTYPE wml PUBLIC "-//WAPFORUM//DTD WML 1.2//EN"
    "http://www.wapforum.org/DTD/wml_1.1.xml">

<wml>

<card id="GetLunch">
  <p>
    <select name="Items" multiple="true">
      <option value="Burger">Burger</option>
      <option value="Fries">Fries</option>
      <option value="Coke">Coke</option>
    </select>

    <do type="accept" label="Order">
      <go href="#Order" />
    </do>

  </p>
</card>

<card id="Order">
  <p>
    You ordered: $Items
  </p>
</card>

</wml>
```

Depending on your microbrowser, the way the **<select>** statement will display selected and unselected items may differ. If, for example, you load GetLunch.wml into the phone simulator, the simulator will display a circle for unselected items and an x for selected items, as shown in Figure 5-9. After you press the accept button, which contains the Order label, the application will display the items you selected.

Figure 5-9 Selecting multiple options within a <select> tag

Hint

Like many WML attributes, the `<select>` tag supports a title attribute, whose value the microbrowser may display when the `<select>` tag is active. By assigning a meaningful name to `<select>` tags using the title attribute, you may simplify troubleshooting an application later, because users who are having difficulty or confusion with the application can refer to the menu by name.

GroceryChecklist.wml

Project 5-1: Checking Off Grocery List Items as You Shop

In Module 2, you created a simple application that displayed a list of items to pick up from the grocery store. This WML application, GroceryChecklist.wml, uses a `<select>` element with the multiple attribute set to "true" to let you check off items as you put them in your cart. To check off an item, you simply highlight the item in the list and then press the accept button.

Step-By-Step

1. Using a text editor, create the file GroceryChecklist.wml. Type the following header information into the file:

```
<?xml version="1.0"?>

<!DOCTYPE wml PUBLIC "-//WAPFORUM//DTD WML 1.2//EN"
    "http://www.wapforum.org/DTD/wml_1.1.xml">

<wml>
```

2. Use a `<card>` tag to create the card CheckList:

```
<card id="CheckList">
  <p>
```

3. Within the card, use the following `<select>` statement to list the items you need to purchase:

```
<select name="Items" multiple="true">
  <option value="Milk">Milk (half gallon)</option>
  <option value="Eggs">Eggs (large)</option>
  <option value="Chicken">Chicken</option>
  <option value="Pizza">Cheese Pizza</option>
  <option value="Beer">Beer</option>
</select>
```

4. Use the `</card>` tag to end your card and the `</wml>` tag to end the deck. Your application should now contain the following statements:

```
<?xml version="1.0"?>

<!DOCTYPE wml PUBLIC "-//WAPFORUM//DTD WML 1.2//EN"
    "http://www.wapforum.org/DTD/wml_1.1.xml">

<wml>

<card id="CheckList">
  <p>
    <select name="Items" multiple="true">
      <option value="Milk">Milk (half gallon)</option>
      <option value="Eggs">Eggs (large)</option>
      <option value="Chicken">Chicken</option>
      <option value="Pizza">Cheese Pizza</option>
      <option value="Beer">Beer</option>
    </select>

  </p>
</card>

</wml>
```

5

Grouping Options Within a <select> Tag

As you have learned, by using the **<select>** tag you can display a menu of options to a user. Often, you may want to create submenus. For example, in the previous fast-food example, you might want to give the user the opportunity to order not just a hamburger, but also a cheeseburger or veggie burger. In such cases, you can create a Burger menu option, which, when the user selects it, displays the Hamburger, Cheeseburger, and Veggie burger options.

To create a submenu within a **<select>** statement, you can create *option groups* by placing the submenu options within an **<optgroup>** element. Within the **<optgroup>** element, you use the title attribute to specify the menu option the user will select to display the submenu. The following statements, for example, create two option groups, one for weekdays and one for the weekend:

```
<select>
  <optgroup title="Weekdays">
    <option value="Monday">Monday</option>
    <option value="Tuesday">Tuesday</option>
    <option value="Wednesday">Wednesday</option>
    <option value="Thursday">Thursday</option>
    <option value="Friday">Friday</option>
  </optgroup>
  <optgroup title="Weekend">
    <option value="Saturday">Saturday</option>
    <option value="Sunday">Sunday</option>
  </optgroup>
</select>
```

The following WML application, BetterMenu.wml, uses option groups to create a better fast-food menu:

```
<?xml version="1.0"?>

<!DOCTYPE wml PUBLIC "-//WAPFORUM//DTD WML 1.2//EN"
```

```
             "http://www.wapforum.org/DTD/wml_1.1.xml">

<wml>

<card id="BetterMenu">
  <p>
    <select name="Items" multiple="true">
      <optgroup title="Burger">
        <option value="Hamburger">Hamburger</option>
        <option value="Cheeseburger">Cheeseburger</option>
        <option value="Veggieburger">Veggie Burger</option>
      </optgroup>

      <option value="Fries">Fries</option>

      <optgroup title="Soda">
        <option value="Coke">Coke</option>
        <option value="Sprite">Sprite</option>
        <option value="Rootbeer">Root beer</option>
      </optgroup>
    </select>

    <do type="accept" label="Order">
      <go href="#Order" />
    </do>

  </p>
</card>

<card id="Order">
  <p>
    You ordered: $Items
  </p>
</card>

</wml>
```

Ask the Expert

Question: My microbrowser does not support option groups. What else can I do?

Answer: If your microbrowser does not support option groups, but you want to provide users with the simplicity of submenus, you simply must spread your select statements across multiple cards. Based on the option the user selects, you will branch to a specific card, which, in turn, uses a second `<select>` tag to create a submenu.

Unfortunately, not all microbrowsers support option groups. Some, for example, will simply ignore the option group names and will, instead, simply display the entire menu list. Others will correctly display the submenu of items when you select an option group title.

1-Minute Drill

● What is the purpose of the `<select>` tag's multiple attribute?

● When a `<select>` tag uses the multiple attribute, how does the microbrowser assign multiple selections to the `<select>` tag variable?

Understanding Field Sets

In the previous section, you learned how to use option groups to organize related menu options. You can similarly use *field sets* to direct the microbrowser to group related card content. (Unfortunately, different microbrowsers support field sets differently, and some microbrowsers do not support them at all.)

Suppose that you have a card that prompts the user to enter personal information, such as his or her name, phone numbers, and address:

```
<card id="GetInput">
 <p>
   Enter your name:
```

● The `<select>` tag's multiple attribute lets the user select multiple options within a select statement.
● When a user selects multiple options within a `<select>` tag, the microbrowser will assign each option's value to the `<select>` tag variable, separating each value with a semicolon.

```
    <input name="Name" />

    Home Phone:
    <input name="HomePhone" />

    Work Phone:
    <input name="WorkPhone" />

    Cell Phone:
    <input name="CellPhone" />

    Street:
    <input name="Street" />

    City:
    <input name="City" />

    State:
    <input name="State" />

    <do type="accept" label="Show">
       <go href="#ShowInfo" />
    </do>

  </p>
</card>
```

Using field sets, you can direct the microbrowser to organize the related information so that it displays related prompts in a manner more meaningful to the user. The following application, FieldSet.wml, uses the `<fieldset>` tag to organize the input prompts. Again, depending on the microbrowser you are using, the application's output may appear differently:

```
<?xml version="1.0"?>

<!DOCTYPE wml PUBLIC "-//WAPFORUM//DTD WML 1.2//EN"
    "http://www.wapforum.org/DTD/wml_1.1.xml">

<wml>

<card id="FieldSetDemo">
  <p>
```

```
     Enter your name:
     <input name="Name" />

     <fieldset title="Phone Information">
        Home Phone:
        <input name="HomePhone" />

        Work Phone:
        <input name="WorkPhone" />

        Cell Phone:
        <input name="CellPhone" />
     </fieldset>

     <fieldset title="Address Information">
        Street:
        <input name="Street" />

        City:
        <input name="City" />

        State:
        <input name="State" />
     </fieldset>

     <do type="accept" label="Show">
        <go href="#ShowInfo" />
     </do>

  </p>
</card>

<card id="ShowInfo">
  <p>
     You entered:<br/>
     $Name<br/>
     $HomePhone<br/>
     $WorkPhone<br/>
```

```
    $CellPhone<br/>
    $Street<br/>
    $City<br/>
    $State<br/>
  </p>
</card>

</wml>
```

Understanding Events

As a WML application executes, a variety of events can occur. For example, a user can enter one card (for which WML generates an onenterforward event), the user can then move to a second card, and possibly later return to the first card (an onenterbackward event). Further, if the application uses a `<select>` tag to display a menu of choices, a user will choose one of several options (an onpick event). Finally, as you will learn in this module, WML lets you set a timer that expires at a specific time interval (which creates an ontimer event).

To improve an application's capabilities, WML lets you specify code that executes when such events occur. Table 5-4 briefly describes the events WML supports.

Event	Description
Onenterbackward	Occurs when the microbrowser reloads a card as the result of a `<prev/>` operation
Onenterforward	Occurs when the microbrowser loads a card for an operation other than `<prev/>`, such as a `<go>` or `<anchor>` operation
Onpick	Occurs when a user chooses an option from within a `<select>` element
Ontimer	Occurs when a user-specified timer occurs

Table 5-4   WML Events

WML Events Can Trigger Specific Tasks

Within an application, WML lets you specify code that executes when an event occurs. Specifically, WML events can launch the tasks listed in Table 5-5.

Reviewing the <go> and <prev/> Events

Throughout this book, you have used the **<go>** tag to direct the microbrowser to load and execute a specific card. Likewise, you have used the **<prev/>** tag to direct the microbrowser to reload and execute the previous card. The following WML application, GoPrev.wml, illustrates the use of the **<go>** and **<prev/>** tags.

To start, the First card displays a message and prompts you to press the accept button. When you press the button, the card uses the **<go>** tag to load the Second card. Within the Second card, if you press the Back button, the card

Event	Purpose
<go>	Directs the microbrowser to load and execute a specific card
<noop>	Directs the microbrowser to do nothing—to perform no operation
<prev>	Directs the microbrowser to reload the previous card
<refresh>	Directs the microbrowser to refresh the display so that it reflects the most recent values assigned to variables

Table 5-5   Tasks an Event Can Launch

will use a **<prev/>** tag to direct the microbrowser to reload the previous card, which, in this case, is the card named First:

```
<?xml version="1.0"?>

<!DOCTYPE wml PUBLIC "-//WAPFORUM//DTD WML 1.2//EN"
    "http://www.wapforum.org/DTD/wml_1.1.xml">

<wml>

<card id="First">
  <p>
    Hello from First<br/>
    Press Go<br/>
    to continue

    <do type="accept" label="Go">
       <go href="#Second" />
    </do>
  </p>
</card>

<card id="Second">
  <p>
    Second says Hello<br/>
    Press Back<br/>
    to continue

    <do type="options" label="Back">
```

5

```
        <prev/>
      </do>
   </p>
</card>

</wml>
```

Understanding the <noop> Tag

Within a WML application, there will be times when you want the application to
ignore a specific event. In such cases, you can use the WML **<noop>** tag, which
directs the microbrowser to do nothing (to perform no operation). Applications
sometimes use the **<noop>** tag, for example, to disable a microbrowser's default
processing. For example, many phones have a Back button. When the user presses
the Back button, the microbrowser performs a **<prev/>** operation by default.
Using the **<noop>** button, you can override this default processing, telling the
microbrowser to do nothing when the user presses the Back button. The following
application, Noop.wml, uses the **<noop>** tag to disable the Back button:

```
<?xml version="1.0"?>

<!DOCTYPE wml PUBLIC "-//WAPFORUM//DTD WML 1.2//EN"
    "http://www.wapforum.org/DTD/wml_1.1.xml">

<wml>

<card id="One">
  <p>
    In card One<br/>

    <do type="accept" label="Go">
       <go href="#Two" />
    </do>
  </p>
</card>

<card id="Two">
  <p>
    Back button disabled
```

```
   <do type="prev">
      <noop/>
   </do>
 </p>
</card>

</wml>
```

Unfortunately, depending on your microbrowser, the microbrowser itself may let the user return to the previous card via the accept key.

1-Minute Drill

● What is an event?

● What are the WML events?

Understanding the <refresh> Tag

When WML applications use the same variables within two or more cards, there will be times when the application must direct the microbrowser to update the current display to reflect possible changes to the values a variable contains. For example, assume one card is displaying a variable's contents and the application branches to a card that changes the variable's value. Next, assume the card returns to the previous card. Because WML typically caches a card's contents, the value the card displays for the variable may reflect the old value, not the update. In such cases, the application can use the **<refresh/>** tag. For example, assume that card One uses a variable named Total to display a user's bill for items he or she has purchased. As the user adds or removes items from his or her shopping cart, the application must update the bill accordingly. Assuming that after a user adds or deletes an item, the application returns to card One, the application should perform a refresh operation to ensure the microbrowser displays the current value of the Total variable.

● As a WML application executes, different things (events) happen. For example, the microbrowser may load a card for the first time or reload a card. To expand an application's processing, you can specify code the microbrowser will execute when specific events occur.

● WML supports the following events: onenterbackward, onenterforward, onpick, and ontimer.

In addition to using the **<refresh>** tag to update the screen display, applications can also use the tag to assign values to one or more variables by placing **<setvar>** tags within the **<refresh>** element, as shown here:

```
<refresh>
<setvar  name="Total"  value="100" />
<setvar  name="Shipping"  value="3-day ground" />
<refresh/>
```

Using the <do> Tag to Respond to Events

Throughout this book, you have used the **<do>** tag in conjunction with the **<go>** tag to move from one card to another. For example, the following application, DoCard2.wml, prompts the user to enter his or her name. Then, the card displays the user's input and prompts the user to press the accept key to continue. After the user presses the accept key, the **<do>** tag directs the microbrowser to load and execute Card2.

Within Card2, the application displays a message telling the user that it is about to override the value of the Name variable. When the user presses the accept key, the card uses a **<setvar>** tag within the **<refresh>** tag to assign and display the new value, as shown in Figure 5-10.

The following statements implement the DoCard2.wml application:

```
<?xml version="1.0"?>

<!DOCTYPE wml PUBLIC "-//WAPFORUM//DTD WML 1.2//EN"
    "http://www.wapforum.org/DTD/wml_1.1.xml">

<wml>

<card id="Card1">
  <p>
    Enter your name:<br/>

    <input name="Name" />

    You entered $Name

    <do type="accept" label="Go">
      <go href="#Card2" />
    </do>
  </p>
</card>
```

```
<card id="Card2">
  <p>
    About to override<br/>
    $Name with Buddy

    <do type="accept" label="Do it">
      <refresh>
        <setvar name="Name" value="Buddy" />
      </refresh>
    </do>

    <do type="options" label="Back">
      <prev/>
    </do>

  </p>
</card>

</wml>
```

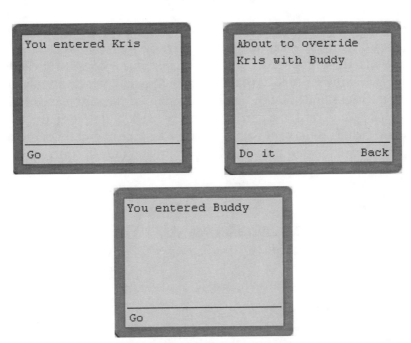

Figure 5-10   Using a <refresh> tag to update the screen display

Responding to Other Events

Depending on the processing a card performs, there may be times when you will want a card to perform specific processing when the application loads the card (as opposed to when the microbrowser reloads a card). As it turns out, each time the microbrowser loads a card, WML generates an onenterforward event. Within a WML application, you can trap the event and perform specific processing when it occurs.

Within an application, you specify the processing a card will perform when the onenterforward event occurs in one of two ways: using the **<card>** tag's onenterforward attribute or using an **<onevent>** tag. For example, the following statement directs the application to load and execute the ShowLogo card when the microbrowser loads the card (should the microbrowser reload the card using a <prev/> tag, for example, the onenterforward event will not occur and the microbrowser, instead, will execute the card's statements):

```
<card id="first" onenterforward="#ShowLogo">
```

The following WML application, CardEvent.wml, uses the **<card>** tag's onenterforward attribute to capture the onenterforward event. When the microbrowser loads the application, the First card's onenterforward attribute directs the microbrowser to load the card named Second, which displays a message to the user stating that the application skipped the card named First.

Within the Second card, the user can press the Back button to return to the previous card (which is the card named First). When the microbrowser reloads the card, the onenterforward event does not occur, and thus the microbrowser displays the card's contents:

```
<?xml version="1.0"?>

<!DOCTYPE wml PUBLIC "-//WAPFORUM//DTD WML 1.2//EN"
    "http://www.wapforum.org/DTD/wml_1.1.xml">

<wml>

<card id="First" onenterforward="#Second">
  <p>
    In the card named First
  </p>
</card>
```

```
<card id="Second">
  <p>
    Skipped First card<br/>
    In the card named Second

    <do type="options" label="Back">
       <prev/>
    </do>

  </p>
</card>

</wml>
```

In addition to using the **\<card\>** tag's onenterforward attribute to handle an event, WML also lets you use the **\<onevent\>** tag. The following example directs the microbrowser to branch to the ShowLogo card when an onenterforward event occurs:

```
<onevent type= "onenterforward">
  <go href="#ShowLogo" />
</onevent>
```

The following WML application, Onevent.wml, uses the **\<onevent\>** tag to perform identical processing to the previous application:

```
<?xml version="1.0"?>

<!DOCTYPE wml PUBLIC "-//WAPFORUM//DTD WML 1.2//EN"
    "http://www.wapforum.org/DTD/wml_1.1.xml">

<wml>

<card id="First">
  <onevent type="onenterforward">
    <go href="#Second" />
  </onevent>

  <p>
    In the card named First
  </p>
</card>
```

```
<card id="Second">
  <p>
    Skipped First card<br/>
    In the card named Second

    <do type="options" label="Back">
      <prev/>
    </do>

  </p>
</card>

</wml>
```

Understanding the onenterbackward Event

As you have learned, by using the **<prev/>** tag, a card can direct the microbrowser to reload and execute the previous card. Depending on the processing your application performs, a card may need to perform specific processing when the microbrowser reloads the card. For such cases, you can specify the card's processing using the onenterbackward event.

As was the case with the onenterforward event, an application specifies its processing for an onenterbackward event using the **<card>** tag's onenterbackward attribute or by using an **<onevent>** tag. For example, the following card uses the **<onevent>** tag to direct the microbrowser to perform a **<refresh>** operation when an onenterbackward event occurs:

```
<card id="EventDemo">
  <onevent type="onenterbackward">
    <refresh/>
  </onenter>

  <p>
    Today is $Date
  </p>
</card>
```

Understanding the onpick Event

Earlier in this module, you learned that by using a **<select>** element, you can display a menu of options to the user. As it turns out, when the user selects an option from within a **<select>** element, an onpick event occurs. The following WML application, Onpick.wml, captures the onpick event, directing the microbrowser to load a card that displays the user's selection. (In Module 7, you will learn how your code can call a WMLScript function that performs processing based on the user's selection.)

To capture the onpick event, the code places an **<onevent>** tag within each **<option>** tag, using a **<go>** element to branch to a specific card when the event occurs. For the first two choices (One and Two), the application branches to the ShowValue card, which simply displays the user's selection. For the third choice, however, the application branches to a card named Special. By capturing onpick events in this way, your WML applications can easily branch to a specific card based on a user's selection.

The following code implements Onpick.wml:

```
<?xml version="1.0"?>

<!DOCTYPE wml PUBLIC "-//WAPFORUM//DTD WML 1.2//EN"
    "http://www.wapforum.org/DTD/wml_1.1.xml">

<wml>

<card id="OnpickDemo">
  <p>
    <select name="UserChoice">
      <option value="One">
        <onevent type="onpick">
            <go href="#ShowValue" />
        </onevent>
        One
      </option>

      <option value="Two">
        <onevent type="onpick">
            <go href="#ShowValue" />
        </onevent>
        Two
      </option>

      <option value="Three">
        <onevent type="onpick">
            <go href="#Special" />
        </onevent>
        Three
      </option>
```

```
     </select>
  </p>
</card>

<card id="ShowValue">
  <p>
    You chose $UserChoice

    <do type="options" label="Back">
      <prev/>
    </do>
  </p>
</card>

<card id="Special">
  <p>
    You chose $UserChoice<br/>
    It's special!

    <do type="options" label="Back">
      <prev/>
    </do>
  </p>
</card>

</wml>
```

Understanding the ontimer Event

Depending on your application's processing, there may be times when you will want the user to perform specific processing within an interval of time. For example, you might want the user to log in to the site within 30 seconds of the login prompt appearing. Within a WML application, you can use the `<timer>` element to start a timed event.

The `<timer>` element will start a clock ticking that counts down to zero. Should the clock reach zero, a timer event will occur. If instead, the user leaves the current card before the clock reaches zero (which means the user has performed his or her processing), the timer stops and the event will not occur. The format of the `<timer>` tag is as follows:

```
<timer  name="Name" value="TenthsOfSeconds" />
```

It is important to note that you specify a timer's interval in tenths of seconds. For example, the following statement specifies a 10 second interval:

```
<timer  name="Delay" value="100" />
```

Within an application, you can use an **<ontimer>** element to catch and handle the timer event. The following application, TimerLogin.wml, for example, displays a main screen that contains company information and a login prompt. If the user selects the login prompt, the application will display prompts for a username and password. If the user fails to provide a username and password within a 30 second period, an ontimer event will occur and the application will return to the main page:

```
<?xml version="1.0"?>

<!DOCTYPE wml PUBLIC "-//WAPFORUM//DTD WML 1.2//EN"
    "http://www.wapforum.org/DTD/wml_1.1.xml">

<wml>

<card id="TimerDemo">
  <p align="center">
    <b>Welcome to<br/>
    Wireless World</b><br/><br/>
  </p>

  <p>
    2112 West Main<br/>
    Houston, Texas 77456<br/>
    212-555-1212
  </p>

  <do type="accept" label="Login">
    <go href="#Login" />
  </do>

</card>


<card id="Login" ontimer="#TimerDemo">
  <timer name="Delay" value="300" />
```

```
  <p>
    Username:
    <input name="Username" />

    Password:
    <input name="Password" />
  </p>

  <do type="accept" label="Go">
    <go href="#ShowInput" />
  </do>
</card>


<card id="ShowInput">
  <p>
    You entered $Username, $Password
  </p>
</card>

</wml>
```

Similarly, the WML application TimerWeather.wml uses a timer to cycle through the weather for each day of the work week. After the user starts the application, the code displays a day's weather information for five seconds and then moves on to the next day. The program continues to cycle through cards using timer events until the user presses the accept key to end the application:

```
<?xml version="1.0"?>

<!DOCTYPE wml PUBLIC "-//WAPFORUM//DTD WML 1.2//EN"
    "http://www.wapforum.org/DTD/wml_1.1.xml">

<wml>

<card id="Weather" title="Weather" onenterforward="#Monday">
  <p align="center">
    Welcome to the<br/><br/>
    Weather Forecast<br/>
  </p>

  <do type="accept" label="View Monday">
    <go href="#Monday" />
  </do>
```

```
</card>

<card id="Monday" title="Monday" ontimer="#Tuesday">
  <timer value="50" />

  <p>
    <img localsrc="sun" src="" alt="Sunny" /><br/><br/>
    Monday<br/>
    Sunny<br/>
    High: 84<br/>
    Low: 58
  </p>

  <do type="accept" label="End">
    <go href="#Weather" />
  </do>
</card>


<card id="Tuesday" title="Tuesday" ontimer="#Wednesday">
  <timer value="50" />

  <p>
    <img localsrc="sun" src="" alt="Sunny" /><br/><br/>
    Tuesday<br/>
    Sunny<br/>
    High: 88<br/>
    Low: 62
  </p>

  <do type="accept" label="End">
    <go href="#Weather" />
  </do>
</card>


<card id="Wednesday" title="Wednesday" ontimer="#Thursday">
  <timer value="50" />

  <p>
    <img localsrc="partcloudy" src="" alt="Cloudy" /><br/><br/>
    Wednesday<br/>
    Partly Cloud<br/>
    High: 76<br/>
    Low: 52
```

5

```
    </p>

  <do type="accept" label="End">
    <go href="#Weather" />
  </do>
</card>


<card id="Thursday" title="Thursday" ontimer="#Friday">
  <timer value="50" />

  <p>
    <img localsrc="cloud" src="" alt="Cloudy" /><br/><br/>
    Thursday<br/>
    Cloudy<br/>
    High: 69<br/>
    Low: 50
  </p>

  <do type="accept" label="End">
    <go href="#Weather" />
  </do>
</card>


<card id="Friday" title="Friday" ontimer="#Monday">
  <timer value="50" />

  <p>
    <img localsrc="rain" src="" alt="Rain" /><br/><br/>
    Friday<br/>
    Rain<br/>
    High: 64<br/>
    Low: 52
  </p>

  <do type="accept" label="End">
    <go href="#Weather" />
  </do>
</card>


</wml>
```

When you load the TimerWeather.wml application into the phone simulator, the simulator will display screens similar to those shown in Figure 5-11.

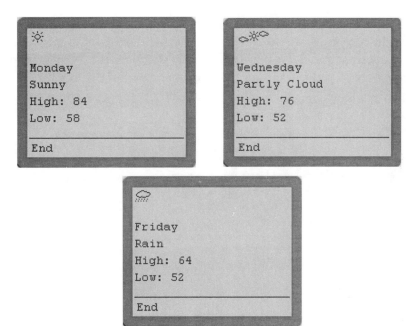

Figure 5-11 | Using a timer to cycle through cards

Hint

If you create applications that use timers, keep in mind that the speed at which phones can load and execute pages will differ. If, for example, your application loads a new image based on a timer that occurs every 10 seconds, the speed at which the phone can download and display the image will affect the rate at which the images appear on the screen display.

Using Templates

As your applications become more complex, you may find that you are placing several of the same tags within each card you create. For example, you might include a <do> tag that provides a Back button the user can press to return to the previous card. Rather than having to cut and paste related statements into each card, you can define a template, whose statements WML includes within each card you create. Using a template, for example, you only need to place the

<do> tag that creates a Back button in one place, and WML will automatically include it in every card. If one card has unique processing—you might, for example, not want a Back button—you simply overwrite the template's code by placing a tag to perform the specific processing within that card.

To define a template, you use place a **<template>** tag within your deck, after the **<wml>** tag, as shown here:

```
<wml>

<template>
  <do type="options" label="Back">
    <prev/>
  </do>
</template>

<card id="SomeCard">
  <p>
    Statements here
  </p>
</card>
```

Using the <meta> Tag

As you examine WML applications, you may periodically encounter a **<meta>** tag, which programmers use to provide information about the deck (called meta-information) to the microbrowser or other applications (such as proxy servers). Today, the most common **<meta>** tag provides the browser with instructions on caching:

```
<meta  http-equiv="Cache-Control" content="max-age=0" forua="true">
```

In this case, the http-equiv attribute specifies that the microbrowser should interpret the meta tag's contents as HTTP header information. In this case, **http-equiv="Cache-Control"** tells the microbrowser that this piece

of meta-information applies to the memory caching system. Next, the
`content=max-age=0` specifies the maximum time the microbrowser should
keep the contents of this deck in its cache. The value 0 directs the microbrowser
not to cache the deck. To direct the microbrowser to cache the deck for 1 minute,
you would use the value 60 (seconds). Finally, the forua attribute, when set to
"true", specifies that the property must reach the microbrowser, as opposed to
another program (such as a proxy server intercepting the statement). When forua
is set to "false", a program other than the microbrowser can process and extract
the meta command. In the future, you may encounter other `<meta>` directives.
Today, however, the cache-control directive is the most common directive
applications use.

5

☑ *Mastery Check*

1. How do the following `<input>` tag format specifiers differ: "5N", "NNNNN", "*N"?

_____

_____

2. What is the purpose of the `<input>` tag's value attribute?

_____

_____

3. Use an `<input>` tag format specifier to prompt the user to enter a currency amount in the form $NN.NN.

4. What is the purpose of noesc in `$(Variable:noesc)`?

_____

_____

5. How do the `<input>` tag's size and maxlength attributes differ?

_____

_____

6. Use a `<select>` element to create the following menu:

```
Wireless Sites

Nokia
Ericsson
Openwave
WAPForum
```

7. Specify the `<onevent>` element that is functionally equivalent to the following `<card>` tag onenterforward attribute:

```
<card id="Test" onenterforward="#ShowDateTime">
```

☑ *Mastery Check*

8. Create a WML application that uses a `<timer>` element to toggle the display between three different cards, every 15 seconds.

9. Use a `<template>` tag to specify generic code that directs each card in a deck to return to the application's first page, after 30 seconds of inactivity. Assume that the first card is named StartDeck.

10. What is the purpose of the WML `<meta>` tag?

_____

_____

5

Module 6

Building Real-World WML Applications

The Goals of This Module

- Create your own Wireless Web site that provides visitors with your phone number, address, and current news

- Create a Wireless Web site for your family that others can view to get contact information for your various family members

- Create a company-wide locator that users can visit to find phone numbers and office-locator information for the company's employees

- Create a WML site that implements a news feed, whose contents you can change to provide users with news about your company or your products, or with news, sports, and entertainment information

In this module, you will build several "real-world" projects that let you put many of the concepts you have examined in the previous modules to use. To start, you will create your own Wireless site containing your contact information, recent news about yourself, and even a photo! Then, you will extend your personal site to include your family members. Next, you will learn how to place a company locator on the Wireless Web, which puts the information within the hand of Web-enabled cellular phone users and may eliminate a company's need to print an expensive directory. Finally, you will learn how to create a Wireless news feed when you build an application that provides users about prime-time TV shows.

-*Hint*---------------------------------

The applications this lesson presents are meant to give you a starting point from which you can create your own applications. Each application presents WML features you have used throughout this book. Take time to examine each application's processing. Then, edit the application to build a custom solution that better meets your needs.

Creating Your Own Wireless Site

One of the easiest ways to get others excited about the Wireless Web is to show them a working and useful site. The following WML application, MyInfo.wml, creates a simple Wireless site others can visit to view your contact information, your recent news, and so on. If you open the application within the phone simulator, the simulator will display the site's main page, which contains links to specific information, as shown in Figure 6-1.

Depending on which link the user selects, the application will display one of the screens shown in Figure 6-2.

Figure 6-1   Viewing the main page of the MyInfo.wml application

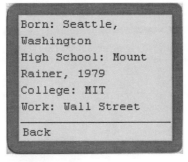

```
John Doe
225 Main Street
Houston, TX 77479

▶[Home: 832-555-1212]
 [Cell: 713-555-1212]

Call
```

```
Born: Seattle,
Washington
High School: Mount
Rainer, 1979
College: MIT
Work: Wall Street

Back
```

```
I recently moved to
Houston, Texas. I
bought a horse named
"Run Away."



Back
```

Figure 6-2   Viewing pages in the MyInfo.wml application

The following statements implement the MyInfo.wml application:

```
<?xml version="1.0"?>

<!DOCTYPE wml PUBLIC "-//WAPFORUM//DTD WML 1.2//EN"
    "http://www.wapforum.org/DTD/wml_1.1.xml">

<wml>

<card id="AboutMe" title="About Me">
  <p align="center">Welcome to</p>
  <p align="center">My Site!</p>
  <p>
    <br/>
    <a href="#Contact">Contact Me</a>
    <a href="#Facts">Facts About Me</a>
    <a href="#RecentNews">News About Me</a>
  </p>
</card>


<card id="Contact" title="Contact Information">
  <p>
```

6

```
      John Doe<br/>
      225 Main Street<br/>
      Houston, TX 77479<br/>
      <br/>
      <a href="wtai://wp/mc;8325551212" title="Call">Home: 832-555-1212</a>
      <a href="wtai://wp/mc;7135551212" title="Call">Cell: 713-555-1212</a>
      Fax: 281-555-1212<br/>
      <br/>
      <a href="wtai://wp/mc;8005551212" title="Call">Work: 800-555-1212</a>
      E-mail: JohnDoe@aol.com

      <do type="prev" label="Back"><prev/></do>
    </p>
</card>


<card id="Facts" title="My Facts">
  <p>
      Born: Seattle, Washington<br/>
      High School: Mount Rainer, 1979<br/>
      College: MIT <br/>
      Work: Wall Street<br/>
      Spouse: None<br/>

      <do type="prev" label="Back"><prev/></do>
  </p>
</card>


<card id="RecentNews" title="News">
  <p>
      I recently moved to Houston, Texas. I bought a horse named &quot;Run Away.&quot;

      <do type="prev" label="Back"><prev/></do>
  </p>
</card>

</wml>
```

Taking a Closer Look at MyInfo.wml

The MyInfo.wml application starts with document type definition entries you have seen in previous applications. Next, within the application's first card (AboutMe), the application uses three **<a>** tags to create links to cards that contain specific information:

```
<a href="#Contact">Contact Me</a>
<a href="#Facts">Facts About Me</a>
<a href="#RecentNews">News About Me</a>
```

As you can see, the application uses fragments (card names following a pound sign) to specify each link. When the microbrowser encounters the **<a>** tags, it will highlight the links on the phone's screen display.

Within the Contact card, the application displays several phone numbers. To let the user automatically dial a phone number, the application uses an **<a>** tag that references the WTAI make call (mc) function:

```
<a href="wtai://wp/mc;8325551212" title="Call">Home: 832-555-1212</a>
```

Because it does not make sense for the user to dial the fax, the card does not use the **<a>** tag for the fax number.

Within each card, the application provides a **<do>** tag that lets the user return to the previous card by selecting the Back button:

```
<do type="prev" label="Back"><prev/></do>
```

To further customize the MyInfo.wml application, you might want to create a WBMP image of yourself, which you could let users view by creating a fourth card named RecentPhoto, as shown here:

```
<card id="RecentPhoto" title="Photo">
  <p>
    Recent Photo<br/>
    <img src="MyPhoto.wbmp" alt="Kodak Moment" />

    <do type="prev" label="Back"><prev/></do>
  </p>
</card>
```

Figure 6-3 illustrates how such a photo might appear within a phone simulator.

Figure 6-3   Extending the MyInfo.wml application to include a recent photo

1-Minute Drill

● What is WTAI?

● What is the purpose of the "?

MyInfoIcons.wml

Project 6-1: Adding a Photo to Your Wireless Web Site

As you have learned, most Web-enabled phones provide built-in images you can display using the <img> tag's localsrc element. In this project, you will enhance the previous MyInfo.wml application by adding localsrc images to the main menu.

Step-By-Step

1. Using a text editor, create the file MyInfoIcons.wml. Within the file, paste the contents of the WML application MyInfo.wml, which this module presents.

2. In the application's source code, edit the contents of the AboutMe card to use the localsrc images "phone1", "head1", and "newspaper":

```
<card id="AboutMe" title="About Me">
  <p align="center">Welcome to</p>
  <p align="center">My Site!</p>
  <p>
    <br/>
    <img localsrc="phone1" src="" alt=""/>
    <a href="#Contact">Contact Me</a>
    <br/><img localsrc="head1" src="" alt=""/>
    <a href="#Facts">Facts About Me</a>
    <br/><img localsrc="newspaper" src="" alt=""/>
    <a href="#RecentNews">News About Me</a>
  </p>
</card>
```

3. Save the application file to disk.

Note that within the <img> tags, the code uses an empty string for the src and alt attributes. This means that if the microbrowser is unable to display the specified local source image, the microbrowser will not display a WBMP image or alternate text.

● WTAI stands for Wireless Telephony Application Interface. Using the WTAI mc (make call) function, a WML application can direct the browser to dial a specified number.

● The special characters " direct the microbrowser to display a double quote character.

Ask the Expert

Question: Why does the MyInfo.wml application not use a `<meta>` tag similar to that discussed in Module 5?

```
<head>
<meta http-equiv="cache-control" content="max-age=0" forua="true" />
</head>
```

Answer: The `<meta>` tag shown here uses the `http-equiv=`
`"cache-control"` attribute to provide the microbrowser with
directives that control how the microbrowser caches WML cards. In
this case, the `content="max-age="` attribute tells the microbrowser
not to cache information, but rather, to reload cards each time they are
called. (The `forua="true"` attribute specifies that the `<meta>` tag's
contents are meant for the phone, and an intermediate agent (a software
program, such as a proxy server) that views the card's contents should
not remove the tag.

By caching cards, the microbrowser improves an application's
performance because it can quickly reload a card from its cache memory,
as opposed to having to download the card across the Wireless Web.
Unfortunately, when you work with variables whose values may change
and thus change the information a card displays, the microbrowser's cache
may not always reflect the correct information. To prevent such errors,
many developers will use the previous `<meta>` tag to disable caching.

The applications this module presents do not use variables. As such,
to improve their performance, you will want the microbrowser to cache
the application's cards. Therefore, the applications will not use the
`<meta>` tag to disable caching.

6

Creating a Wireless Site for Family Information

If your family is like most, you probably have a wide variety of information
that you often need when you are out and about. By creating a Wireless site
that contains such information, you can access the information at any time,
from any place, using a Web-enabled cellular phone. You might, for example,
want to maintain a list of phone numbers for your children's friends. You may
also want to track birthdays or other events.

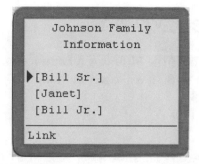

Figure 6-4 Providing access to information specific to various family members

The FamilyInfo.wml application extends the previous application to provide links to information for various family members. When you load the application into the phone simulator, the program will display its main page, which contains links to information for various members of the family, as shown in Figure 6-4.

Depending on the link the user selects, the application will display information about the corresponding family member, as shown in Figure 6-5.

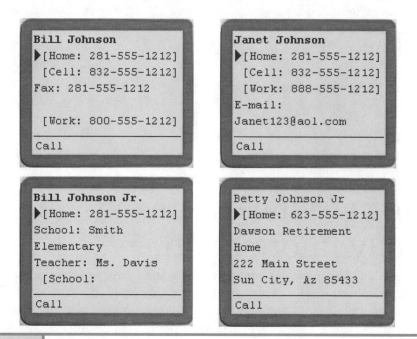

Figure 6-5 Displaying family member information

The following statements implement the FamilyInfo.wml application:

```
<?xml version="1.0"?>

<!DOCTYPE wml PUBLIC "-//WAPFORUM//DTD WML 1.2//EN"
    "http://www.wapforum.org/DTD/wml_1.1.xml">

<wml>

<card id="JohnsonFamily" title="Johnson">
  <p align="center">Johnson Family</p>
  <p align="center">Information</p>
  <p>
    <br/>
    <a href="#Dad">Bill Sr.</a>
    <a href="#Mom">Janet</a>
    <a href="#Billy">Bill Jr.</a>
    <a href="#Granny">Grandma</a>
  </p>
</card>


<card id="Dad" title="Bill Sr.">
  <p>
    <b>Bill Johnson</b><br/>
    <a href="wtai://wp/mc;2815551212" title="Call">Home: 281-555-1212</a>
    <a href="wtai://wp/mc;8325551212" title="Call">Cell: 832-555-1212</a>
    Fax: 281-555-1212<br/>
    <br/>
    <a href="wtai://wp/mc;8005551212" title="Call">Work: 800-555-1212</a>
    E-mail: BillJohnson@aol.com<br/>
    <br/>
    Medications:<br/>
    Prozac<br/>
    Allergic to penicillin<br/>
    <br/>
    Insurance: 11344-15
  </p>

  <do type="prev" label="Back"><prev/></do>
</card>


<card id="Mom" title="Janet">
  <p>
    <b>Janet Johnson</b><br/>
    <a href="wtai://wp/mc;2815551212" title="Call">Home: 281-555-1212</a>
    <a href="wtai://wp/mc;8325551212" title="Call">Cell: 832-555-1212</a>
    <br/>
    <a href="wtai://wp/mc;8885551212" title="Call">Work: 888-555-1212</a>
    E-mail: Janet123@aol.com<br/>
    <br/>
    Medications:<br/>
```

6

```
   Aspirin<br/>
   <br/>
   Insurance: 11344-25
  </p>

  <do type="prev" label="Back"><prev/></do>
</card>


<card id="Billy" title="Bill Jr.">
  <p>
    <b>Bill Johnson Jr.</b><br/>
    <a href="wtai://wp/mc;2815551212" title="Call">Home: 281-555-1212</a>
    School: Smith Elementary<br/>
    Teacher: Ms. Davis<br/>
    <a href="wtai://wp/mc;7135551212" title="Call">School: 713-555-1212</a>
    <br/>
    Medications:<br/>
    Ritalin<br/>
    <br/>
    Insurance: 11344-15a
  </p>

  <do type="prev" label="Back"><prev/></do>
</card>

<card id="Granny" title="Grandma">
  <p>
    Betty Johnson Jr<br/>
    <a href="wtai://wp/mc;6235551212" title="Call">Home: 623-555-1212</a>
    Dawson Retirement Home<br/>
    222 Main Street<br/>
    Sun City, AZ 85433<br/>
    <br/>
    Medications:<br/>
    Paxil<br/>
    Digoxin<br/>
    Aricept<br/>
    Coumaden<br/>
    <br/>
    Insurance: Medicare 334-xx-4444A
  </p>

  <do type="prev" label="Back"><prev/></do>
</card>

</wml>
```

Taking a Closer Look at FamilyInfo.wml

The FamilyInfo.wml application is an extension of the MyInfo.wml application
previously discussed. As such, the application's processing is quite similar. The

application uses <a> tags to create links to each family member's card, and within the cards, the application uses the WTAI make call function to dial the phone numbers the user selects.

Ask the Expert

Question: The FamilyInfo.wml application contains information I would not want the public to access, such as current medications. Is there a way to password-protect such information?

Answer: In Module 7, you will learn how to use the WMLScript scripting language to perform conditional (if-then) processing. Using WMLScript, for example, your application can prompt the user to enter a password. If the password the user enters is valid, the application can then display your confidential information. Otherwise, if the user enters an invalid password, the application can prevent the user from accessing the information.

Question: I used <a> tags to create links in my cards, but the phone numbers aren't lined up with other unlinked numbers. How can I align the numbers?

Answer: When you use an <a> tag to create a link to a card, many microbrowsers will indent the link's text, which may misalign your screen's text, as shown in Figure 6-6.

To align such text, you can place the   special character in front of the card's other text, to use the space character to achieve better alignment. The following card, for example, aligns text using the space character:

```
<card id="AlignText">
  <p align="center">My Phone</p>
  <p align="center">Information</p>
  <p>
    <br/>
    <a href="wtai://wp/mc;2815551212" title="Call">Home: 281-555-1212</a>
    <a href="wtai://wp/mc;8325551212" title="Call">Cell: 832-555-1212</a>
      Fax: 281-555-1212<br/>
    <a href="wtai://wp/mc;8005551212" title="Call">Work: 800-555-1212</a>
      Phil@Yahoo.com
  </p>
</card>
```

6

Figure 6-6   Misaligned text due to a link

Creating a Wireless Company Locator

Today, most large companies, the military, universities, and a wide range of organizations publish phone-book-like locators, the content of which is very well suited for the Wireless Web. By placing such locator information on a Wireless Web site, people can access the information from any location using a Web-enabled cell phone. Further, as information changes, a developer can quickly update the information within the WML application and the locator can be kept up to date. The following Locator.wml application implements a simple company locator. When you load the application into the phone simulator, the application will display links that correspond to last names, as shown in Figure 6-7.

If, for example, you select the link that corresponds to names that start with letters in the range F–J, the application will display a list of corresponding names,

| **Figure 6-7** | Using a Wireless company locator |

as shown in Figure 6-8. If you then select a name from the list, the application will display the individual's location information.

6

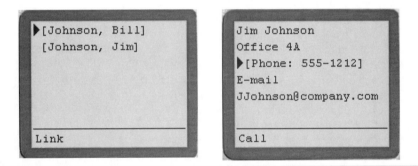

| **Figure 6-8** | Displaying an individual's locator information |

The following code implements the Locator.wml application:

```
<?xml version="1.0"?>

<!DOCTYPE wml PUBLIC "-//WAPFORUM//DTD WML 1.2//EN"
    "http://www.wapforum.org/DTD/wml_1.1.xml">

<wml>

<card id="Locator" title="Company Name">
  <p align="center">Welcome</p>
  <p align="center">Company Locator</p>
  <p>
    <br/>
    <a href="#A_E">Names A-E</a>
    <a href="#F_J">Names F-J</a>
    <a href="#K_O">Names K-O</a>
    <a href="#P_T">Names P-T</a>
    <a href="#U_Z">Names U-Z</a>
  </p>
</card>


<card id="A_E" title="Employee A-E">
  <p>
    <a href="#Anderson">Anderson, Bill</a>
    <a href="#Barker">Barker, Joe</a>
    <a href="#Davis">Davis, Betty</a>
    <do type="prev" label="Back"><prev/></do>
  </p>
</card>


<card id="F_J" title="Employee F-J">
  <p>
    <a href="#JohnsonB">Johnson, Bill</a>
    <a href="#JohnsonJ">Johnson, Jim</a>
    <do type="prev" label="Back"><prev/></do>
  </p>
</card>


<card id="K_O" title="Employee K-O">
  <p>
```

```wml
      <a href="#Kleiner">Kleiner, Betty</a>
      <do type="prev" label="Back"><prev/></do>
   </p>
</card>


<card id="P_T" title="Employee P-T">
   <p>
     <a href="#Stevens">Stevens, Sandra</a>
     <a href="#Taylor">Taylor, Tim</a>
     <do type="prev" label="Back"><prev/></do>
   </p>
</card>


<card id="U_Z" title="Employee U-Z">
   <p>
     <a href="#Zoogle">Zoogle, Zig</a>
     <do type="prev" label="Back"><prev/></do>
   </p>
</card>

<card id="Anderson" title="Anderson">
   <p>
     Bill Anderson<br/>
     Office 3C<br/>
     <a href="wtai://wp/mc;5551212" title="Call">Phone: 555-1212</a>
     E-mail BAnderson@company.com
     <do type="prev" label="Back"><prev/></do>
   </p>
</card>

<card id="Barker" title="Barker">
   <p>
     Joe Barker<br/>
     Office 3D<br/>
     <a href="wtai://wp/mc;5551212" title="Call">Phone: 555-1212</a>
     E-mail JBarker@company.com
     <do type="prev" label="Back"><prev/></do>
   </p>
</card>

<card id="Davis" title="Davis">
   <p>
```

6

```
      Betty Davis<br/>
      Office 3E<br/>
      <a href="wtai://wp/mc;5551212" title="Call">Phone: 555-1212</a>
      E-mail BDavis@company.com
      <do type="prev" label="Back"><prev/></do>
    </p>
</card>

<card id="JohnsonB" title="Johnson, B">
  <p>
      Bill Johnson<br/>
      Office 3F<br/>
      <a href="wtai://wp/mc;5551212" title="Call">Phone: 555-1212</a>
      E-mail BJohnson@company.com
      <do type="prev" label="Back"><prev/></do>
  </p>
</card>

<card id="JohnsonJ" title="Johnson, J">
  <p>
      Jim Johnson<br/>
      Office 4A<br/>
      <a href="wtai://wp/mc;5551212" title="Call">Phone: 555-1212</a>
      E-mail JJohnson@company.com
      <do type="prev" label="Back"><prev/></do>
  </p>
</card>


<card id="Kleiner" title="Kleiner">
  <p>
      Betty Kleiner<br/>
      Office 4B<br/>
      <a href="wtai://wp/mc;5551212" title="Call">Phone: 555-1212</a>
      E-mail BKleiner@company.com
      <do type="prev" label="Back"><prev/></do>
  </p>
</card>

<card id="Stevens" title="Stevens">
  <p>
```

```
    Sandra Stevens<br/>
    Office 4C<br/>
    <a href="wtai://wp/mc;5551212" title="Call">Phone: 555-1212</a>
    E-mail SStevens@company.com
    <do type="prev" label="Back"><prev/></do>
  </p>
</card>

<card id="Taylor" title="Taylor">
  <p>
    Tim Taylor<br/>
    Office 4D<br/>
    <a href="wtai://wp/mc;5551212" title="Call">Phone: 555-1212</a>
    E-mail TTaylor@company.com
    <do type="prev" label="Back"><prev/></do>
  </p>
</card>

<card id="Zoogle" title="Zoogle">
  <p>
    Zig Zoogle<br/>
    Office 6C<br/>
    <a href="wtai://wp/mc;5551212" title="Call">Phone: 555-1212</a>
    E-mail Zoogie@company.com
    <do type="prev" label="Back"><prev/></do>
  </p>
</card>

</wml>
```

Taking a Closer Look at Locator.wml

The WML code in the Locator.wml application is actually quite similar to the code in the FamilyInfo.wml and MyInfo.wml applications previously discussed. What you should note within the application is how the code uses menus to organize the data. In this case, the menus group a range of names. However, you could use the same processing to group a range of cities, a range of products, and so on. By letting the user select menu options to "drill down" to the information they desire, the user can quickly traverse data without having to type on the phone's numeric keypad.

Ask the Expert

Question: The menus work well within the Locator.wml application because the number of entries in the list is quite short. As the number of entries increases, traversing many menus may become quite time consuming. Is there an easy way to implement a search engine the user can use to type an individual's name?

Answer: In Module 9, you will learn how to use the WMLScript scripting language to create a simple search engine. In Module 10, you will learn how to build a Wireless application that interacts with a database, allowing the user to query the database, which in turn, builds the WML result.

Creating a News Feed

Companies use news feeds on the Wireless Web to provide users with current news, sports, weather, and financial information. A news feed is simply a site that makes information readily available to users who visit the site. Figure 6-9 illustrates several such Wireless sites.

The following WML application, PrimeTimeTV.wml, creates a simple news feed that provides users with information about prime-time television shows. Using such an application, users can plan their evenings knowing whether or not their favorite program is a rerun. The application's true purpose, however, is to illustrate how you might use WML to structure a news feed.

When you load the application into the phone simulator, the simulator will display a menu from which you can select the time you desire, as shown in Figure 6-10.

After you select a time, the application will display a listing of shows on the network stations, as shown in Figure 6-11. If you select a specific show, the application will display information about the show's episode.

Figure 6-9   News feeds on the Wireless Web

Figure 6-10   Using a menu to select television programs for a specific time

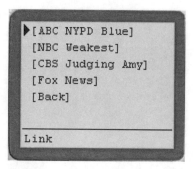

Figure 6-11 Displaying information about a specific TV show

The following statements implement the PrimeTimeTV.wml application:

```
<?xml version="1.0"?>

<!DOCTYPE wml PUBLIC "-//WAPFORUM//DTD WML 1.2//EN"
    "http://www.wapforum.org/DTD/wml_1.1.xml">

<wml>

<card id="TV" title="Prime Time">
  <p align="center">Prime Time TV</p>
  <p align="center">Thursday</p>
  <p>
    <br/>
    <a href="#TV7_00">7:00PM</a>
    <a href="#TV8_00">8:00PM</a>
    <a href="#TV9_00">9:00PM</a>
  </p>
</card>


<card id="TV7_00" title="7:00PM">
  <p>
    <a href="#Millionaire">ABC Millionaire</a>
    <a href="#Fitzgeralds">NBC Fitzgeralds</a>
    <a href="#JAG">CBS JAG</a>
    <a href="#Seventies">Fox 70s Show</a>

    <do type="options" label="Back"><prev/></do>
  </p>
```

```
    </card>

    <card id="TV8_00" title="8:00PM">
      <p>
        <a href="#Dharma">ABC Dharma and Greg</a>
        <a href="#Frasier">NBC Frasier</a>
        <a href="#Minutes">CBS 60 Minutes II</a>
        <a href="#DarkAngel">Fox Dark Angel</a>

        <do type="options" label="Back"><prev/></do>
      </p>
    </card>

    <card id="TV9_00" title="9:00PM">
      <p>
        <a href="#NYPD">ABC NYPD Blue</a>
        <a href="#Weakest">NBC Weakest</a>
        <a href="#Amy">CBS Judging Amy</a>
        <a href="#FoxNews">Fox News</a>

        <do type="options" label="Back"><prev/></do>
      </p>
    </card>

    <card id="Millionaire" title="Millionaire">
      <p>
        Regis asks hard questions to celebrity guests hoping to win money for charity.

        <do type="options" label="Back"><prev/></do>
      </p>
    </card>

    <card id="Fitzgeralds" title="Fitzgeralds">
      <p>
        Patrick convinces Fitzgerald to invest in an Irish restaurant.
        <do type="options" label="Back"><prev/></do>
      </p>
    </card>

    <card id="JAG" title="JAG">
      <p>
        Mac and Harm handle the case of a Petty Officer who illegally smuggled an Arab princess
    into the U.S. and married her.

        <do type="options" label="Back"><prev/></do>
      </p>
    </card>

    <card id="Seventies" title="70s">
```

6

```
  <p>
    Kitty recruits Eric, Red, Kelso, and Hyde to help at her church fund-raiser.

    <do type="options" label="Back"><prev/></do>
  </p>
</card>

<card id="Dharma" title="Dharma">
  <p>
    Dharma is rattled by her pregnant mom's plans for the new baby.

    <do type="options" label="Back"><prev/></do>
  </p>
</card>

<card id="Frasier" title="Frasier">
  <p>
    A Wine Club dispute uncorks a feud between Niles and Frasier.

    <do type="options" label="Back"><prev/></do>
  </p>
</card>

<card id="Minutes" title="60 Minutes">
  <p>
    Bradley reports on the shootings at Colorado's Columbine High School.

    <do type="options" label="Back"><prev/></do>
  </p>
</card>

<card id="DarkAngel" title="Dark Angel">
  <p>
    Max plans to steal a set of computer disks but is sidetracked by Cindy's felonious
ex-lover, who draws attention from a shadowy pharmaceutical firm.

    <do type="options" label="Back"><prev/></do>
  </p>
</card>

<card id="NYPD" title="NYPD">
  <p>
    Greg and Baldwin mess up a case involving a holdup at a bodega resulting in a freak death.

    <do type="options" label="Back"><prev/></do>
  </p>
</card>

<card id="Weakest" title="Weakest">
  <p>
```

```
    Game show contestants try not to be "the weakest link."

    <do type="options" label="Back"><prev/></do>
  </p>
</card>

<card id="Amy" title="Amy">
  <p>
    Maxine fights feelings of apathy as the Gray family says goodbye to one member of the
family and participates in the birth of another.

    <do type="options" label="Back"><prev/></do>
  </p>
</card>

<card id="FoxNews" title="Fox News">
  <p>
    National and local news.

    <do type="options" label="Back"><prev/></do>
  </p>
</card>

</wml>
```

6

Ask the Expert

Question: The PrimeTimeTV.wml application lists only information about a few shows. I can imagine that an application that provides a complete listing of all shows for a week's time would become very large and cumbersome to work with. Is there an easier way to implement such an application?

Answer: In Module 10, you will learn how to build a Wireless application that interacts with a database. In this case, the database can maintain information about each show. As the user moves through the menu options, the application can interact with the database to create cards that display information specific to the show.

☑ *Mastery Check*

1. To align text on a page, there may be times when you will use the ` ` special character. Why can't you simply use a space character to align the text?

   _____

   _____

2. How would you modify the Locator.wml application to display information about the following restaurant franchise locations?

   Super Burger
   Chicago
           1133 Michigan Avenue, 800-555-1212
           4441 Delaware, 888-555-1212
   New York
           13 Broadway, 212-555-1212
           4544 Park Avenue, 888-555-1212
           33 Lincoln, 800-555-1212
   Houston
           121 Rodeo Way, 713-555-1212

3. When should you consider using the `<meta>` tag to disable caching within a microbrowser?

   _____

   _____

Module 7

Automating WML Applications Using WMLScript

The Goals of This Module

- Learn how to create a WMLScript file and how to access the script from within WML

- Understand how to create WMLScript functions that perform a specific task

- Use variables within the WMLScript functions to store information as the script executes

- Understand and use the WMLScript arithmetic operators

- Use the `if` statement to let scripts make decisions

- Use iterative control structures, such as the `for` and `while` loops to repeat a set of statements a given number of times, or while a specific condition is "true"

- Learn how to pass information (parameters) between WMLScript functions

- Access WML variables from within WMLScript

As you have learned, WML makes it easy for you to create applications that display information. However, WML itself is not well suited for applications that must perform arithmetic operations, make decisions, or repeat a set of operations a specific number of times. Fortunately, you can use WMLScript for such cases. This module introduces you to WMLScript, a scripting language you can use to automate WML applications, much like Web designers use JavaScript and VBScript to automate HTML Web sites.

Place WMLScript Statements Within a .wmls File

When you create an application that uses WMLScript, you will work with two types of files: .wml and .wmls. As you have learned, files with the .wml extension will contain WML card decks. In contrast, files with the .wmls extension contain WMLScript functions. A WMLScript file is a text file that contains the definitions for one or more functions.

Hint

Within a WMLScript, you organize your processing into small pieces of code called functions, much like you would organize a large WML application using cards. Each function must have a unique name and should perform a specific task.

Depending on your application's processing and design, the application may start with a WML card, which, in turn, will use statements that reside within a .wmls file. As shown in Figure 7-1, a WML application will normally call a WMLScript function, which resides in a .wmls file, to perform specific processing. Normally, after the WMLScript completes its processing, it will return control to the original card.

Depending on the processing the WML application performs, it may call several different WMLScript functions, each of which performs a specific task. One function, for example, may calculate a company's payroll. A second function might perform general-ledger accounting operations to place the payroll entries

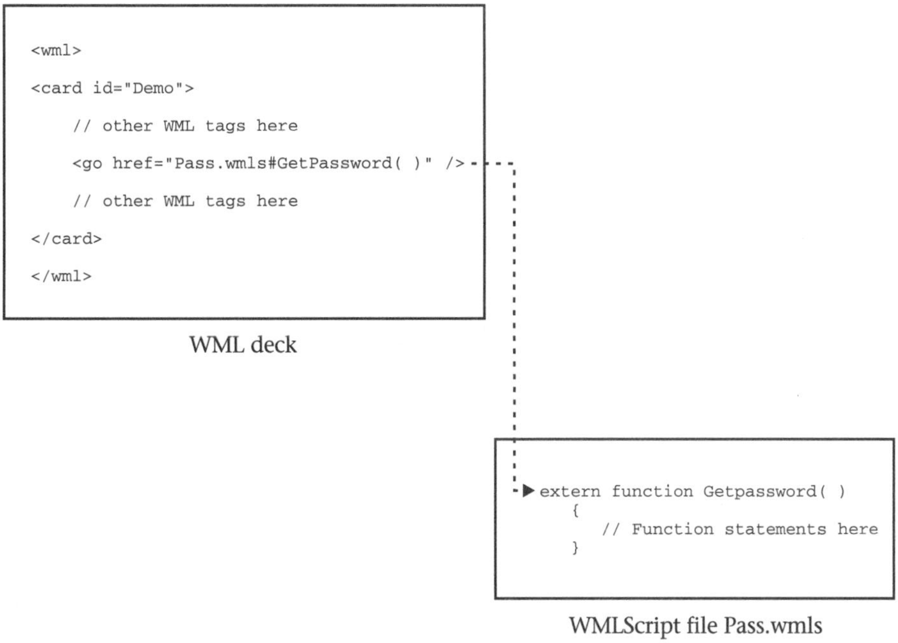

```
<wml>

<card id="Demo">

    // other WML tags here

    <go href="Pass.wmls#GetPassword( )" />

    // other WML tags here

</card>

</wml>
```

WML deck

```
extern function Getpassword( )
    {
        // Function statements here
    }
```

WMLScript file Pass.wmls

Figure 7-1 WMLScript function to perform specific processing

on the books. A third function might issue the payroll checks electronically. The .wmls functions a WML application calls may reside in one .wmls file, or they may reside in many different files.

Hint

Just as the microbrowser executes WML tags that reside within a WML card deck, the microbrowser also executes WMLScript statements. Although microbrowsers may implement WMLScript operations slightly differently, most newer microbrowsers will fully support the concepts this module presents.

```
<wml>
<card id="Demo">
    // other WML tags here
    <go href="Pass.wmls#GetPassword( )" />
    // other WML tags here
</card>
</wml>
```

WML deck

```
use url Remote "Validate.wmls";
extern function Getpassword( )
    {
        var Password;

        Password = GetUserInput( );

        Remote.ValidatePassword(Password);
    }
extern function GetUserInput( )
    {
        return(Dialogs.prompt("Password");
    }
```

WMLScript file Pass.wmls

```
extern function ValidatePassword(Password)
    {
            if (Password== "SecretData")
                WMLBrowser.go("Secret.wml");
            else
                WMLBrowser.go("BadPassword.wml");
    }
```

WMLScript file Validate.wmls

Figure 7-2 A WMLScript function may call other functions and may direct the microbrowser to load a specific WML card

Understanding WMLScript Functions

As programs become large and complex, programmers often break the programs into smaller, more manageable pieces, called functions—much like you might break a large WML application into multiple cards.

Within a WMLScript file, each function must have a unique name. Like WML, WMLScript is case-dependent, which means it considers the names DeterminePayroll, determinepayroll, and Determinepayroll to be different. Within a function, you specify the WMLScript statements that perform the function's task within left and right braces, {}. The function statements will follow the function name, as shown here:

```
extern function FunctionName(optional_parameters)
  {
    // Statements here
  }
```

The **extern** keyword that precedes the function name tells the microbrowser that other applications, such as a WML application, external to the WMLScript file can use the function. To use a function, a WML application simply refers to the function by name, preceding the function name with the name of the WMLScript file and a pound sign (#). For example, to use the function PhoneHome that resides in the WMLScript file AutoDial.wmls, a WML application would use a **<go>** tag similar to the following:

```
<go href="AutoDial.wmls#PhoneHome()" />
```

Later in this module, you will learn that WML applications can pass information, which programmers refer to as parameters, to WMLScript functions. For example, a WML application might pass a phone number to a function named PlaceCallingCardCall that resides in the AutoDial.wmls file using the following **<go>** tag:

```
<go href="AutoDial.wmls#PlaceCallingCardCall('555-1212')" />
```

7

1-Minute Drill

● What is a function?

● What is the difference between a file with the .wml extension and a file with the .wmls extension?

● How does a WML application use a WMLScript function?

Understanding WMLScript Reserved Words

When you name a function within a WMLScript file, and when you create variables to store information while the function executes, you must choose function and variable names that do not conflict with the WMLScript reserved words listed in Table 7-1. Reserved words are words that have special meaning within WMLScript. The word **function**, for example, identifies the start of a function's statements, just as the word **extern** tells the microbrowser that the function is externally accessible. If you try to use reserved words for function or variable names, the microbrowser will not compile the WMLScript code and, instead, will display syntax error messages.

access	Agent	break	case	catch	class
const	continue	debugger	default	delete	div
do	Domain	else	enum	equiv	export
extends	Extern	false	finally	for	function
header	http	if	import	in	invalid
isvalid	Lib	meta	name	new	Null
path	Private	public	return	sizeof	struct
super	Switch	this	throw	true	try
typeof	url	use	user	var	void
while	With				

Table 7-1   WMLScript Reserved Words

● A function is a small, uniquely named piece of code that performs a specific task.
● A file with the .wml extension contains a WML deck. A file with the .wmls extension contains WMLScript functions.
● A WML application calls a WMLScript function by specifying the function's name and the name of the WMLScript file within a <go> tag's href attribute.

?—Ask the Expert

Question: Most programming languages provide a run-time library—a collection of built-in functions that perform common tasks. Does WMLScript provide a run-time library?

Answer: Yes. WMLScript provides several different libraries that you will examine in detail in Module 8. In fact, you will use several of the library functions to perform specific tasks throughout this module.

To use a WMLScript library function, you specify the library name, followed by a period and the name of the function you desire. You place the information you want to pass to the function within parentheses following the function name. For example, you will use the Dialogs library's `alert` function to display a message to the user from within a WMLScript function, as shown here:

```
Dialogs.alert("Message to user");
```

You will also use the WMLBrowser library's `go` function to direct the microbrowser to load a specific WML card or deck:

```
WMLBrowser.go("SomeFile.wml");
```

Looking at a Simple Example

As mentioned earlier, to call a WMLScript function, a WML application uses the `<go>` tag's href attribute to specify the name of the WMLScript file, followed by a pound sign (#) and the function name. The following WML application, WMLSDemo.wml, calls the WMLScript function Demo, which resides in the WMLScript file Sample.wmls. The Demo function displays the message "Hello, Wireless World!"

```
<?xml version="1.0"?>

<!DOCTYPE wml PUBLIC "-//WAPFORUM//DTD WML 1.2//EN"
    "http://www.wapforum.org/DTD/wml_1.1.xml">

<wml>

<card id="WMLSDemo">
```

```
<p>
   About to call function
</p>

<do type="accept" label="Go">
   <go href="Sample.wmls#Demo()" />
</do>

</card>

</wml>
```

The following statements implement the Sample.wmls file:

```
extern function Demo()
{
   Dialogs.alert("Hello, Wireless World!");
}
```

When the application first starts, it displays a message telling you that it is about to call the function. After you press the accept button, the application will call the function, which, in turn, displays the message. To display the message, the function uses the Dialogs library's **alert** function. To simplify your programming tasks, WMLScript provides several libraries of functions your scripts can use. The Dialogs library's **alert** function lets you display a message to the phone's screen.

In Module 8, you will examine the various library functions in detail. For now, simply understand that you can use the **alert** function shown here to display messages to the screen.

HelloMessages.wmls

Project 7-1: Revisiting Hello, Wireless World!

This WMLScript application, HelloMessages.wmls, will create two functions. The first function, Hello, will simply display the message "Hello," on the phone's screen. The function will then call the second function, Message, which will display the text "Hello, Wireless World!" To call the functions, you will create a WML application named CallTwoFunctions.wml, which uses the <go> tag to the call the first function.

Step-By-Step

1. Using a text editor, create the file HelloMessages.wmls. Within the file, create the Hello function, which uses the `Dialogs.alert` function to display a message and then calls the Message function by specifying the function's name followed by parentheses:

```
extern function Hello()
{
    Dialogs.alert("Hello,");
    Message();
}
```

2. Within the HelloMessages.wmls file, create the second function, Message, which contains the following statements:

```
extern function Message()
{
    Dialogs.alert("Hello, Wireless World!");
}
```

3. Using the text editor, create the WML application CallTwoFunctions.wml, which uses a <go> tag to call the WMLScript function "Hello":

```
<?xml version="1.0"?>

<!DOCTYPE wml PUBLIC "-//WAPFORUM//DTD WML 1.2//EN"
    "http://www.wapforum.org/DTD/wml_1.1.xml">

<wml>

<card id="CallTwoFunctions">
  <p>
    About to call the function
  </p>

  <do type="accept" label="Go">
    <go href="HelloMessages.wmls#Hello()" />
  </do>
```

7

```
</card>

</wml>
```

4. Load the CallTwoFunctions.wml application into the phone simulator.

Hint

When your scripts become more complex, the number of statements they contain may make the scripts difficult to understand. Because other programmers may eventually have to understand, and possibly change, your scripts, you must write your scripts in the most readable manner possible. You can increase your script's readability by using meaningful variable names, indenting and aligning statements, using blank lines to separate related statements, and providing comments that explain the script's processing.

Using Comments to Explain Your Script's Processing

As you create scripts, you can place notes within your source file that explain the script's processing. Programmers refer to such notes as *comments*. By placing comments throughout your code, you not only help other programmers understand your script, but you might also help yourself remember, after you have not looked at the script for several months, why your script uses specific statements. Comments exist only to aid programmers in understanding your code. When WMLScript compiles a script, it ignores the comments.

To place a comment within your WMLScript code, you simply place two forward slashes (//) within your script statements before the comment, as shown here:

```
// This is a comment
```

When the WMLScript compiler encounters the double slashes, the compiler ignores all text remaining on that line. At a minimum, you should place comments at the start of each script to specify who wrote the script, when, and why, as shown here:

```
// Script: Payroll.wmls
// Programmer: Kris Jamsa
// Written: 6-10-01
//
// Purpose: Calculates the monthly payroll and interacts with the
// payroll server to generate electronic checks.
```

Like the C and C++ programming languages, WMLScript also supports block comments that begin with a slash and an asterisk (/*) and end with an asterisk and a slash (*/), as shown here:

```
/*
  This is line one of a block comment
  This is line two of a block comment
  This is the last line of a block comment
*/
```

When the WMLScript compiler encounters a block comment, the compiler will ignore all the text that appears between the /* and */.

As your script performs specific processing, you should place comments in front of, or next to, specific statements to explain their purpose. For example, consider the following assignment statement:

```
Weekly_hours = 168;    // Number of hours in a week
```

The comment to the right of the assignment statement provides additional information to someone reading your script. In this case, the comment tells another programmer who is reading your code that the value 168 represents the number of hours in a week.

New programmers often have difficulty determining when and what to comment. In general, you cannot have too many comments in your scripts. Make sure, however, that your comments are meaningful. The following comments provide no additional information to a programmer who is reading your code:

```
Phone = "555-1212";    // Assign 555-1212 to the variable Phone
Salary = 33000.00;     // Assign 33,000.00 to the variable Salary
```

7

Note

Within WMLScript, you must place a semicolon at the end of each statement. The WMLScript compiler uses the semicolon to identify the end of a statement. If you omit the semicolon, the WMLScript compiler will generate a syntax error.

Storing Information in WMLScript Variables

To perform meaningful work, scripts must store information while they execute. For example, a script that prints a file must know the file's name and possibly the number of copies you want to print. As the script runs, it will store such information in your device's memory (RAM), and to store and retrieve information from specific memory locations, your scripts use *variables*. In the simplest sense, a variable is the name of a memory location that can store a specific value. The following sections examine how to create and use variables within WMLScript.

Hint

Think of a variable as a box that can contain a value. When you assign a value to the variable, you place a value into the box. When you later use the variable's value, the computer will simply look at the value in the box.

1-Minute Drill

● What is the purpose of comments within WMLScript?

● How do you create a comment within WMLScript?

● Comments are text that explain how and why the script performs specific operations. Comments exist only to help programmers understand the code—the WMLScript compiler ignores comments.

● To create a comment within WMLScript, you can use two slashes (//)—the compiler will ignore the text to the right of the slashes. You can also use a block comment (/* comment */) to document your code.

Declaring Variables Within Your Script

Scripts use variables to store information. Unlike other programming languages that require you to specify the type of value a variable will store (such as an integer or counting number, a floating-point number with a decimal point, or character string that contains alphanumeric characters and punctuation symbols), WMLScript does not require that you specify a variable's type. Instead, WMLScript only requires that you declare the name of each variable you plan to use. A WMLScript variable can store an integer, floating-point, Boolean ("true" or "false"), or character string value. In addition, a variable may store a special value that represents "invalid data" which may be the result of an error.

Before your script can use a variable, your script must *declare* the variable. In other words, your script must introduce the variable to the WMLScript compiler. To declare a variable in your script, you must specify the name your script will use to refer to the variable, following the **var** keyword. For example, the following statement creates a variable named UserName:

```
var  UserName;
```

Within a WMLScript function, each variable you create must have a unique name. When you create variables, choose a name that meaningfully describes to someone reading your script the information the variable will store. For example, your script might use variables such as UserName, UserPhoneNumber, and so on. Note the semicolon that follows the variable name in the preceding variable declaration. WMLScript considers a variable's declaration a statement, so you must place a semicolon at the end of the declaration.

When you select variable names, you can use a combination of letters, numbers, and underscores (_). The first character of your variable names must be a letter or underscore. You cannot begin a variable name with a number. Also, WMLScript considers uppercase and lowercase letters as different.

The following statements use the **var** keyword to declare three variables:

```
var  UserName;
var  UserPhone;
var  UserEmailAddress;
```

7

When you declare more than one variable, WMLScript lets you declare all the variables in one statement by separating the variable names with commas. The following statement, for example, declares the same three variables:

```
var  UserName, UserPhone, UserEmailAddress;
```

Assigning a Value to a Variable

After you declare a variable, you can use the WMLScript *assignment operator* (the equal sign) to assign a value to a variable. The following statements assign values to several different variables. Note that you use a semicolon to end each statement:

```
UserName = "Amanda";
UserPhone = "281-555-1212";
UserEmailAddress = "Duh@Wireless.com";
UserAge = 18
UserAllowance = 9.85;
```

These statements assign three character string values (contained in double quotes), one integer value (18), and one floating-point value (9.85). When you assign a character string to a variable, you must place the value within quotes. When you assign numeric values, you omit the quotes. WMLScript considers a numeric value with quotes around it a character string. Also, do not include commas within numeric values (such as 100,000 or 238,857). If you include the commas, the WMLScript compiler will generate and display syntax error messages.

When you declare a variable, it is often convenient to assign the variable's initial value at the same time (programmers refer to this process as "initializing a variable"). To make it easy for you to initialize variables, WMLScript lets you assign values when you declare variables, as shown here:

```
var  SearchEngineName = "Yahoo.com";
var  SearchEngineURL = "www.yahoo.com";
var  Limit = 100;
```

Using the Value a Variable Contains

After you assign a value to a variable, your scripts can use the variable's value simply by referring to the variable name. The following script, Variables.wmls, creates the **ShowVariables** function, which assigns values to three variables and then displays each variable's value:

```
extern function ShowVariables()
{
   var Name = "Amanda";
   var Phone = "555-1212";
   var City = "Houston";

   Dialogs.alert("Name: " + Name);
   Dialogs.alert("Phone: " + Phone);
   Dialogs.alert("City: " + City);
}
```

To display each variable's value, the function calls the Dialogs library's **alert** function. If you examine the values the **ShowVariables** function passes to Dialogs.alert, you will find that **ShowVariables** is passing one character string. When you use the plus operator (+) with character strings, WMLScript will *concatenate* the values, meaning that it will append the second string's contents to the first. In this case, the operation **"Name:" + Name** results in the character string "Name: Amanda".

To call the **ShowVariables** function, create the following WML application, ShowVar.wml, which uses a **<go>** tag to access the function:

```
<?xml version="1.0"?>

<!DOCTYPE wml PUBLIC "-//WAPFORUM//DTD WML 1.2//EN"
    "http://www.wapforum.org/DTD/wml_1.1.xml">

<wml>

<card id="ShowVar">
  <p>
    About to call function
  </p>
```

7

```
<do type="accept" label="Go">
   <go href="Variables.wmls#ShowVariables()" />
</do>

</card>

</wml>
```

When you load the ShowVar.wml application into the phone simulator, the simulator will display a message telling you it is about to call the function. After you press the accept button, the application will call the function, which, in turn, displays the values of the three variables.

Hint

Several of the previous examples have used decimal (base 10) values, such as 1, 3, and 9.99. Depending on your script's processing, there may be times when you must work with octal (base 8) or hexadecimal (base 16) values. To specify an octal value, you simply start the value with a 0, such as 0177. To specify a hexadecimal value, you start the value with 0x, such as 0xFF.

1-Minute Drill

- What is a variable?
- How do you create a variable in WMLScript?
- How do you assign a value to a variable?

Understanding Floating-Point Precision

Within WMLScript, you can assign a value to an integer variable in the range –2,147,483,648 to 2,147,483,647. When you assign a value to an integer variable

---

- A variable is a named storage location within which WMLScript can store information as a script executes.
- To create a variable in WMLScript, you use the var keyword to specify the name you will use for the variable.
- To assign a value to a variable in WMLScript, you use the assignment operator (=). The following statement assigns the value 10 to the variable Hours:

   Hours = 10;

that falls outside the range of values the variable can store, an overflow error occurs, which means the variable's value will not match the value it intended to assign. You must also understand that devices do not have unlimited *precision* (accuracy) with which they can store numbers. For example, when you work with floating-point numbers (values that have a decimal point), there are times when the device cannot represent the number in its exact format. Such precision errors can be difficult for you to detect within your scripts.

The following script, Precision.wmls, creates the function **PrecisionError**, which assigns small values to floating-point:

```
extern function PrecisionError()
{
  var A = 0.09999999999999999;
  var B = 0.10000000000000001;

  Dialogs.alert("A contains: " + A);
  Dialogs.alert("B contains: " + B);
}
```

Unfortunately, because the microbrowser has a limited ability to represent numbers, the script's variables do not actually contain the value the script assigns, but rather, the value 0.1. When you load the script into the phone simulator, the script will display the values shown in Figure 7-3. As you can see, the values the script assigns to the variables, and the values the variables actually contain, are not exactly the same. Such precision errors occur because the device must represent numbers using a fixed number of ones and zeros.

In many cases, the device can represent numbers exactly. At other times, as shown in this script, the computer's representation of a number is close, but not exact. As you program, you must keep precision in the back of your mind. Depending on the values your scripts are working with, precision errors that are very difficult to detect may arise.

To run the **PrecisionError** function, create the following WML application, ShowPrecision.wml:

```
<?xml version="1.0"?>

<!DOCTYPE wml PUBLIC "-//WAPFORUM//DTD WML 1.2//EN"
    "http://www.wapforum.org/DTD/wml_1.1.xml">
```

7

```
<wml>

<card id="ShowPrecision">
  <p>
    About to call function
  </p>

  <do type="accept" label="Go">
    <go href="Precision.wmls#PrecisionError()" />
  </do>

</card>

</wml>
```

Performing Arithmetic Operations

As your scripts become more complex, you will perform arithmetic operations such as addition, subtraction, multiplication, and division on the values your variables contain. Regardless of your script's purpose, most WMLScript functions will add, subtract, multiply, or divide values. Table 7-2 lists the WMLScript basic math operators.

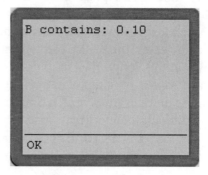

Figure 7-3   Floating-point values are not always exact

Operator	Purpose	Example
+	Addition	total = cost + tax;
−	Subtraction	change = payment − total;
*	Multiplication	tax = cost * tax_rate;
/	Division	average = total / count;

Table 7-2   The WMLScript Basic Math Operators

The following script, BasicMath.wmls, creates the **MathDemo** function, which displays the result of several simple arithmetic operations:

```
extern function MathDemo()
{
  var A = 10;
  var B = 5;
  var Result;

  Result = A + B;
  Dialogs.alert("A + B = " + Result);

  Result = A - B;
  Dialogs.alert("A - B = " + Result);

  Result = A * B;
  Dialogs.alert("A * B = " + Result);

  Result = A / B;
  Dialogs.alert("A / B = " + Result);
}
```

Take a close look at the **Dialogs.alert** script statements. Note that each expression first appears within quotes, which causes the script to output the characters describing the operation (such as A + B =) on your screen. Next, the script displays the result of the operation.

To call the **MathDemo** function, create the following ShowMath.wml application:

```
<?xml version="1.0"?>

<!DOCTYPE wml PUBLIC "-//WAPFORUM//DTD WML 1.2//EN"
```

```
          "http://www.wapforum.org/DTD/wml_1.1.xml">

<wml>

<card id="ShowMath">
  <p>
    About to call function
  </p>

  <do type="accept" label="Go">
    <go href="BasicMath.wmls#MathDemo()" />
  </do>

</card>

</wml>
```

Incrementing a Variable's Value by 1

As you program, a common operation you will perform is to add 1 to the value of a variable. For example, assume your script uses the variable named AppointmentCount to keep track of the number of appointments it has displayed. Each time your script displays an appointment, your script will add 1 to AppointmentCount's current value.

Using the WMLScript assignment operator, your script can increment AppointmentCount's value as shown here:

```
AppointmentCount = AppointmentCount + 1;
```

In this case, the script first obtains AppointmentCount's value and then adds 1 to that value. Then the script stores the result of the addition back to the variable AppointmentCount.

Because incrementing a variable's value is a common operation within scripts, WMLScript provides an *increment operator*, the double plus sign (++). The increment operator provides a shorthand way to add 1 to a variable's value. The following statements, for example, both increment AppointmentCount's value by 1:

```
AppointmentCount = AppointmentCount + 1;
AppointmentCount++;
```

The following script, IncrementOperator.wmls, uses the increment operator to increment AppointmentCount's value by 1:

```
extern function DemoIncrement()
 {
   var AppointmentCount = 0;

   Dialogs.alert("Starting value = " + AppointmentCount);

   AppointmentCount++;

   Dialogs.alert("After increment = " + AppointmentCount);
 }
```

To run the **DemoIncrement** function, create the following ShowIncrement .wml application:

```
<?xml version="1.0"?>

<!DOCTYPE wml PUBLIC "-//WAPFORUM//DTD WML 1.2//EN"
    "http://www.wapforum.org/DTD/wml_1.1.xml">

<wml>

<card id="ShowIncrement">
  <p>
    About to call function
  </p>

  <do type="accept" label="Go">
     <go href="IncrementOperator.wmls#DemoIncrement()" />
  </do>

</card>

</wml>
```

7

Using Prefix (Before) and Postfix (After) Increment Operators

When you use the increment operator, you can place the operator before or after the variable, as shown here:

```
++Variable;
Variable++;
```

In the first case, the operator appears in front of the variable, making the operator a *prefix increment operator*. In contrast, the second case places the operator after the variable and is a *postfix increment operator*. As you program, you must understand that WMLScript treats these two operators differently.

The prefix operator (**++Variable**) directs WMLScript to increment the variable's value before the value is used in the current statement. For example, consider the following assignment statement:

```
NewCount = ++Count;
```

The assignment statement directs WMLScript to first increment the variable Count's value and then to assign the new value to the variable NewCount. Using the prefix increment operator makes the previous statement equivalent to the following two statements:

```
Count = Count + 1;
NewCount = Count;
```

In contrast, the postfix operator directs WMLScript to first use the variable's value in the statement and then to increment the variable's value by 1:

```
NewCount = Count++;
```

Using the postfix operator in this case makes the previous statement equivalent to the following two statements:

```
NewCount = Count;
Count = Count + 1;
```

It is important that you understand the prefix and postfix increment operators, because you will see them in most WMLScript scripts.

As you have just learned, the double plus sign (++) is the WMLScript increment operator. In a similar way, the double minus sign (– –) is the WMLScript *decrement operator*. As was the case with the increment operator, WMLScript supports prefix and postfix decrement operators that work just like their increment operator counterparts, with the difference that they decrement the variable's value by 1. The following statement, for example, directs WMLScript to first use the value stored in the variable DaysRemaining and then to decrement the variable's value by 1:

```
SaleDays = DaysRemaining--;
```

The previous statement uses the postfix decrement operator and is equivalent to the following two statements:

```
SaleDays = DaysRemaining;
DaysRemaining = DaysRemaining - 1;
```

In contrast, the following statement directs WMLScript to first decrement the DaysRemaining variable's current value and then to assign that value:

```
SaleDays = --DaysRemaining;
```

The previous statement uses the prefix decrement operator and is equivalent to the following two statements:

```
DaysRemaining = DaysRemaining - 1;
SaleDays = DaysRemaining;
```

Other WMLScript Operators

The previous sections focused on the common WMLScript arithmetic operators and the increment and decrement operators. As you examine WMLScript code, you may also encounter one or more of the operators listed in Table 7-3. Within WMLScript, the bitwise operators behave in the same manner as related operators you may have encountered in other programming languages, such as C and C++.

Operator	Function
div	Integer division; returns the integer result of a division
%	Modulo operator; returns the remainder of an integer division
~	One's complement operator; inverts a value's bits
&	Bitwise AND operator; ANDs the ones bits between two values
|	Bitwise OR operator; ORs the ones bits between two values
^	Bitwise exclusive OR; exclusive ORs the bits between two values
<<	Bitwise left shift; shifts a value's bits left by the number of positions specified
>>	Bitwise right shift; shifts a value's bits right by the number of positions specified

Table 7-3   Other WMLScript Arithmetic Operators

Understanding Operator Precedence

When you perform arithmetic operations, you must be aware that WMLScript performs operations in a specific order, based on *operator precedence*. In other words, WMLScript considers some operators more important than others, and WMLScript will perform the important operations first. For example, based on its operator precedence, WMLScript will perform a multiplication operation before it will perform an addition.

To better understand operator precedence, consider the following expression:

```
Result = 6 + 1 * 3;
```

Depending on the order in which WMLScript performs the multiplication and addition operations, different results could occur, as shown here:

```
Result = 6 + 1 * 3;          Result = 6 + 1 * 3;
       = 7 * 3;                     = 6 * 3;
       = 21;                        = 18;
```

To avoid such mix-ups, WMLScript assigns a precedence to each operator to determine the order in which operations are performed. Because WMLScript performs operations in a consistent order, your scripts will perform arithmetic calculations in a consistent manner.

Table 7-4 lists the WMLScript operator precedence. The operators that appear in the top box have the highest precedence. Within each box, operators have the same precedence. If you examine the table, you will find that WMLScript assigns a higher precedence to multiplication than to addition (so the correct result in the previous example is 18).

Operator	Name	Example
++	Prefix increment	++variable
«− −	Prefix decrement	«− −variable
~	Ones complement	~expression
!	Not operator	! expression
+	Unary plus	+1
−	Unary minus	−1
typeof	Variable's type	typeof variable
isvalid	Validity check	isvalid variable
*	Multiplication	expression * expression
/	Division	expression / expression
%	Modulo	expression % expression
div	Integer division	expression div expression
>>	Bitwise right shift	expression << expression
<<	Bitwise left shift	expression >> expression
>>>	Bitwise right shift with 0 fill	expression >>> expression

Table 7-4 WMLScript Operator Precedence

Operator	Name	Example
&	Bitwise AND	expression & expression
|	Bitwise OR	expression | expression

Table 7-4   WMLScript Operator Precedence (*continued*)

Controlling the Order in Which WMLScript Performs Arithmetic Operations

As you have learned, WMLScript assigns a different precedence to different operators, which controls the order in which WMLScript performs operations. Unfortunately, there may be times when the order in which WMLScript performs arithmetic operations does not match the order you want. For example, assume that your script must add two weights and then multiply the result by a shipping rate (of $1.25), as shown here:

```
ShippingCost = Weight_a + Weight_b * 1.25;
```

Unfortunately, in this case, WMLScript will perform the multiplication first (**Weight_b * 1.25**) and then will add the value of Weight_a.

When your scripts must perform arithmetic operations in a specific order, you can place expressions within parentheses. When WMLScript evaluates expressions, it always first performs the operations your script groups within parentheses. For example, consider the following expression:

```
Result = (5 + 3) * (1 + 4);
```

WMLScript will evaluate this expression as shown here:

```
Result = (5 + 3) * (1 + 4);
       = (8) * (1 + 4);
       = 8 * (5);
       = 8 * 5;
       = 40;
```

By grouping expressions within parentheses in this way, you can control the order in which WMLScript performs arithmetic operations. Given the previous example, your script can add the two weights within parentheses, as shown here:

```
ShippingCost = (Weight_a + Weight_b) * 1.25;
```

1-Minute Drill

● How do the WMLScript prefix and postfix operators differ?

● Why does WMLScript assign an operator precedence?

● How can you override the WMLScript operator precedence?

Calling a WMLScript Function from Another Function

As your WMLScript code executes, it is not uncommon for one WMLScript function to use another. For example, to process a company's payroll, the WMLScript `CalculatePayroll` function might call the `GetSalary` function to determine an employee's salary, the `DetermineWithholdings` function to determine the corresponding taxes and other withholdings, as well as the `DetermineVacationTime` function to calculate the number of vacation days the employee has accumulated. When one function uses another function, the first function is said "to call" the second.

● The prefix operators (++variable and − −variable) direct WMLScript to first increment (or decrement) a variable's value and then to use the variable's new value. The postfix operators (variable++ and variable− −), direct WMLScript to first use the variable's value and then to increment (or decrement) the variable's value.

● WMLScript assigns an operator precedence to ensure that WMLScript performs arithmetic operations consistently.

● To override WMLScript's operator precedence, you can place expressions within parentheses, and these expressions will be evaluated first.

7

Within WMLScript, one function can call another by simply specifying the second function's name, followed by parentheses that contain information (parameters) that the first function is passing to the second. For example, to determine an employee's salary, the `CalculatePayroll` function might call the `GetSalary` function, passing the name of the desired employee as a parameter.

Depending on the processing the function performs, a function may return a result to the caller. The following function, `AddNumbers`, for example, returns the sum of the numbers 10 and 90:

```
extern function AddNumbers()
   {
      return(10 + 90);
   }
```

To return a value, the function uses the **return** statement. When WMLScript encounters the **return** statement within a function, WMLScript will stop executing the function's statements and will return the specified value to the calling function. Normally, the calling function will assign the return value to a variable, using an assignment operator as shown here:

```
Result = AddNumbers();
```

The following WMLScript file, FunctionCall.wmls, contains two functions. The first function, **ShowResult**, calls the **AddNumbers** function and displays the returned value. The second function, **AddNumbers**, simply returns the sum of the values 10 and 90, as previously shown:

```
extern function ShowResult()
  {
     var Result;

     Result = AddNumbers();

     Dialogs.alert("Result: " + Result);
  }
// Because the function is not called by a source outside
// of the WMLScript file, we did not precede its name with
// the extern keyword
```

```
function AddNumbers()
{
   return(10 + 90);
}
```

To call the **ShowResult** function, create the ShowResult.wml application, as shown here:

```
<?xml version="1.0"?>

<!DOCTYPE wml PUBLIC "-//WAPFORUM//DTD WML 1.2//EN"
    "http://www.wapforum.org/DTD/wml_1.1.xml">

<wml>

<card id="ShowResult">
  <p>
    About to call function
  </p>

  <do type="accept" label="Go">
    <go href="FunctionCall.wmls#ShowResult()" />
  </do>

</card>

</wml>
```

Other than to show you how a function returns a value, the **AddNumbers** function is of little use. A better function would add two numbers it receives from the caller. Before a function can access values passed to it from the caller, the function must declare parameter variables to hold the values by specifying the parameter variable names within the parentheses that follow the function name.

The following function, **AddTwoNumbers**, defines two parameter variables, A and B, to which WMLScript will assign the values passed to the function by the caller:

```
extern function AddTwoNumbers(A, B)
{
   return(A + B);
}
```

As you can see, in the **return** statement the function adds the values the two parameter variables contain.

The following WMLScript application, AddParameters.wmls again uses two functions. The first, **ShowResult** calls the **AddTwoNumbers** function, passing the values to add. After the **AddTwoNumbers** function returns the result, the **ShowResult** function displays the sum:

```
extern function ShowResult()
 {
   var Result;

   Result = AddTwoNumbers(5, 13);

   Dialogs.alert("Result: " + Result);
 }

function AddTwoNumbers(A, B)
 {
   return(A + B);
 }
```

When you pass information to a function using parameters, you must make sure that the number of values you pass to the function matches the number of parameter values the function expects to receive. In this case, the **ShowResult** function does not expect any parameters and the **AddTwoNumbers** function expects two.

To call the **ShowResult** function, create the following ShowAddTwo.wml application:

```
<?xml version="1.0"?>

<!DOCTYPE wml PUBLIC "-//WAPFORUM//DTD WML 1.2//EN"
    "http://www.wapforum.org/DTD/wml_1.1.xml">

<wml>

<card id="ShowAddTwo">
  <p>
    About to call function
  </p>

  <do type="accept" label="Go">
```

```
      <go href="AddParameters.wmls#ShowResult()" />
   </do>

</card>

</wml>
```

Passing WML Variables and Other Values as Parameters to a WMLScript Function

In the previous section, you learned how to pass parameters from one WMLScript function to another. Similarly, when a WML application calls a WMLScript function, the WML application can specify parameter values for the function within the <go> tag.

The following WML application, PassParameters.wml, displays a Go prompt for you to press the accept button. After you press the button, the application will call the WMLScript **ShowParameters** function, which resides within the Parameters.wmls file:

```
<?xml version="1.0"?>

<!DOCTYPE wml PUBLIC "-//WAPFORUM//DTD WML 1.2//EN"
    "http://www.wapforum.org/DTD/wml_1.1.xml">

<wml>

<card id="PassParameters">
  <p>
    About to call function
  </p>

  <do type="accept" label="Go">
    <go href="Parameters.wmls#ShowParameters(10, 20)" />
  </do>

</card>

</wml>
```

7

The following WMLScript file, Parameters.wmls, implements the **ShowParameters** function:

```
extern function ShowParameters(A, B)
{
  Dialogs.alert("A: " + A);
  Dialogs.alert("B: " + B);
}
```

In the previous example, the WML application passed two numeric constants to the **ShowParameters** function. You can, however, pass the values contained in WML variables as parameters.

The following WML application, PassVariables.wml, uses two **<input>** tags to prompt you for numeric values. The application then passes the variables to the **ShowParameters** function for display:

```
<?xml version="1.0"?>

<!DOCTYPE wml PUBLIC "-//WAPFORUM//DTD WML 1.2//EN"
    "http://www.wapforum.org/DTD/wml_1.1.xml">

<wml>

<card id="PassVariables">
  <p>
    Enter a value
    <input name="First" />

    Enter a second value
    <input name="Second" />
  </p>

  <do type="accept" label="Go">
    <go href="Parameters.wmls#ShowParameters($First, $Second)" />
  </do>

</card>

</wml>
```

> *Hint*
>
> When you pass a WML variable to a function as a parameter, the function cannot use the parameter variable to change the value of the WMLScript variable by assigning a value to the parameter variable. However, by using the WMLBrowser library's `setvar` function, a WMLScript function can change the value of an existing WML variable, or it can create a new variable whose value is accessible within other WML cards.

Using Conditional Processing to Make Decisions

A script is a list of instructions the microbrowser executes to accomplish a specific task. All the simple WMLScript scripts you have seen so far in this book have started with the first statement in a function and have executed each statement, in order, to the end of the function. As your scripts become more complex, there will be times when you will want the scripts to execute one set of statements if one condition is true and, possibly, another set if the condition is false. In other words, you will want your scripts to make decisions and act accordingly. Programs that make decisions perform *conditional processing*. In other words, based on one or more conditions, the script will execute specific statements.

Using Relational Operators to Compare Two Values

To make decisions, your scripts must first perform some type of test. For example, one script might test whether the password a user enters is correct, and a second script might test whether the phone number a user enters has the correct number of digits.

To perform such tests, your scripts will use the WMLScript relational operators. *Relational operators* let your scripts test how one value "relates" to another. In other words, using relational operators, your scripts can test whether one value is equal to, greater than, or less than a second value. When your scripts use relational operators to compare two values, the result of the comparison is either "true" or "false"—meaning that the two values are either equal (true) or they are not equal (false). Each of the `if` statements that the scripts in this book present will use the relational operators listed in Table 7-5.

7

Operator	Test	Example
==	If two values are equal	(Password == "Secret")
!=	If two values are not equal	(Digits != 8)
>	If the first value is greater than the second	(Age > 21)
<	If the first value is less than the second	(Age < 17)
>=	If the first value is greater than or equal to the second	(Weight >= 100.0)
<=	If the first value is less than or equal to the second	(Balance <= 0.0)

Table 7-5   The WMLScript Relational Operators

Using the if Statement to Test a Condition

The WMLScript if statement lets your scripts perform a test and then execute statements based on the result of the test. The if statement normally performs a test using a WMLScript relational operator. If the test result is true, the script executes the statement that follows the if. On the other hand, if the test result is false, the script ignores (skips) the statement that follows.

The format of the if statement is as follows:

```
if (condition_is_true)
   statement;
```

The following statement uses an if statement to determine whether the value stored in the variable Age is greater than or equal to (>=) 21. If the value is greater than or equal to 21, the application will load the WML card deck SellBeer.wml. If the value is less than 21, the microbrowser will continue its execution with the first statement that follows the if statement:

```
if (Age >=21)
  WMLBrowser.go("SellBeer.wml");
```

The following script, DemoIf.wmls, defines the **Check21** function, which uses the if statement to compare the value stored in the variable Age to 21. If the age is greater than or equal to 21, the script will displays a message to the user. Otherwise, if the value is less than 21, the script will simply end:

```
extern function Check21()
{
  var Age = 25;

  if (Age >= 21)
    Dialogs.alert("Check out www.freebeer.com");
}
```

As you can see, the script uses the WMLScript greater-than-or-equal-to relational operator (>=) to perform the test. If the value comparison results in true, the script will execute the statement that follows—in this case, displaying the message. If the comparison results in false, the script will not display the message. Experiment with this script, changing the age to a value that is less than 21.

To call the Check21 function, create the following ShowIfDemo.wml application:

```
<?xml version="1.0"?>

<!DOCTYPE wml PUBLIC "-//WAPFORUM//DTD WML 1.2//EN"
    "http://www.wapforum.org/DTD/wml_1.1.xml">

<wml>

<card id="ShowIfDemo">
  <p>
    About to call function
  </p>

  <do type="accept" label="Go">
    <go href="DemoIf.wmls#Check21()" />
  </do>

</card>

</wml>
```

Understanding Simple and Compound Statements

There will be times when your scripts must only perform one statement if the condition for an **if** statement is true. At other times, your script must perform several statements when a condition is true. When your script only performs one statement following an `if`, the statement is a *simple statement*:

```
if (Age >= 21)
  WMLBrowser.go("SellBeer.wml");
```

For your script to perform several statements when a condition evaluates as true, you must group the statements within left and right braces, {}. The statements that appear within the braces make up a *compound statement*, as shown here:

```
if (Password >= "Secret")
  {
    Dialogs.alert("Invalid Password");
    WMLBrowser.go("InvalidPassword.wml")
  }
```

It is not important that you remember the terms "simple" and "compound" statements, but rather, that you know that you must group related statements within the left and right braces.

Using the Else Statement for False Conditions

In the previous section, you used an `if` statement to determine whether a user's age was greater than or equal to 21. If the condition was true, the script displayed a message to the user. If the condition was false, meaning the age was less than 21, the script did not display a message; it simply ended. In most cases, your scripts will want to specify one set of statements that executes when the condition is true and a second set that executes if the condition is false. To provide the statements that execute when the condition is false, your scripts must use the `else` statement.

The format of the `else` statement is as follows:

```
if (condition_is_true)
   statement;
else
   statement;
```

The following script, IfElse.wmls, changes the Check21 function to use an `if` statement to test whether the value of the Age variable is greater than or equal to 21. If the condition is true, the script will display a message telling the user the phone number of a microbrewery. If the condition is false, the script will display a message telling the user to "Just say no!"

```
extern function Check21()
{
  var Age = 15;

  if (Age >= 21)
    Dialogs.alert("Check out www.freebeer.com");
  else
    Dialogs.alert("Just say no!");
}
```

Hint

If you examine the scripts this chapter presents, you will find that the scripts indent the statements that follow an if, else, or left brace. By indenting your statements one or two spaces in this way, you make it easy for someone who is reading your script to determine how statements relate to the if, and which statements relate to the else. WMLScript itself does not care about the indentation, but programmers who are reading and trying to understand your code will.

To call the new Check21 function, create the following ShowIfElse.wml application:

```
<?xml version="1.0"?>

<!DOCTYPE wml PUBLIC "-//WAPFORUM//DTD WML 1.2//EN"
    "http://www.wapforum.org/DTD/wml_1.1.xml">

<wml>

<card id="ShowIfElse">
  <p>
    About to call function
  </p>

  <do type="accept" label="Go">
    <go href="IfElse.wmls#Check21()" />
```

7

```
    </do>

</card>

</wml>
```

Using Logical Operators to Test Two or More Conditions

The if statement lets your scripts test specific conditions. As your scripts become more complex, there will be times when you will test more than one condition. For example, your script might test whether a user's age is greater than 20 and less than 50. Likewise, you might test whether a user owns a dog or a cat. To perform such operations, you will use the WMLScript logical AND operator (**&&**) and the logical OR operator (| |). When your scripts use the logical AND or logical OR operator to test more than one condition, you will place each condition within parentheses, as shown here:

```
if ((UserOwnsaDog) || (UserOwnsaCat))
   // Statements
```

The preceding if statement uses the logical OR operator to test whether the user owns a dog or a cat.

Similarly, the following statement uses a logical AND operator to determine whether a user's age is in the range 20 to 50:

```
if ((Age >= 20) && (Age <= 50))
   // Statements
```

When your scripts use the logical AND operator (**&&**), all the conditions within the statement must be true for the entire condition to evaluate as true. If any condition is false, the entire condition becomes false. For example, if the user's age is not greater than or equal to 20, the previous condition is false. Likewise, if the user's age is greater than 50, the condition is false. In order for the condition to be true, the user must be both 20 or older and 50 or younger.

For a condition that uses the logical OR operator to evaluate as true, only one condition must be true. In the previous dog or cat example, if the user owns a dog, the condition is true. If the user owns a cat, the condition is true. And, if the user owns both a dog and a cat, the condition is true. The only time the condition would be false is if the user does not own either a dog or a cat.

Understanding How WMLScript Represents True and False

Within WMLScript, a variable can store the value "true" or "false". Your applications, therefore, can use the variable's value within an **if** statement as previously shown:

```
UserOwnsaDog = true;

if (UserOwnsaDog)
   // Statements
```

In addition to the Boolean true and false values, WMLScript considers the following values as either true or false:

- The integer value 0 is false. Any other integer is true.

- An empty string ("") is false. Any other string is true.

- The floating-point value 0.0 is false. Any other floating-point value is true.

The following **if** statement, for example, uses the fact that WMLScript considers an empty string as false to test if the string variable Name contains a value:

```
if (Name)
   // Statements - the variable contains a value
else
   // Statements - the variable is empty
```

Using the WMLScript Not Operator

Just as there are times you want a script to perform specific statements when a condition is true, there may be times when you want your script to perform a set of statements when a condition is *not* true. The WMLScript Not operator, the exclamation point (!), lets your scripts test whether a condition is not true. For example, the following statement tests whether the user does not own a PC:

```
if (! Owns_a_PC)
  // Statement
```

The Not operator converts a false condition to true and a true condition to false. For example, assume that the user does not own a PC. The variable Owns_a_PC would contain the value false. When WMLScript performs the condition using the Not operator, WMLScript uses the variable's current value (false), and applies the Not operator, which makes the false value true. The entire condition then evaluates as true, and the script performs the corresponding statements.

The following statement uses the Not operator to test whether a user's password is not equal to "Secret":

```
if (Password != "Secret")
  // Statement
```

Performing If-Else Processing

This module's scripts have used **if** and **else** to specify one set of statements the script is to perform when a condition is true, and another set of statements the script will perform if the condition is false. There may be times, however, when your scripts must test several different related conditions. For example, assume that your script must determine a user's area code. To do so, your script must test for the many different cities. The following statement uses a series of **if-else** statements to illustrate a simplified example of the processing your script might perform:

```
if (City == "New York")
  AreaCode = 212;
else if (City == "Houston")
  AreaCode = 281;
else if (City == "Phoenix")
  AreaCode = 602;
else if (City == "Seattle")
  AreaCode = 206;
else
  AreaCode = 0;      // Program does not know city's area code
```

When the script performs the first **if** statement, it first tests whether the city is New York. If so, the script assigns the AreaCode variable the value 212. If the city is not New York, the script performs the following **else if** to test whether the city is Houston. The script will perform this processing for each city until it finds a matching city or it reaches the final **else** statement. If the script does not find a matching city, it assigns the variable AreaCode the value 0.

Using Iterative Processing to Repeat Specific Statements

In the previous sections, you learned how to use the WMLScript **if** statement to make decisions within your scripts. Closely related to decision making within your scripts is the ability to repeat one or more statements a specific number of times, or until a known condition occurs. In the following sections, you will use the WMLScript iterative constructs to repeat one or more statements. Depending on your script's processing, you may use the **for** or **while** loops to repeat script statements.

7

Using the for Statement to Repeat Statements a Specific Number of Times

One of the most common operations your scripts will perform is to repeat one or more statements a specific number of times. For example, a script might repeat the same statements to display five different WBMP images. The WMLScript **for** statement makes it very easy for your scripts to repeat one or more statements a specific number of times.

When your script uses a **for** statement, it must specify a variable, called a *control variable*, that keeps track of the number of times the loop executes. For example, the following **for** loop uses the variable Count to keep track of the number of times the script has executed the loop. In the following example, the loop will execute five times:

```
for (Count = 1; Count <= 5; Count++)
  // Statements;
```

The **for** statement consists of four parts: an initialization, a test condition, the statements that are to repeat, and an increment. To begin, the statement **Count = 1;** assigns the control variable's starting value. The **for** loop performs this initialization one time, when the loop first starts. Next, the loop tests the condition **Count <= 5**. If the condition is true, the **for** loop will execute the statements that follow. If the condition is false, the loop will end, and the script will continue its execution with the first statement that follows the loop. If the condition is true, and the **for** loop executes the statements, the loop will then increment the variable Count using the statement Count++. Finally, the script tests the condition **Count <= 5** again. If the condition is still true, the script will execute the statements, and the process of incrementing and then testing the variable count will repeat.

The following script, ForDemo.wmls, creates the OneToFive function, which uses the **for** loop to display the values 1 through 5:

```
extern function OneToFive()
{
  var Count;

  for (Count = 1; Count <= 5; Count++)
    Dialogs.alert("Count = " + Count);
}
```

As you can see, the **for** loop initializes the variable Count to the value 1. The loop then tests if Count's value is less than or equal to 5. If so, the **for** loop will execute the corresponding statement and then increment Count, repeating the test. Experiment with the script, changing the value 5 to 1, 10, and even 0 (which causes the loop's first condition to fail because Count's initial value (1) will be greater than 0.

To call the OneToFive function, create the following ShowFor.wml application:

```
<?xml version="1.0"?>

<!DOCTYPE wml PUBLIC "-//WAPFORUM//DTD WML 1.2//EN"
    "http://www.wapforum.org/DTD/wml_1.1.xml">

<wml>

<card id="Showfor">
  <p>
```

```
   About to call function
 </p>

 <do type="accept" label="Go">
    <go href="ForDemo.wmls#OneToFive()" />
 </do>

</card>

</wml>
```

Within a **for** loop, you are not restricted to incrementing the value by 1. The following **for** loop, for example, displays every fifth number from 0 through 25:

```
for (count = 0; count <= 25; count += 5)
  Dialogs.alert("Count = " + Count);
```

Note the statement the **for** loop uses to increment the variable Count:

```
Count += 5;
```

When you want to add a value to a variable's current value and then assign the result to the same variable, WMLScript lets your scripts do so in one of two ways. First, assuming your script must add the value 5 to Count, your script can do as shown here:

```
Count = Count + 5;
```

Second, WMLScript lets you use the shorthand notation shown here to add the value 5 to the variable Count:

```
Count += 5;
```

Because it is easier to write, programmers commonly use this shorthand notation within loops.

When you use a **for** loop, WMLScript does not limit your loops to counting up. The following **for** loop, for example, counts down from 10 to 1, by ones:

```
for (count = 10; count >= 1; count--)
  // Statements
```

7

As you can see, the **for** loop initializes the variable Count to 10. With each iteration, the loop decrements the variable's value by 1. When the Count contains the value 0, the loop ends.

WML also does not restrict a **for** loop to using integer values for the control variable. The following statement, for example, uses a floating-point value, which the loop initializes to 0.0 and then increments by 0.10:

```
for (Value = 0.0; Value <= 1.0; Value += 0.10)
  // Statements
```

A **for** loop ends when it reaches its ending condition and your script continues execution at the first statement that follows the **for** loop. Unfortunately, due to errors within scripts, there are times when a loop never reaches its ending condition and, therefore, loops forever (or until you end the script). Programmers refer to such unending loops as infinite loops—loops that have no way of ending. The following **for** statement, for example, creates an infinite loop:

```
for (Count = 0; Count < 10; WrongVariable++)
  // Statements
```

As you can see, the **for** loop uses the variable Count as its control variable. Within the loop's increment section, however, the script increments the wrong variable. As a result, the loop never increments the variable Count and Count will never have a value greater than or equal to 10. Thus, the loop becomes a never-ending infinite loop.

Using a While Loop to Repeat Statements While a Condition is True

The WMLScript **for** loop lets your scripts repeat one or more statements a specific number of times. In some cases, however, your scripts must repeat statements as long as a specific condition is true. For situations in which your scripts must loop as long as a specific condition is true, but not necessarily a specific number of times, your scripts can use the WMLScript **while** statement. The general format of the **while** statement is as follows:

```
while (Condition_Is_True)
   statement;
```

When your script encounters a **while** statement, your script first tests the specified condition. If the condition is true, the script will execute the **while** loop's statements. After the last statement in the loop executes, the **while** loop again tests the condition. If the condition is still true, the loop's statements will repeat, and this process will continue. When the condition finally becomes false, the loop will end, and your script will continue its execution at the first statement that follows the loop.

The following script, WhilePassword.wmls, uses a **while** loop to repeatedly prompt the user to enter a password, until the user enters the password "Secret":

```
extern function GetPassword()
{
  var Password = "";  // Assign an initial value != "Secret"

  while (Password != "Secret")
    Password = Dialogs.prompt("Password", "");

  Dialogs.alert("You're in!");
}
```

7

To call the GetPassword function, create the following ShowWhile.wml application:

```
<?xml version="1.0"?>

<!DOCTYPE wml PUBLIC "-//WAPFORUM//DTD WML 1.2//EN"
    "http://www.wapforum.org/DTD/wml_1.1.xml">

<wml>

<card id="Showwhile">
  <p>
    About to call function
  </p>

  <do type="accept" label="Go">
    <go href="WhilePassword.wmls#GetPassword()" />
```

```
    </do>
</card>
</wml>
```

Accessing WML Variables from Within WMLScript

Earlier in this module, you learned how to pass parameters from a WML application to a WMLScript function. In addition to using parameters, a WMLScript function can also access and change the value stored in a WML variable. To access a WML variable's value, the WMLScript function uses the WMLBrowser library's **getVar** function, as shown here:

```
Value = WMLBrowser.getVar("VariableName");
```

To change the value in a WML variable, the WMLScript function uses the WMLBrowser library's setVar function. The following statement, for example, assigns the string "Hello, Wireless World!" to the WML variable Message. If the Message variable did not previously exist, the statement will create it. If the Message variable exists, the statement will overwrite the variable's contents:

```
WMLBrowser.setVar("Message", "Hello, Wireless World!");
```

The following WML application, GetMessage.wml, uses an **<input>** tag to prompt the user for a message. The application then calls the WMLScript ChangeMessage function, which resides in the WMLScript file Message.wmls. The function, in turn, uses the WMLBrowser library getVar function to get the value of the WML Message variable for display. ChangeMessage then uses the WMLBrowser library's setVar function to change the message. Finally, the function uses the WMLBrowser library's go function to direct the microbrowser to load the ShowMessage card from within the GetMessage.wml application.

The following statements implement the GetMessage.wml application:

```
<?xml version="1.0"?>

<!DOCTYPE wml PUBLIC "-//WAPFORUM//DTD WML 1.2//EN"
    "http://www.wapforum.org/DTD/wml_1.1.xml">

<wml>

<card id="GetMessage">
  <p>
    Enter message
    <input name="Message" />
  </p>

  <do type="accept" label="Go">
    <go href="Message.wmls#ChangeMessage()" />
  </do>

</card>

<card id="ShowMessage">
  <p>
    Final message: $Message
  </p>
</card>

</wml>
```

The following statements implement the Message.wmls script:

```
extern function ChangeMessage()
 {
   var Message;

   Message = WMLBrowser.getVar("Message");

   Dialogs.alert("Original Message: " + Message);

   WMLBrowser.setVar("Message", "Hello, Wireless World!");

   WMLBrowser.go("GetMessage.wml#ShowMessage");
 }
```

7

Using the use access Pragma to Restrict Access to a WMLScript File

After you place a WMLScript file on line, there may be times when you want to restrict which applications can use the file's contents. You may not, for example, want other programmers to take advantage of WMLScript functions you have written for specific applications. To restrict which applications can access the functions a WMLScript file contains, you can use the **use access** pragma. In general, the term *pragma* is simply another name for a compiler directive.

The **use access** pragma lets you restrict access to functions within a WMLScript file to WML and WMLScript files that reside on a specific host. For example, to restrict access to WML and WMLScript files that reside on the domain www.WirelessLookup.com, you would place the following **use access** pragma at the top of your WMLScript file:

```
use access domain "WirelessLookup.com" path "";
```

You may further want to restrict access to those WML and WMLScript files that reside within a specific directory path on the host. In such cases, you can specify the path within the **use access** pragma, as shown here:

```
use access domain "WirelessLookup.com" path "/Wireless/Demos";
```

Using the use Pragma to Simplify Access to External Functions

Within a WMLScript application, it is possible for a function to call another function that resides within a different WMLScript file. For example, assume the file SystemUtilities.wmls contains the GetDate function, as shown here:

```
extern function GetDate()
{
   return("January 31, 2001");
}
```

Before a function in a different WMLScript file can call the GetDate function, the other WMLScript file must place a **use** pragma similar to the following at the top of the file:

```
use url Util "SystemUtilities.wmls";
```

In this case, the **use** pragma creates a library named Util. Within the WMLScript file, functions can use the Util library name within a function call. For example, the following statement calls the GetDate function:

```
Result = Util#GetDate();
```

The following WMLScript file uses the Util library to call the GetDate function:

```
use url Util "SystemUtilities.wmls";

extern function TestPragma()
{
   var Result;

   Result = Util#GetDate();
   Dialogs.alert(Result);
}
```

7

☑Mastery Check

1. How does a WML application call a WMLScript function?

   _____

   _____

2. How do WMLScript variables differ from variables used in other programming languages?

   _____

   _____

3. How do you declare a variable within WMLScript?

   _____

   _____

4. What is the output of the following expression:

   Result = 3 + 2 * 5 – 3;

5. What is a parameter?

   _____

   _____

6. Create a WMLScript function named Cube that returns the cube of the value passed to the function as a parameter.

7. What is a pragma?

   _____

   _____

8. Create an `if` statement to test whether the variable Salary contains a value in the range 35,000 to 75,000.

9. Create a `for` loop that displays the numbers 0.25, 0.50, 0.75, and 1.0.

10. When should you use a `for` loop as opposed to a `while` loop?

   _____

   _____

Module 8

Using the WMLScript Libraries

The Goals of This Module

- Learn how to call the WMLScript library functions
- Learn how to use the Dialogs library functions to simplify input and output operations
- Learn how to use the Float library functions to perform arithmetic operations
- Learn how to use the String library functions to manipulate character strings and delimited strings
- Learn how to use the URL library functions to parse key information from a URL address
- Learn how to use the WMLBrowser library functions to interact with the WML context

In Module 7, you learned that by using WMLScript you can add significant processing capabilities to your WML applications. You created your own WMLScript functions, each of which performed a specific task. To make it easier for your applications to perform common operations, WMLScript provides its own built-in functions that you can use easily and quickly. By taking advantage of these WMLScript functions, you reduce the amount of programming you must perform.

Understanding Libraries, Functions, and Parameters

WMLScript organizes its built-in functions in libraries. In general, a library is a collection of functions (software that performs a specific task) that another programmer has written, and which your applications can use. By making use of a library's functions, you reduce the amount of code you must write, and thus your program development time. Each library contains functions that correspond to a specific set of operations. For example, the WMLScript Dialogs library provides a collection of functions your applications can use to interact with the user (to perform a dialog with the user). Likewise, the Float library provides functions your applications can use to perform floating-point operations. This module examines the WMLScript built-in functions in detail.

Often, you will pass information to a function, that programmers refer to as parameters. When your code calls a function, you will place the parameter values within parentheses after the function name. For example, to pass the value 100 to the Float library's sqrt function, you would use `Float.sqrt(100)`. Depending on the function, the number of parameters an application can pass to the function will differ. The sqrt function supports only one parameter. In contrast, the pow function supports two parameters, which you separate using a comma: `Float.pow(10, 2)`. Some functions, such as the WMLBrowser library's getCurrentCard function do not support parameter values. In such cases, you call the function with an empty set of parentheses: `WMLBrowser.getCurrentCard()`.

Each section in this module will briefly introduce a library's functions. Then, the section will present WML and WMLScript source code that uses the function to accomplish a specific task. Take time to experiment with the applications this module presents, and you will quickly recognize the power of the WMLScript built-in library functions.

Using the WMLScript Dialogs Library

One of the most difficult challenges programmers face when they create applications is the user interface. In Module 5, you learned how to use the `<input>` tag to perform input operations within WML applications. To improve your application's input and output capabilities, WMLScript provides the Dialogs library, which contains the three functions described in Table 8-1.

Alerting the User of a Problem or Event

As your WML applications become more complex, there will be many times when your application will display a message to which the user must respond. Using the WMLScript Dialogs library alert function, an application can display a message and then pause the application's processing until the user responds. After the user presses the accept key, the alert function returns control to the calling function. The format of the alert function is as follows:

```
Dialogs.alert("Important User Message");
```

8

For example, assume that the user enters an invalid password. In such cases, you will want to notify the user of the invalid password and then let the user re-enter the password. The following WML application, UseAlert.wml, prompts

Function	Example	Purpose
alert	Dialogs.alert("Message");	Waits for the user to acknowledge a message.
confirm	Dialogs.response = confirm("Message", "Yes", "No");	Waits for the user to confirm a message by selecting one of two options. Returns the value "true" if the user selects the first option and "false" for the second.
prompt	value = Dialogs.prompt("Message", "Default Value");	Prompts the user for a response, providing a default value.

Table 8-1   Functions Provided by the WMLScript Dialogs Library

the user to enter a password. After the application has the password, it calls the ValidatePassword function, which resides in the Password.wmls WMLScript file:

```
<?xml version="1.0"?>

<!DOCTYPE wml PUBLIC "-//WAPFORUM//DTD WML 1.2//EN"
    "http://www.wapforum.org/DTD/wml_1.1.xml">

<wml>

<card id="UseAlert" title="UseAlert">
 <p>
   Enter password:
   <input name="Password" type="password" />

   <do type="accept">
     <go href="Password.wmls#ValidatePassword('$(Password)')" />
   </do>
 </p>
</card>

</wml>
```

The Password.wmls file contains the following statements:

```
extern function ValidatePassword(UserPassword)
{

  if ($UserPassword == "Password")
    Dialogs.alert("Password is correct");
  else
    {
      Dialogs.alert("Invalid Password");
      WMLBrowser.newContext();
      WMLBrowser.go("UseAlert.wml");
    }
}
```

If the password is valid (in this case, if the user enters the password text "Password"), the WMLScript uses the alert function to display a message stating that the password is correct.

If the password is invalid, the WMLScript uses the alert function to display a message to the user stating that the password was invalid, as shown in Figure 8-1. Then the script calls the WMLBrowser library's newContext function, which

Figure 8-1 Using the alert function to display a message to which the user must respond

erases the value of any variables in the WML context. If you do not clear the context in this way, the WML context will retain the previous password when the script returns control to the WML card UseAlert.wml, which it uses to again prompt the user for a password. As you can see, the script uses the WMLBrowser library's go function to reload the card into the microbrowser.

Hint

Typing on a cell phone's keypad is difficult under the best circumstances. When a WML application uses the type="password" attribute within an <input> tag, the browser will not display the characters the user types, but rather, will instead display asterisk (*) characters. Although the asterisk character prevents another user from viewing a user's password, the asterisks make it impossible for the user to know whether he or she typed the correct character. Because of the cell phone's small screen size and the user's ability to move the screen out of the view of others, most applications should display password characters on the screen as the user types, as opposed to displaying asterisks.

Confirming an Operation with the User

Applications will often display a question to the user that requires a Yes or No response, rather than just pressing the accept key as in the previous example. Using the Dialogs library's confirm function, an application can display a question and two user options (such as Yes or No, or Continue or Stop). The confirm function returns the value "true" if the user selects the first option and "false" if the user selects the second option. The format of the confirm function is as follows:

```
Result = Dialogs.confirm("Invalid Password", "Retry", "Cancel");
```

The following WMLScript file, ConfirmPassword.wmls, changes the previous application slightly to use the confirm function to verify that the user wants to re-enter a password:

```
extern function ValidatePassword(UserPassword)
  {
    var result;  // Value returned by confirm function

    if (UserPassword == "Password")
      Dialogs.alert("Password is correct");
    else
      {
        result = Dialogs.confirm("Invalid Password -- Retry",
                                 "Yes", "No");

        if (result)
          {
            WMLBrowser.newContext();
            WMLBrowser.go("UseConfirm.wml");
          }
        else
          WMLBrowser.go("BadPassword.wml");
      }
  }
```

If the user enters the correct password, the script uses the alert function to display a message that tells the user that his or her password was correct. If the user enters an invalid value, the script uses the confirm function to determine whether the user wants to try a different password. If the user selects No, the script uses the go function to load the WML card deck BadPassword.wml. If the user selects Yes, the script clears the current WML context (erasing the previous password), and then uses the go function to reload the UseConfirm.wml card.

Hint

Using the WMLBrowser.newContext function, you can erase the current WML context, which clears the history stack and erases existing variables. You can also erase the WML context by placing a `newcontext="true"` attribute within a WML `<card>` tag. When the browser loads a card that contains the `newcontext="true"` attribute, the browser will erase the current context.

To use the new password verifier, create the WML application UseConfirm.wml containing the following statements:

```
<?xml version="1.0"?>

<!DOCTYPE wml PUBLIC "-//WAPFORUM//DTD WML 1.2//EN"
    "http://www.wapforum.org/DTD/wml_1.1.xml">

<wml>

<card id="UseConfirm" title="UseConfirm">
 <p>
   Enter password:
   <input name="Password" type="password" />

   <do type="accept">
     <go href=
       "ConfirmPassword.wmls#ValidatePassword('$(Password)')" />
   </do>
 </p>
</card>

</wml>
```

When you load the UseConfirm.wml application into the simulator, the application will prompt you for a password. If you enter the password text "Password", the application will continue. Otherwise, the application will

| **Figure 8-2** | Using the confirm function to prompt the user to re-enter a password or cancel |

display the message shown in Figure 8-2, which lets you choose to re-enter or cancel the operation.

If you choose to re-enter the password, the confirm function will return the value "true" to the WMLScript code, which will reload the UseConfirm.wml card, prompting you to re-enter the password. If you choose to cancel the operation, the function returns the value "false" to the function, which causes the WMLScript code to call the BadPassword.wml card, which simply displays the message "Invalid user password – Access denied", as shown here:

```
<?xml version="1.0"?>

<!DOCTYPE wml PUBLIC "-//WAPFORUM//DTD WML 1.2//EN"
    "http://www.wapforum.org/DTD/wml_1.1.xml">
<wml>

<card id="BadPassword" title="BadPassword">
 <p>
    Invalid user password<br/>
    Access denied
 </p>
</card>

</wml>
```

Prompting the User for Input

In Module 5, you used the `<input>` tag within a WML application to prompt the user for input. In WMLScript you can use the Dialogs library's prompt function to prompt the user for input. The prompt function displays to the user the prompt you specify. In addition, the prompt function lets you specify a default value. The format of the prompt function is as follows:

```
Result = Dialogs.prompt("Prompt", "Default value");
```

For example, the following WML application, UsePrompt.wml, calls the WMLScript GetFavoriteFood, which resides within the WMLScript file Food.wmls, to prompt the user for his or her favorite food:

```
<?xml version="1.0"?>

<!DOCTYPE wml PUBLIC "-//WAPFORUM//DTD WML 1.2//EN"
```

```
Enter Favorite Food
Italian|




OK              alpha
```

Figure 8-3 | Using the prompt function to get user input

Ask the Expert

Question: Do all microbrowsers support the WMLScript libraries?

Answer: Unfortunately, no. Although WMLScript offers what is said to be a "standard set of functions," you will encounter functions that simply do not work with specific phones or phone simulators.

Question: How can I know which functions work and which ones do not work with various browsers?

Answer: You cannot. That is why, when you develop your applications, you should test them using as many phones and simulators as you can.

Question: What should I do if a function does not work on a specific phone?

Answer: Normally, when a WMLScript function does not work, the browser will not return a value for the function. For example, assume you find that for a specific microbrowser, the Float library's pow function does not return a value. At the start of your application, you can test the function by comparing the function's result to a known result. For example, the following statements invoke the pow function with values that should result in the value 25. If the function's return value does not equal 25, the statements load the NoSupport.wml card, which lets the application exit gracefully:

```
if (Float.pow(5, 2) != 25)
  WMLScript.go("NoSupport.wml");
```

8

Using the WMLScript Float Library

A floating-point number is a number that contains a decimal point, such as 3.815 or 99.99. Floating-point numbers are difficult for small processors, such as those in cellular phones, to manipulate, because the processor must represent the floating-point number using a fixed number of bits. For example, a processor can represent numbers in the range 0 to 255 using eight bits:

Bit Combination	Value
0000 0000	0
0000 0001	1
0000 0010	2
0000 0011	3
...	...
1111 1101	253
1111 1110	254
1111 1111	255

Likewise, a processor can represent numbers in the range 0 to 65,535 using 16 bits. The challenge floating-point numbers present is that the processor must represent very small fractional components using a fixed number of bits. To represent the value 0.5, the processor needs only one bit:

$$1 \times 2^{-1} = 0.5$$

Likewise, to represent the numbers 0.25 or 0.75, the processor needs two bits:

$$1 \times 2^{-1} = 0.5 \qquad\qquad 0 \times 2^{-1} = 0$$
$$1 \times 2^{-2} = 0.25 \qquad\qquad 1 \times 2^{-2} = 0.25$$
$$============== \qquad ==============$$
$$0.75 \qquad\qquad\qquad 0.25$$

To represent a very complex floating-point number, or a repeating fraction, such as 0.333333333, the processor needs a very large number of bits. To avoid the complexity of manipulating floating-point numbers, many small processors simply do not support floating-point operations.

In the following project, you will learn how to use the WMLScript Lang library's float function to determine whether a device supports floating-point operations. If you find that the device supports floating-point operations, your applications can take advantage of the WMLScript Float library, which provides

Function	Example	Purpose
ceil	integer_value = Float.ceil(55.4);	Returns the largest integer value that is not smaller than the specified floating-point value.
floor	integer_value = Float.floor(55.4);	Returns the smallest integer value that is not larger than the specified floating-point value.
int	integer_value = Float.int(55.4);	Returns the integer portion of a floating-point value.
maxfloat	float_value = Float.maxfloat();	Returns the largest floating-point value the system supports.
minfloat	float_value = Float.minfloat();	Returns the smallest floating-point value the system supports.
pow	float_value = Float.pow(5, 2);	Returns the result of the value raised to the specified power.
round	integer_value = Float.round(99.9);	Returns the specified value rounded to the nearest integer.
sqrt	float_value = Float.sqrt(100);	Returns the square root of the specified value.

Table 8-2   Functions Provided by the WMLScript Float Library

functions that perform common arithmetic operations. Table 8-2 briefly describes functions built into the WMLScript Float library.

8

`CheckFloat.wml`

Project 8-1: Checking a Phone for Floating-Point Support

Before you use the Float library to perform floating-point operations, you should use the Lang.float function to determine whether the microbrowser supports floating-point operations. This project creates the CheckFloat.wml WML application, which calls the CheckFloatingPoint function that resides within the WMLScript file CheckFloatingPoint.wmls.

Step-By-Step

1. Using a text editor, create the CheckFloat.wml file. Enter the following header information into the file:

```
<?xml version="1.0"?>

<!DOCTYPE wml PUBLIC "-//WAPFORUM//DTD WML 1.2//EN"
```

```
        "http://www.wapforum.org/DTD/wml_1.1.xml">

<wml>
```

2. Use a <card> tag to create the CheckFloat card:

```
<card id="CheckList">
  <p>
```

3. To pass control to the WMLScript CheckFloatingPoint function, the card will trap the onenterforward event that occurs when the card is first loaded. Within the card, use the following <onevent> statement to trap the event:

```
<onevent type="onenterforward">
    <go href="CheckFloatingPoint.wmls#CheckFloatingPoint()" />
</onevent>
```

4. Use the </card> tag to end the card and the </wml> tag to end the deck. The card's contents should appear as follows:

```
<?xml version="1.0"?>

<!DOCTYPE wml PUBLIC "-//WAPFORUM//DTD WML 1.2//EN"
    "http://www.wapforum.org/DTD/wml_1.1.xml">

<wml>

<card id="CheckFloat">
  <onevent type="onenterforward">
    <go href="CheckFloatingPoint.wmls#CheckFloatingPoint()" />

  </onevent>
</card>

</wml>
```

5. Using a text editor, create the CheckFloatingPoint.wmls file. Enter the following statements in the file to create the CheckFloatingPoint function, which uses the Lang.float() function to determine whether floating-point operations are supported:

```
extern function CheckFloatingPoint()
 {
```

```
    if (Lang.float())
      Dialogs.alert("Floating Point is OK");
    else
      Dialogs.alert("Browser does not support floating point");
}
```

6. Save the file's contents to disk. Using a phone simulator, load and execute the WML application CheckFloat.wml.

Hint

As your applications execute across the Wireless Web, an application may run on a wide range of phone types, with a myriad of microbrowsers. As a rule, if your application performs arithmetic operations, you should use the Lang.float function when your application first starts to determine whether the current device supports floating-point operations. If the device does not support floating-point operations, your application should exit gracefully by displaying a meaningful message to the user.

Determining the Range of Values Your Device Supports

8

Within WMLScript, a floating-point value can store a value in the range 1.17549435e-38 to 3.40282347e+38. However, depending on the device you are using, the range of floating-point values a device can store may differ. The WML Float library's minFloat and maxFloat functions return the smallest and largest values the current device can support. The following WML file, FloatRange.wml, uses these functions to determine the current device capabilities:

```
<?xml version="1.0"?>

<!DOCTYPE wml PUBLIC "-//WAPFORUM//DTD WML 1.2//EN"
    "http://www.wapforum.org/DTD/wml_1.1.xml">

<wml>

<card id="FloatRange" title="FloatRange">
 <p>
    Press OK to display<br/>
    floating-point range
```

```
   <do type="accept">
     <go href="FloatingPointRange.wmls#SetFloatRange()" />
   </do>
 </p>
</card>

</wml>
```

As you can see, the WML code calls the function SetFloatRange, which resides in the file FloatingPointRange.wmls. Within the function, the code assigns the minimum and maximum values to the variables MinFloat and MaxFloat.

```
extern function SetFloatRange()
 {
    WMLBrowser.setVar("MinFloat", Float.minFloat());
    WMLBrowser.setVar("MaxFloat", Float.maxFloat());
    WMLBrowser.refresh();
    WMLBrowser.go("ShowFloatRange.wml");
 }
```

The code then loads the ShowFloatRange.wml WML card, which displays each variable's value:

```
<?xml version="1.0"?>

<!DOCTYPE wml PUBLIC "-//WAPFORUM//DTD WML 1.2//EN"
    "http://www.wapforum.org/DTD/wml_1.1.xml">

<wml>

<card id="ShowFloatRange" title="ShowFloatRange">
 <p>
    Min $(MinFloat) <br/>
    Max $(MaxFloat)
 </p>
</card>

</wml>
```

When you load the FloatRange.wml application into the phone simulator, the phone simulator will prompt you to press the accept button to display the range of floating-point values. After you press the accept button, the application will display output something like that shown in Figure 8-4.

Figure 8-4   Using the Float library to determine the smallest and largest floating-point values a device supports

Rounding and Truncating Values

When applications work with floating-point values, the applications will often, for simplicity, either round a value up or truncate the value into an integer. The WML Float library's round function returns the integer value that is closest to the floating-point value. In contrast, the Float library's int function creates an integer value by discarding the floating-point digits. The following WML file, RoundIntDemo.wml, illustrates the use of the round and int functions:

```
<?xml version="1.0"?>

<!DOCTYPE wml PUBLIC "-//WAPFORUM//DTD WML 1.2//EN"
    "http://www.wapforum.org/DTD/wml_1.1.xml">

<wml>

<card id="RoundIntDemo">
 <p>
   Enter a floating-point value:
   <input name="Value" />

   <do type="accept">
     <go href="RoundInt.wmls#IntRound($(Value))" />
   </do>
 </p>
</card>

</wml>
```

8

As you can see, the WML code prompts you to enter a floating-point value. The code then calls the WMLScript function IntRound, which resides in the file RoundInt.wmls. Within the function, the code uses the round and int functions and assigns the result of each function to the variables RoundResult and IntResult, respectively. The function then calls the WML application ShowIntRound.wml to display the result:

```
extern function IntRound(Value)
 {
    WMLBrowser.setVar("IntResult", Float.int(Value));
    WMLBrowser.setVar("RoundResult", Float.round(Value));

    WMLBrowser.refresh();
    WMLBrowser.go("ShowIntRound.wml");
 }
```

The following code statements implement ShowIntRound.wml:

```
<?xml version="1.0"?>

<!DOCTYPE wml PUBLIC "-//WAPFORUM//DTD WML 1.2//EN"
    "http://www.wapforum.org/DTD/wml_1.1.xml">

<wml>

<card id="ShowIntRound">
 <p>
    $(Value) int: $(IntResult) <br/>
    $(Value) round: $(RoundResult) <br/>
 </p>
</card>

</wml>
```

When you run the RoundIntDemo.wml application in the phone simulator, you will see output similar to that shown in Figure 8-5.

Depending on your application's purpose, there may be times when the application requires finer floating-point value conversion than the round and int functions provide. In such cases, you can use the Float library's floor and ceil functions. The floor function returns the greatest integer value that is not larger than the floating-point value. In contrast, the ceil function returns the smallest integer value that is not less than the floating-point value. The

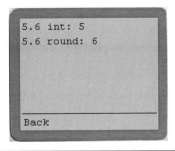

```
5.6 int: 5
5.6 round:  6




Back
```

Figure 8-5   Using the Float library to round and truncate floating-point numbers

following WML file, FloorCeilDemo.wml, calls the GetFloorCeil function that resides in the WMLScript file FloorCeil.wmls:

```xml
<?xml version="1.0"?>

<!DOCTYPE wml PUBLIC "-//WAPFORUM//DTD WML 1.2//EN"
    "http://www.wapforum.org/DTD/wml_1.1.xml">

<wml>

<card id="FloorCeilDemo">
 <p>
   Enter a floating-point value:
   <input name="Value" />

   <do type="accept">
     <go href="FloorCeil.wmls#GetFloorCeil($(Value))" />
   </do>
 </p>
</card>

</wml>
```

Within the GetFloorCeil function, the code uses the floor and ceil functions and assigns the result of each function to the variables FloorResult and CeilResult, respectively. The function then calls the WML application ShowFloorCeil.wml to display the result:

```
extern function GetFloorCeil(Value)
  {
```

8

```
WMLBrowser.setVar("FloorResult", Float.floor(Value));
WMLBrowser.setVar("CeilResult", Float.ceil(Value));

WMLBrowser.refresh();
WMLBrowser.go("ShowFloorCeil.wml");
}
```

The following statements implement ShowFloorCeil.wml:

```
<?xml version="1.0"?>

<!DOCTYPE wml PUBLIC "-//WAPFORUM//DTD WML 1.2//EN"
    "http://www.wapforum.org/DTD/wml_1.1.xml">

<wml>

<card id="ShowFloorCeil">
 <p>
    $(Value) floor: $(FloorResult) <br/>
    $(Value) ceil: $(CeilResult) <br/>
 </p>
</card>

</wml>
```

When you run the FloorCeilDemo.wml application within the phone simulator, you will see output similar to that shown in Figure 8-6.

1-Minute Drill

● How do the Float library functions floor and ceil differ? What result will each give for the value 99.9?

● How do the Float library functions int and round differ? What result will each give for the value 99.9?

● What values will the round and ceil functions return for the value 99.4?

● The floor function returns an integer that is nearest to, but not greater than the specified value. The ceil function returns an integer that is nearest to, but not less than the specified value. For the value 99.9, floor will return 99 and ceil will return 100.

● The int function returns the integer part of a floating-point number. The round function rounds a floating-point number using standard rounding rules. For the value 99.9, int will return 99 and round will return 100.

● For the value 99.4, round will round down the value to 99 and the ceil will return the value 100, which is the integer nearest to, but not less than 99.4.

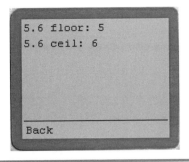

Figure 8-6   Using the Float library Floor and ceil functions

Raising One Value to the Power of Another

As you create applications that perform arithmetic operations, a common task
the application must perform is to raise one value to the power of another. For
example, to calculate the area of a circle, you use the expression Area = pi * r^2.
In other words, the area equals pi times the value of the radius raised to the
power of 2.

The Float library's pow function calculates the result of one value raised to
another. The following WML file, powerDemo.wml, illustrates the use of the
pow function to calculate the area of a circle:

8

```
<?xml version="1.0"?>

<!DOCTYPE wml PUBLIC "-//WAPFORUM//DTD WML 1.2//EN"
    "http://www.wapforum.org/DTD/wml_1.1.xml">

<wml>

<card id="PowerDemo" title="Area">
 <p>
   Enter Radius:
   <input name="Radius" />

   <do type="accept">
     <go href="Area.wmls#CalculateArea($(Radius))" />
   </do>
 </p>
</card>

</wml>
```

When you run the powerDemo.wml application, it will prompt you to enter the radius of a circle. The code will then call the calculateArea function that resides in the Area.wmls file. The calculateArea function will calculate the area using the pow function. The code will then launch the ShowArea.wml file.

```
extern function CalculateArea(Radius)
 {
    WMLBrowser.setVar("Area", (22.0 / 7.0) *
                      Float.pow(Radius, 2));
    WMLBrowser.refresh();
    WMLBrowser.go("ShowArea.wml");
 }
```

The following statements implement ShowArea.wml, which displays the radius and area, as shown in Figure 8-7.

```
<?xml version="1.0"?>

<!DOCTYPE wml PUBLIC "-//WAPFORUM//DTD WML 1.2//EN"
    "http://www.wapforum.org/DTD/wml_1.1.xml">

<wml>

<card id="ShowArea" title="ShowArea">
 <p>
    Radius $(Radius)<br/>
    Area $(Area)
 </p>
</card>

</wml>
```

Figure 8-7 Using the Float library's power function to calculate the area of a circle

Calculating a Value's Square Root

Just as there are times when your application must calculate the result of one value raised to the power of another, there will be times when your applications must determine a value's square root. The Float library's sqrt function returns the square root of the value it receives as a parameter. The following WML file, sqrtDemo.wml, prompts the user for a value and then calls the SquareRoot function, which resides in the WMLScript file Sqrt.wmls:

```
<?xml version="1.0"?>

<!DOCTYPE wml PUBLIC "-//WAPFORUM//DTD WML 1.2//EN"
    "http://www.wapforum.org/DTD/wml_1.1.xml">

<wml>

<card id="SqrtDemo" title="sqrt">
 <p>
   Enter a value:
   <input name="Value" />

   <do type="accept">
     <go href="Sqrt.wmls#SquareRoot($(Value))" />
   </do>
 </p>
</card>

</wml>
```

The following code implements the SquareRoot function:

```
extern function SquareRoot(Value)
 {
   WMLBrowser.setVar("Result", Float.sqrt(Value));
   WMLBrowser.refresh();
   WMLBrowser.go("ShowSquareRoot.wml");
 }
```

As you can see, after the function calculates the square root, the function assigns the result to the variable Result and then loads the card ShowSquareRoot.wml to display the result. The code for ShowSquareRoot.wml follows:

```
<?xml version="1.0"?>
```

```
<!DOCTYPE wml PUBLIC "-//WAPFORUM//DTD WML 1.2//EN"
    "http://www.wapforum.org/DTD/wml_1.1.xml">

<wml>

<card id="ShowSqrt" title="ShowSqrt">
 <p>
    Value $(Value)<br/>
    Square Root $(Result)
 </p>
</card>

</wml>
```

You can only take the square root of a positive number. A negative number, such as –25, does not have a square root in real numbers (imaginary numbers are not supported by the Float library). For simplicity, the previous SquareRoot function did not test for a negative number. Using the following statements, however, you can direct the code to handle a negative number gracefully:

```
if (value >= 0)
    WMLBrowser.setVar("Result", Float.sqrt(Value));
else
    WMLBrowser.setVar("Result", "Invalid negative value");
```

Using the WMLScript Lang Library

The WMLScript Lang library contains a set of arithmetic functions, as well as two functions an application can use to end its processing. Table 8-3 briefly describes the functions built into the WMLScript Lang library.

Function	Example	Purpose
abort	Lang.abort("Invalid input");	Displays an error message and ends the current WMLScript, returning control to the browser
abs	Result = Lang.abs(-3);	Returns the absolute value of the specified number
characterSet	CharSet = Lang.characterSet();	Returns an integer number that corresponds to the current character set

Table 8-3   Functions Provided by the WMLScript Lang Library

Function	Example	Purpose
exit	`Lang.exit(99);`	Ends the current session, returning a status value to the browser
float	`floatSupport = Lang.float();`	Returns "true" if the browser supports floating-point operations and "false" otherwise
isFloat	`canConvert = Lang.isFloat("3.43Hz");`	Returns "true" if the specified value can be converted to a floating-point number, or "false" otherwise
isInt	`canConvert = Lang.isInt("1GHz");`	Returns "true" if the specified value can be converted to an integer number, or "false" otherwise
max	`bigger = Lang.max(5, 100);`	Returns the larger of two specified values
maxInt	`value = Lang.maxInt();`	Returns the largest integer value the system supports
min	`smaller = Lang.min(5, 100);`	Returns the smaller of two specified values
parseFloat	`float_value = Lang.parseFloat("1.33GHz");`	Returns the floating-point portion of a value
parseInt	`integer_value = Lang.parseInt("800Mb");`	Returns the integer portion of a value
random	`integer_value = Lang.random(100);`	Returns a random integer number in the range 0 to the specified value
seed	`Lang.seed(555);`	Uses the specified value to control the random-number generator's sequence

8

Table 8-3   Functions Provided by the WMLScript Lang Library *(continued)*

Aborting the Current Application

Depending on how you structure your code, you may encounter situations for which you need a WMLScript routine to end its processing and to return control to the browser. For such cases, you can use the Lang library's exit or abort functions. As a rule, you should use the exit function to end a script under normal circumstances and the abort function for error conditions.

The abort function lets you display an error message to the user, which the browser displays before the application ends:

```
Lang.abort("Invalid user input");
```

In contrast, the exit function lets you return an error status value to the browser:

```
Lang.exit(99);
```

The following WML application, abortDemo.wml, uses the abort function to end the application's processing when the user enters an invalid password. When you run this application, you may find that various microbrowsers will respond to the abort function differently. In fact, some microbrowsers may not respond at all:

```
<?xml version="1.0"?>

<!DOCTYPE wml PUBLIC "-//WAPFORUM//DTD WML 1.2//EN"
    "http://www.wapforum.org/DTD/wml_1.1.xml">

<wml>

<card id="AbortDemo" title="Abort">
 <p>
    Enter password:
    <input name="Password" type="password" />

    <do type="accept">
      <go href=
        "AbortPassword.wmls#ValidatePassword('$(Password)')" />
    </do>
 </p>
</card>

</wml>
```

As you can see, the application calls the ValidatePassword function, which resides in the WMLScript file AbortPassword.wmls. If the user does not enter the password text "Password", the function uses the abort function to end the application's processing:

```
extern function ValidatePassword(UserPassword)
 {

    if (UserPassword == "Password")
      Dialogs.alert("Password is correct");
```

```
    else
       Lang.abort("Invalid Password -- Aborting");
}
```

Ask the Expert

Question: Under what conditions should an application use the exit or abort functions?

Answer: Ideally, your applications should never use the exit and abort functions. That is because the function returns control to the microbrowser, whose processing your application cannot control. Rather than using the abort or exit functions to end an application, you should instead write your own code that ends the application gracefully, perhaps simply by calling a WML card that explains to the user that the application experienced a fatal processing error, and which then gives the user directions on how to proceed.

Determining a Value's Absolute Value

When your applications perform arithmetic operations, there may be times when you must calculate a value's absolute value. In general, the absolute value specifies a number's distance from zero on a number line. For example, 2 is two whole numbers from zero on the number line, and hence the absolute value of 2 is 2. Likewise, the number –3 appears three whole numbers from zero on the number line, so the absolute value of –3 is 3. The absolute value is always a positive number.

Within a WMLScript application, you can use the Lang library's abs function to return a value's absolute value. The following WML application, absDemo.wml, prompts the user to enter a positive or negative integer number. The code then passes the value to the WMLScript CalcAbsolute function, which resides in the WMLScript file ReturnAbsolute.wmls:

```
<?xml version="1.0"?>

<!DOCTYPE wml PUBLIC "-//WAPFORUM//DTD WML 1.2//EN"
    "http://www.wapforum.org/DTD/wml_1.1.xml">
```

8

```
<wml>

<card id="absDemo" title="Abs">
 <p>
   Enter a value:
   <input name="Value" />

   <do type="accept">
     <go href="ReturnAbsolute.wmls#CalcAbsolute($(Value))" />
   </do>
 </p>
</card>

</wml>
```

Within the WMLScript function ReturnAbsolute, the code uses the Lang library's abs function to determine the value's absolute value:

```
extern function CalcAbsolute(Value)
 {
   WMLBrowser.setVar("AbsoluteValue", Lang.abs(Value));
   WMLBrowser.refresh();
   WMLBrowser.go("ShowAbsolute.wml");
 }
```

After the code calculates the absolute value, the code assigns the result to the variable AbsoluteValue and launches the card ShowAbsolute.wml, which displays the result:

```
<?xml version="1.0"?>

<!DOCTYPE wml PUBLIC "-//WAPFORUM//DTD WML 1.2//EN"
    "http://www.wapforum.org/DTD/wml_1.1.xml">

<wml>

<card id="ShowAbsolute" title="ShowAbs">
 <p>
   Value $(Value)<br/>
   Absolute Value $(AbsoluteValue)
 </p>
</card>

</wml>
```

Determining the Current Character Set

If you create applications for worldwide distribution, there will be times when your applications must know the browser's current character set. Using the Lang library's characterSet function, you can retrieve the MIBenum value, a unique value that identifies a coded character set. The following WML application, CharacterSet.wml, calls the WMLScript getCharacterSet function to get the current MIBenum value:

```
<?xml version="1.0"?>
<!DOCTYPE wml PUBLIC "-//WAPFORUM//DTD WML 1.2//EN"
    "http://www.wapforum.org/DTD/wml_1.1.xml">

<wml>

<card id="CharacterSet">
  <onevent type="onenterforward">
    <go href="GetCharacterSet.wmls#GetCharacterSet()" />
  </onevent>
</card>

</wml>
```

The WMLScript getCharacterSet function, which resides in the file getCharacterSet.wmls, uses the Lang library's characterSet function:

```
extern function GetCharacterSet()
 {
   WMLBrowser.setVar("MIBenum", Lang.characterSet());

   WMLBrowser.refresh();
   WMLBrowser.go("ShowCharacterSet.wml");
 }
```

After the function determines the current character set, it assigns the MIBenum number to the variable MIBenum, which the WML application ShowCharacterSet.wml displays:

```
<?xml version="1.0"?>

<!DOCTYPE wml PUBLIC "-//WAPFORUM//DTD WML 1.2//EN"
    "http://www.wapforum.org/DTD/wml_1.1.xml">
```

8

```
<wml>

<card id="ShowCharacterSet">
 <p>
   Character Set: [$(MIBenum)]
 </p>
</card>

</wml>
```

Note

The Internet Assigned Numbers Authority (IANA) is an organization that controls (standardizes) the use of numeric values on the Internet. The IANA, for example, specifies that browser applications use port 80. The IANA also assigns unique values, called MIBenum values, to character sets. For specifics on IANA character-set numbers, visit the IANA Web site at www.iana.org/numbers.htm.

Testing for a Valid Integer or Floating-Point Number

When a WML application prompts a user for numeric data, the application should verify that the user entered a valid number.

To help your applications verify data, the WMLScript Lang library provides the isInt and isFloat functions, which return the value "true" or "false" based on whether or not the value the application passes to the function can be successfully converted to an integer or floating-point value, respectively. The value does not have to be a valid integer or floating-point number, but rather, the function determines whether the value can be converted to a valid value. For example, the value "33ff" can become a valid integer value if you truncate the "ff" characters.

The following WML application, isIntFloatDemo.wml, prompts you to enter a number. The code then calls the WMLScript function CheckIntFloat to determine the type of value you entered:

```
<?xml version="1.0"?>

<!DOCTYPE wml PUBLIC "-//WAPFORUM//DTD WML 1.2//EN"
    "http://www.wapforum.org/DTD/wml_1.1.xml">

<wml>
```

```
<card id="isIntFloatDemo">
 <p>
   Enter a value:
   <input name="Value" />

   <do type="accept">
     <go href="CheckIntFloat.wmls#CheckIntFloat('$(Value)')" />
   </do>
 </p>
</card>

</wml>
```

The CheckIntFloat function, which resides within the file CheckIntFloat.wmls, uses the isInt and isFloat functions to check whether the value is an integer or floating-point number. The function then assigns the "true" or "false" values to the variables Integer and Float and calls the WML application ShowIntFloat.wml to display the result:

```
extern function CheckIntFloat(Value)
 {
    WMLBrowser.setVar("Integer", Lang.isInt(Value));
    WMLBrowser.setVar("Float", Lang.isFloat(Value));

    WMLBrowser.refresh();
    WMLBrowser.go("ShowIntFloat.wml");
 }
```

The following code implements ShowIntFloat.wml:

```
<?xml version="1.0"?>

<!DOCTYPE wml PUBLIC "-//WAPFORUM//DTD WML 1.2//EN"
    "http://www.wapforum.org/DTD/wml_1.1.xml">

<wml>

<card id="ShowIntFloat">
 <p>
    $(Value) ok for integer: $(Integer) <br/>
    $(Value) ok for float: $(Float) <br/>
 </p>
</card>

</wml>
```

1-Minute Drill

● Why does the Lang library's isFloat function consider the string "8.333PSI" a valid number?

Determining Maximum and Minimum Values

When you create applications that perform arithmetic operations, there may be times when your application must determine the maximum and minimum of two values. In such cases, your applications can use the Lang library's max and min functions. The following WML file, MinMaxDemo.wml, illustrates the use of min and max functions:

```
<?xml version="1.0"?>

<!DOCTYPE wml PUBLIC "-//WAPFORUM//DTD WML 1.2//EN"
    "http://www.wapforum.org/DTD/wml_1.1.xml">

<wml>

<card id="MinMax" title="MinMax">
 <p>
    Press OK to display the minimum
    and maximum of 1, 5, and 3<br/>

    <do type="accept">
      <go href="MinMax.wmls#GetMinAndMax(1, 5, 3)" />
    </do>
 </p>
</card>

</wml>
```

● The isFloat function considers a string that contains a number that the parseFloat function can extract as a valid number. The string "8.333PSI" contains the number 8.333. If you pass the string to the Lang library's parseFloat function, the function will return the value 8.333 and will discard the characters "PSI". The isFloat function will consider the following to be valid numbers "8", "8.3", "8.3Mb".

As you can see, the application calls the function GetMinAndMax, which assigns the minimum and maximum values to the variables Minimum and Maximum, respectively. The GetMinAndMax function resides within the MinMax.wmls file shown here:

```
extern function GetMinAndMax(a, b, c)
{
   var min, max;

   min = Lang.min(Lang.min(a, b), Lang.min(b, c));
   max = Lang.max(Lang.max(a, b), Lang.max(b, c));

   WMLBrowser.setVar("Minimum", min);
   WMLBrowser.setVar("Maximum", max);

   WMLBrowser.refresh();
   WMLBrowser.go("ShowMinMax.wml");
}
```

After the function calculates the minimum and maximum values, it loads the card ShowMinMax.wml, shown here:

```
<?xml version="1.0"?>

<!DOCTYPE wml PUBLIC "-//WAPFORUM//DTD WML 1.2//EN"
    "http://www.wapforum.org/DTD/wml_1.1.xml">

<wml>

<card id="ShowMinMax" title="ShowMinMax">
 <p>
   Min $(Minimum)<br/>
   Max $(Maximum)
 </p>
</card>

</wml>
```

When you load the MinMaxDemo.wml application in the phone simulator, the simulator will display output similar to that shown in Figure 8-8.

8

Figure 8-8 Performing arithmetic operations using Lang library functions

Parsing a String for an Integer or Floating-Point Value

Depending on the application's purpose and the wording of its prompts for input, the format used to enter data may vary greatly from one user to the next. For example, if you prompt the user to enter the speed of his or her processor, one user might enter 733, while a second user might enter 733MHz. To simplify the script's processing of user input, the Lang library provides the parseInt and parseFloat functions, which return a value that corresponds to the first digits in a string, up to the first nonnumeric character. For example, if a string contains the characters "733MHz", the parseInt function would return the value 733.

The following application, parseDemo.wml prompts the user to enter text that contains an integer value:

```
<?xml version="1.0"?>

<!DOCTYPE wml PUBLIC "-//WAPFORUM//DTD WML 1.2//EN"
    "http://www.wapforum.org/DTD/wml_1.1.xml">

<wml>

<card id="parseDemo">
 <p>
    Enter an integer value:
    <input name="Value" />
```

```
   <do type="accept">
    <go href="ParseValue.wmls#ShowValue('$(Value)')" />
   </do>
  </p>
</card>

</wml>
```

As you can see, the application then calls the ShowValue function that resides within WMLScript file parseValue.wmls. The ShowValue function uses the parseInt function to extract the integer value:

```
extern function ShowValue(Value)
 {
    WMLBrowser.setVar("IntegerResult", Lang.parseInt(Value));

    WMLBrowser.refresh();
    WMLBrowser.go("ShowParseResult.wml");
 }
```

As you can see, after the function parses the value, it assigns the result to the variable IntegerResult and then calls the WML application ShowParseResult.wml to display the output:

```
<?xml version="1.0"?>

<!DOCTYPE wml PUBLIC "-//WAPFORUM//DTD WML 1.2//EN"
    "http://www.wapforum.org/DTD/wml_1.1.xml">

<wml>

<card id="ShowParseResult">
 <p>
    Value $(Value) <br/>
    Result $(IntegerResult)
 </p>
</card>

</wml>
```

Take time to experiment with the application, as shown in Figure 8-9.

8

Figure 8-9 Parsing a user's integer input

Generating a Random Number

Depending on your application's purpose, there may be times when the application must generate a random number. For example, if a wireless application is trying to call a number that is currently busy, you may want the application to wait a random amount of time before it tries to redial. To generate a random number, your applications can use the Lang library's random function.

The random function returns a value between 0 and the value you specify. For example, to generate a random number in the range 0 to 10, a WMLScript application would invoke the random function as follows:

```
random_number = Lang.random(10);
```

Likewise, to create a random number from 0 to 5,000, the application would use:

```
random_number = Lang.random(5000);
```

The random function returns an integer value. If you need a floating-point value, such as a value in the range 0 to 1.0, you could use the random function to generate a number in the range 0 to 100 and then divide that result by 100.0, as shown here:

```
Result = Lang.random(100) / 100.0;
```

The following WML application, randomDemo.wml, calls the RandomNumbers function, which illustrates the use of the random function, as shown in Figure 8-10.

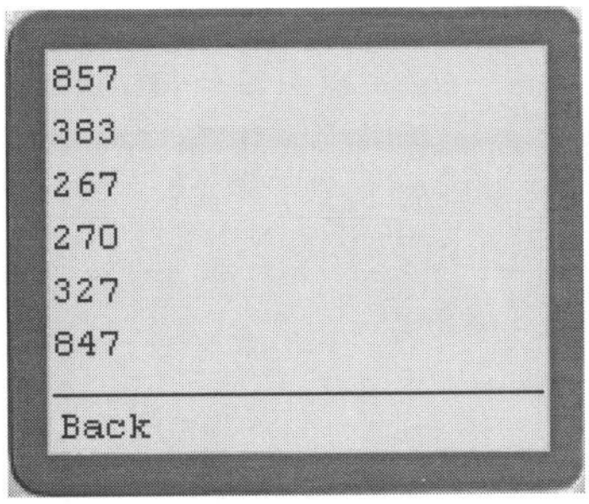

```
857
383
267
270
327
847

Back
```

Figure 8-10   Using the Lang library's random function to generate random numbers

After you start the application, the file's script will generate and display ten random numbers:

```
<?xml version="1.0"?>

<!DOCTYPE wml PUBLIC "-//WAPFORUM//DTD WML 1.2//EN"
    "http://www.wapforum.org/DTD/wml_1.1.xml">

<wml>

<card id="RandomDemo">
  <onevent type="onenterforward">
    <go href="Random.wmls#RandomNumbers()" />
  </onevent>
</card>

</wml>
```

The RandomNumbers function, which resides in the Random.wmls file, uses the random function to generate ten random numbers in the range 0 to 1,000, which the function assigns to the variables A1 to A10:

```
extern function RandomNumbers()
  {
    WMLBrowser.setVar("A1", Lang.random(1000));
    WMLBrowser.setVar("A2", Lang.random(1000));
    WMLBrowser.setVar("A3", Lang.random(1000));
    WMLBrowser.setVar("A4", Lang.random(1000));
```

```
WMLBrowser.setVar("A5", Lang.random(1000));
WMLBrowser.setVar("A6", Lang.random(1000));
WMLBrowser.setVar("A7", Lang.random(1000));
WMLBrowser.setVar("A8", Lang.random(1000));
WMLBrowser.setVar("A9", Lang.random(1000));
WMLBrowser.setVar("A10", Lang.random(1000));

WMLBrowser.refresh();
WMLBrowser.go("ShowRandom.wml");
}
```

The code passes the value 1,000 as a parameter to the random function to direct the function to return values in the range 0 to 1,000. To restrict the function's values to the range 0 to 100, you would pass the value 100 to the function, as shown here:

```
Result = Lang.random(100);
```

The following statements implement ShowRandom.wml, which displays the random numbers:

```
<?xml version="1.0"?>

<!DOCTYPE wml PUBLIC "-//WAPFORUM//DTD WML 1.2//EN"
    "http://www.wapforum.org/DTD/wml_1.1.xml">

<wml>

<card id="ShowRandom">
 <p>
    $(A1)<br/>
    $(A2)<br/>
    $(A3)<br/>
    $(A4)<br/>
    $(A5)<br/>
    $(A6)<br/>
    $(A7)<br/>
    $(A8)<br/>
```

```
    $(A9)<br/>
    $(A10)<br/>
 </p>
</card>

</wml>
```

When programmers build applications that require random numbers, a challenge the programmers often face when they try to test the applications is in controlling some of the program's randomness. By using the Lang library's seed function, you can direct a program to always start with the same series of random numbers, which may significantly simplify your testing. The following statements change the RandomNumbers function just shown to use the seed function. By using the same seed each time you run the program, you can force the program to generate the same sequence of random numbers, which may help you in testing your code:

```
extern function RandomNumbers()
 {
   Lang.seed(1000);
   WMLBrowser.setVar("A1", Lang.random(1000));
   WMLBrowser.setVar("A2", Lang.random(1000));
   WMLBrowser.setVar("A3", Lang.random(1000));
   WMLBrowser.setVar("A4", Lang.random(1000));
   WMLBrowser.setVar("A5", Lang.random(1000));
   WMLBrowser.setVar("A6", Lang.random(1000));
   WMLBrowser.setVar("A7", Lang.random(1000));
   WMLBrowser.setVar("A8", Lang.random(1000));
   WMLBrowser.setVar("A9", Lang.random(1000));
   WMLBrowser.setVar("A10", Lang.random(1000));

   WMLBrowser.refresh();
   WMLBrowser.go("ShowRandom.wml");
 }
```

Run the program and write down the first five numbers the program generates. Then, run the program a second time. Because the program seeds the random-number generator, the program will create the same set of values every time.

1-Minute Drill

● How would you generate a random number in the range 0 to 5?

● How would you generate a random number in the range 0.0 to 0.5?

● When should you seed a random-number generator?

Using the WMLScript String Library

WMLScript stores strings as an array of Unicode characters. As you create WMLScript applications, you will perform a variety of string-manipulation operations, such as extracting a user's first or last name from a string, or parsing a phone number into an area code and seven-digit number. To help you perform string operations, WMLScript provides the String library. Table 8-4 briefly describes the functions built into the WMLScript String library.

Note

Many of the String library functions require that you specify an index value to a character or element within a string. The functions in the String library use zero-based indexing, which means the functions consider the first character in a string to be at offset 0, the second character at offset 1, and so on. If you are working with a delimited string, such as "First/Second/Third/Fourth" the functions will equate element 0 with the string First, element 1 with the string Second, and so on.

● To generate a random number in the range 0 to 5, you simply pass the value 5 to the Lang library's random function.

● To generate a floating-point random number in the range 0.0 to 0.5, you simply pass the value 5 to the Lang library's random function and then divide the result by 10.0 to create a fraction.

● By seeding a random-number generator, you can control the sequence of numbers the random-number generator creates. With test applications that use random numbers, you can control "randomness" by having the application generate the same series of numbers each time it runs.

Function	Example	Purpose
charAt	`letter = String.charAt("ABC", 1);`	Returns the character within a string at the specified index (the first character is at offset 0)
compare	`Bigger = String.compare("ABC", "ABCD");`	Returns –1 if the first string is smaller than the second, 1 if the first string is larger than the second, and 0 if the strings are the same length
elements	`count = String.elements("A/B/C/D", "/");`	Returns the number of elements in a delimited string
elementAt	`value = String.elementAt("A/B/C/D", 1, "/");`	Returns the element within a delimited string at the specified index (the first element is at offset 0)
find	`value = String.find("Wireless", "less");`	Returns the zero-based offset to a specified substring within a string, or the value –1 if the substring does not exist
format	`result = String.format("Result: %d", 999);`	Assigns a value to a string using format specifiers
insertAt	`new_string = String.insertAt("A/C/D", "B", 1, "/");`	Inserts an element into a delimited string at the specified zero-based index
length	`len = String.length("ABC");`	Returns the number of characters in a string
isEmpty	`boolean_value = String.isEmpty(String);`	Returns "true" if the specified string is empty (contains no characters) or "false" otherwise
removeAt	`new_string = String.removeAt("A/C/D", 1, "/");`	Removes an element from a delimited string at the specified zero-based index
replace	`new_string = String.replace("September, 2001", "September", "October");`	Replaces the first substring specified with the second

8

Table 8-4   Functions Provided by the WMLScript String Library

Function	Example	Purpose

replaceAt	`new_string =`
	`String.replaceAt("A/C/C",`
	`"B", 1, "/");`
		Replaces an element in a delimited string at the specified zero-based index

squeeze	`new_string =` `String.squeeze(" A B C ");`	Replaces multiple successive whitespace characters with a single space
subString	`new_string = String.subString` `("Wireless", 4, 4);`	Returns a substring from within a string
trim	`new_string =` `String.trim(" A B C ");`	Removes leading and trailing whitespace characters from a string
toString	`result = String.toString` `(999.99);`	Converts a value into its string representation

Table 8-4 Functions Provided by the WMLScript String Library (*continued*)

Determining the Character at a Specific Location in a String

When your applications manipulate strings, there may be times when you must copy a single character from within the string. For example, your application might examine a phone number to determine if the first digit is an 8 or a 9, which may correspond to the number the user must dial from a company (or hotel) phone to access an outside line. To copy a single character from within a string, applications can use the String library's charAt function. Using the function, the application specifies the index location that corresponds to the character the application desires. The first character in a string is at the index offset of 0. The second character is at offset 1, and so on.

The following WML file, charAtDemo.wml, illustrates the use of the charAt function to display the first, second, and third letters within the string "Wireless":

```
<?xml version="1.0"?>

<!DOCTYPE wml PUBLIC "-//WAPFORUM//DTD WML 1.2//EN"
    "http://www.wapforum.org/DTD/wml_1.1.xml">

<wml>
```

```
<card id="CharAt" title="CharAt">
  <onevent type="onenterforward">
    <go href="charAt.wmls#GetCharacter('Wireless')" />
  </onevent>
</card>

</wml>
```

As you can see, the application calls the function GetCharacter, which resides within the WMLScript file charAt.wmls:

```
extern function GetCharacter(String)
  {
    WMLBrowser.setVar("First", String.charAt(String, 0));
    WMLBrowser.setVar("Second", String.charAt(String, 1));
    WMLBrowser.setVar("Third", String.charAt(String, 2));

    WMLBrowser.refresh();
    WMLBrowser.go("ShowCharacters.wml");
  }
```

As you can see, to display the application's output, the WMLScript GetCharacter function calls the ShowCharacters.wml card, as shown here:

```
<?xml version="1.0"?>

<!DOCTYPE wml PUBLIC "-//WAPFORUM//DTD WML 1.2//EN"
    "http://www.wapforum.org/DTD/wml_1.1.xml">

<wml>

<card id="ShowChars" title="charat">
  <p>
    First $(First)<br/>
    Second $(Second)<br/>
    Third $(Third)<br/>
  </p>
</card>

</wml>
```

When you load the charAtDemo.wml application in the phone simulator, the simulator will display output similar to that shown in Figure 8-11.

8

```
First W
Second i
Third r




Back
```

Figure 8-11 Extracting specific characters from the string "Wireless"

1-Minute Drill

- What is zero-based indexing?
- How can you determine the second character in the string "ABC"?

Comparing Two Character Strings

When WMLScript-based applications manage data, it is not uncommon for the scripts to organize (sort) the data in some way. The String library's compare function compares two strings based on their lexicographic relationship (similar to alphabetical order) and returns the value 0 if the strings are identical, −1 if the first string is less than the second, and 1 if the first string is greater. The following WML file, compareDemo.wml, prompts you to enter two strings. The application then calls the WMLScript function CompareStrings, which resides in the CompareStrings.wmls file:

```
<?xml version="1.0"?>
```

- Zero-based indexing means the first character in a string is residing at offset 0 (as opposed to the first character residing at offset 1). Using zero-based indexing for the string "ABC", the letter A resides at offset 0, the letter B at offset 1, and the letter C at offset 2.
- To determine the second character within a string, you can use the String library's charAt function, as shown here:

  ```
  Character = String.charAt("ABC", 1);
  ```

- Remember, because of zero-based indexing, the second character resides at offset 1.

```
<!DOCTYPE wml PUBLIC "-//WAPFORUM//DTD WML 1.2//EN"
    "http://www.wapforum.org/DTD/wml_1.1.xml">

<wml>

<card id="CompareDemo" title="Area">
 <p>
   Enter first string:
   <input name="String1" />

   Enter second string:
   <input name="String2" />

   <do type="accept">
     <go href="CompareStrings.wmls#CompareStrings('$(String1)',
'$(String2)')" />
   </do>
 </p>
</card>

</wml>
```

The CompareStrings function uses the compare function to examine the strings. The code then assigns the text "Is greater," "Is less," or "Is equal" to the variable Comparison, depending on how the first string relates to the second. The code then calls the WML card ShowCompare.wml to display the result:

```
extern function CompareStrings(String1, String2)
 {
   var result;

   result = String.compare(String1, String2);

   if (result == 0)
     WMLBrowser.setVar("Comparison", "Is equal");
   else if (result == 1)
     WMLBrowser.setVar("Comparison", "Is greater");
   else if (result == -1)
     WMLBrowser.setVar("Comparison", "Is less");

   WMLBrowser.refresh();
   WMLBrowser.go("ShowCompare.wml");
}
```

8

The following statements implement ShowCompare.wml:

```
<?xml version="1.0"?>

<!DOCTYPE wml PUBLIC "-//WAPFORUM//DTD WML 1.2//EN"
    "http://www.wapforum.org/DTD/wml_1.1.xml">

<wml>

<card id="ShowCompare">
 <p>
   $(String1)<br/>
   $(Comparison)<br/>
   $(String2)
 </p>
</card>

</wml>
```

When you load the compareDemo.wml application into the phone simulator, the simulator will display output similar to that shown in Figure 8-12.

Formatting a String's Contents

When your application displays numeric data to the user, there may be times when you will want to format the data in some way. For example, you might

Figure 8-12 Comparing strings within WMLScript

want to restrict the number of digits to the right of the decimal place to two if the application is displaying a floating-point value that represents a dollar amount. Using the String library's format function, you can perform such formatting.

The format function's general format is as follows:

```
String_Result = String.format("Format Specifier", value);
```

Within the string that contains the format specifier, you use **%d** to specify an integer value, **%f** for a floating-point number, and **%s** for a string:

```
String_Result = String.format("Value: %d", 1001);
String_Result = String.format("Value: %f", 3.856);
String_Result = String.format("Value: %s", Age * 10);
```

In addition to specifying a type of value, you can also specify the number of digits for integer and floating-point numbers. For example, the following statement allocates eight digits for an integer number:

```
String_Result = String.format("Value: %8d", 1001);
```

Because the value 1,001 does not require eight digits, the format function will place four spaces in front of the number. To specify seven digits in total, with two digits to the right of the decimal point, you would use the following statement:

```
String_Result = String.format("Price: $ %7.2f", ItemCost);
```

Depending on your application, there may be times when you will want to precede an integer value with leading zeros. In such cases, you will use a format specifier such as **%7.4d**, which directs the format function to allow space for seven digits and, if necessary, to use leading zeros to ensure the output contains at least four digits.

8

1-Minute Drill

● Given the value 12, how would you display the following output?

```
Result = 12
Result = 0012
Result = 12.00
```

Working with Delimited Strings

When applications place multiple fields within the same string, the applications normally parse (separate) the fields using a specific delimiter, such as a space, tab, comma, or semicolon. The following strings illustrate various separators:

```
"Bill Smith 800-238-5555"
"Bill,Smith,800-238-5555"
"Bill;Smith;800-238-5555"
"Bill/Smith/800-238-5555"
```

Before an application can parse such delimited data, the application must know the number of elements the string contains. Using the String library's elements function, the application can determine the number of fields in a string based on a specific delimiter. The following WML file, elementsDemo.wml, calls the WMLScript countElements function, which counts the number of elements a string contains and then assigns the count to the variable ElementCount. The function then loads the ShowElementCount.wml card to display the result:

```
<?xml version="1.0"?>

<!DOCTYPE wml PUBLIC "-//WAPFORUM//DTD WML 1.2//EN"
    "http://www.wapforum.org/DTD/wml_1.1.xml">
```

● To format the output, you can use the String library's format function as follows:

```
output_string = String.format("Result = %d", 12);
output_string = String.format("Result = %4.4d", 12);
output_string = String.format("Result = %4.2f", 12);
```

```
<wml>

<card id="ElementDemo">

  <onevent type="onenterforward">
    <go href="CountElements.wmls#CountElements('A/B/C', '/')" />
  </onevent>

</card>

</wml>
```

The CountElements function resides in the WMLScript
CountElements.wmls file:

```
extern function CountElements(String, Delimiter)
 {
    WMLBrowser.setVar("ElementCount", String.elements(String,
Delimiter));
    WMLBrowser.setVar("String", String);

    WMLBrowser.refresh();
    WMLBrowser.go("ShowElementCount.wml");
 }
```

The following statements implement ShowElementCount.wml:

```
<?xml version="1.0"?>

<!DOCTYPE wml PUBLIC "-//WAPFORUM//DTD WML 1.2//EN"
    "http://www.wapforum.org/DTD/wml_1.1.xml">

<wml>

<card id="ShowElementCount">
 <p>
    String $(String) <br/>
    Elements $(ElementCount)
 </p>
</card>

</wml>
```

8

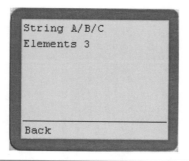

Figure 8-13 Counting the number of elements in a string

When you load the elementsDemo.wml application into the phone simulator, the simulator will display the output shown in Figure 8-13.

Hint

When you work with delimited strings, you will normally use a delimiter such as a space, comma, or a slash. However, the WMLScript String library functions do not care which character you use. You could, for example, use an equal sign (=), a dash (-), or even the letter "a" as a delimiter. In general, the delimiter you choose need only be a character that does not appear within the strings you want to delimit. However, to make your programs easier for others to understand, you should choose a standard delimiter.

If your application works with strings that contain delimited elements, there may be times when you will want to copy a specific element's contents to a different character string. In such cases, you can use the String library's elementAt function, which returns the element that corresponds to an index value that you specify. If the index value exceeds the number of items in the string, the function will return the last item.

The following WML file, elementAtDemo.wml, calls the GetElementAt WMLScript function, which illustrates the use of the elementAt function:

```
<?xml version="1.0"?>

<!DOCTYPE wml PUBLIC "-//WAPFORUM//DTD WML 1.2//EN"
    "http://www.wapforum.org/DTD/wml_1.1.xml">

<wml>
```

```
<card id="ElementAtDemo">

  <onevent type="onenterforward">
    <go href="GetElementAt.wmls#GetElementAt('A/B/C', '/', 1)" />
  </onevent>

</card>

</wml>
```

The GetElementAt function, which resides in the WMLScript file GetElementAt.wmls, assigns the value of the second element (offset 1) to the variable Element. The code then loads the WML application ShowElementAt.wml to display the result:

```
extern function GetElementAt(String, Delimiter, Offset)
 {
    WMLBrowser.setVar("Element", String.elementAt(String, Offset,
Delimiter));
    WMLBrowser.setVar("String", String);

    WMLBrowser.refresh();
    WMLBrowser.go("ShowElementAt.wml");
 }
```

The following statements implement ShowElementAt.wml:

```
<?xml version="1.0"?>

<!DOCTYPE wml PUBLIC "-//WAPFORUM//DTD WML 1.2//EN"
    "http://www.wapforum.org/DTD/wml_1.1.xml">

<wml>

<card id="ShowElementAt">
 <p>
    String: $(String) <br/>
    Element 2: $(Element)
 </p>
</card>

</wml>
```

8

As your WMLScript applications become more complex, there will be times when your applications must locate a substring from within a string (such as an area code from within a phone number), replace one substring within another, or simply remove a substring. The WML String library provides a series of functions your applications can use to manipulate substrings.

To start, the find function locates the first occurrence of a substring within a string, and returns the zero-based index of the substring's first character. For example, if you use the find function to search the string "Wireless" for the substring "less", the value 4 will be returned. If the substring does not exist within the string, the find function will return the value –1. The following statement illustrates the use of the find function to locate the start of the string ".com" in the URL www.WirelessLookup.com:

```
Result = String.find("www.WirelessLookup.com", ".com");
```

To remove an element from a string, your application can use the String library's removeAt function. The following WML file, removeAtDemo.wml, calls the WMLScript RemoveStringAt function, which illustrates the use of the removeAt function:

```
<?xml version="1.0"?>

<!DOCTYPE wml PUBLIC "-//WAPFORUM//DTD WML 1.2//EN"
    "http://www.wapforum.org/DTD/wml_1.1.xml">

<wml>

<card id="RemoveAtDemo">

  <onevent type="onenterforward">
    <go href=
      "RemoveStringAt.wmls#RemoveStringAt('A/B/C', '/', 1)" />
  </onevent>

</card>

</wml>
```

The RemoveStringAt function, which resides in the RemoveStringAt.wmls file, uses the removeAt function to remove a delimited string. The function then assigns the resulting string to the variable NewString and calls the WML application ShowRemoveAt.wml to display the result:

```
extern function RemoveStringAt(String, Delimiter, Offset)
 {
    WMLBrowser.setVar("NewString", String.removeAt(String,
                    Offset, Delimiter));
    WMLBrowser.setVar("String", String);

    WMLBrowser.refresh();
    WMLBrowser.go("ShowRemoveAt.wml");
 }
```

The following statements implement ShowRemoveAt.wml:

```
<?xml version="1.0"?>

<!DOCTYPE wml PUBLIC "-//WAPFORUM//DTD WML 1.2//EN"
    "http://www.wapforum.org/DTD/wml_1.1.xml">

<wml>

<card id="ShowRemoveAt">
 <p>
    String: $(String) <br/>
    New String: $(NewString)
 </p>
</card>

</wml>
```

There may also be times when an application must insert items into a delimited string. To do so, the application can use the insertAt function. The following statement, for example, uses the **String.insertAt** function to insert the letter "B" into the string "A/C/D", yielding "A/B/C/D":

```
Result = String.insertAt("A/C/D", "B", 1, "/");
```

If your application must update fields that reside within a delimited string, the application can take advantage of the String library's replaceAt function. The following statement, for example, uses the **String.replaceAt** function

8

to replace the lowercase letter "b" in the string "A/b/C/D" with an uppercase "B":

```
Result = String.replaceAt("A/b/C/D", "B", 1, "/");
```

Just as there will be times when an application must locate or copy a substring within a string, there will also be times when an application must replace one substring with another. For example, an application might replace an invalid area code with a new code. In such cases, the application can use the String library's replace function. The following statement uses the replace function to replace "Yahoo" in the string "Yahoo.com" with "Wirelesslookup":

```
Result = String.replace("Yahoo.com", "Yahoo", "WirelessLookup");
```

Testing for an Empty String

As a script performs string-manipulation operations, there may be times when an operation results in an empty string. Using the String library's isEmpty function, the script can determine whether a string is empty and then continue its processing accordingly. The isEmpty function returns "true" when a string is empty and "false" otherwise.

```
if (String.isEmpty(InputString))
  WMLBrowser.go("GetInput.wml");
else
  WMLBrowser.go("ProcessData.wml");
```

1-Minute Drill

● What is an empty string?

● When might you encounter an empty string?

● An empty string is a character string that contains no characters.
● When you use an <input> tag to prompt the user for input, WML will assign the characters the user enters to a variable. There may be times when the user does not type in any characters, but simply presses the accept button. In such cases, the <input> tag variable will contain an empty string.

Determining a String's Length

Your applications will sometimes need to know a string's length. The String library's length function returns the number of characters a string contains.

The following WML file, lengthDemo.wml, prompts the user to enter a string and then calls the GetLength function, which resides in the WMLScript GetLength.wmls file. The GetLength function, in turn, calls the length function to determine the number of characters the string contains:

```
<?xml version="1.0"?>

<!DOCTYPE wml PUBLIC "-//WAPFORUM//DTD WML 1.2//EN"
    "http://www.wapforum.org/DTD/wml_1.1.xml">

<wml>

<card id="getLength" title="Length">
 <p>
   Enter a string:
   <input name="String" />

   <do type="accept">
     <go href="GetLength.wmls#GetLength('$(String)')" />
   </do>
 </p>
</card>

</wml>
```

Within the GetLength function, the code assigns the number of characters the string contains to the variable StringLength. The function then calls the ShowLength.wml card to display the output:

```
extern function GetLength(String)
 {

   WMLBrowser.setVar("StringLength", String.length(String));

   WMLBrowser.refresh();
   WMLBrowser.go("ShowLength.wml");
 }
```

8

The following statements implement ShowLength.wml:

```
<?xml version="1.0"?>

<!DOCTYPE wml PUBLIC "-//WAPFORUM//DTD WML 1.2//EN"
    "http://www.wapforum.org/DTD/wml_1.1.xml">

<wml>

<card id="ShowLength">
 <p>
   String: $(String)<br/>
   Length: $(StringLength)
 </p>
</card>

</wml>
```

Removing Whitespace from Within a String

When a user performs a keyboard input, or when an application parses a string into specific components, it is not uncommon for the string to be left with leading or trailing blanks (or other whitespace characters, such as a tab), or with multiple successive whitespace characters within the string. To help an application "clean up" character strings, the WML String library provides the trim and squeeze functions. The trim function removes leading and trailing whitespace characters within a string. Similarly, the squeeze function replaces consecutive occurrences of a whitespace character with one occurrence. The following WML file, TrimSqueeze.wml, calls the TrimString function that resides in the WMLScript file Trim.wmls:

```
<?xml version="1.0"?>

<!DOCTYPE wml PUBLIC "-//WAPFORUM//DTD WML 1.2//EN"
    "http://www.wapforum.org/DTD/wml_1.1.xml">

<wml>

<card id="TrimDemo">
  <onevent type="onenterforward">
    <go href="Trim.wmls#TrimString('   W i r e l e s s   ')" />
```

```
    </onevent>
  </card>

  </wml>
```

The TrimString function removes whitespace from the parameter String and then assigns the result to the variable TrimmedString. The function then loads the WML application showTrim.wml to display the result:

```
extern function TrimString(OriginalString)
  {
    WMLBrowser.setVar("String", OriginalString);
    WMLBrowser.setVar("TrimmedString",
                      String.trim(OriginalString));
    WMLBrowser.setVar("SqueezedString",
                      String.squeeze(OriginalString));

    WMLBrowser.refresh();
    WMLBrowser.go("ShowTrim.wml");
  }
```

The following statements implement showTrim.wml:

```
<?xml version="1.0"?>

<!DOCTYPE wml PUBLIC "-//WAPFORUM//DTD WML 1.2//EN"
    "http://www.wapforum.org/DTD/wml_1.1.xml">

<wml>

<card id="ShowTrim">
 <p>
   String: [$(String)]<br/>
   Trimmed: [$(TrimmedString)]<br/>
   Squeezed: [$(SqueezedString)]
 </p>
</card>

</wml>
```

When you load the TrimSqueeze.wml application into the phone simulator, the simulator will display the output shown in Figure 8-14.

8

```
String: [   W i r e l
e s s   ]
Trimmed: [W i r e l e
s s]
Squeezed: [ W i r e l
e s s ]

Back
```

Figure 8-14 Removing leading and trailing whitespace

1-Minute Drill

● What is whitespace?

● Why should your applications worry about whitespace?

Extracting a Substring from Within a String

Your application may need to copy a portion of a string's contents. For example, assume that the string PhoneNumber contains "800-555-1212", and the application wants to copy the area code, which is three characters long and starts at the index value 0. To do so, the application can use the subString function, as shown here:

```
PhoneNumber = "800-555-1212";
AreaCode = subString(PhoneNumber, 0, 3);
```

Converting a Result to a String

When an application performs specific processing and then displays a result, the application may first convert the result to a string so it can then specify formatting options. To convert a value (or expression) to a string, an

---

● In general, whitespace is characters such as spaces, tabs, carriage-returns, and linefeeds, which separate other characters. When an application uses an <input> tag to prompt a user for information, there may be times when the user inadvertently types an extra space before or after the value he or she inputs.

● If the user inadvertently types a space before or after their password, the additional whitespace will cause the if statement not to match the password.

application can use the String library's toString function. The toString function is similar to WMLScript's automatic conversion with the exception that toString provides better support for invalid parameters. The following statement assigns the string representation of the value 81 to the variable result:

```
result = String.toString(3*27);
```

Using the WMLScript URL Library

Within WML card decks, developers often place links to other decks that reside on the local or a remote system. Depending on the application's processing, the application may prompt the user to enter the URL that he or she desires. To help your applications validate and manipulate URL information, WMLScript provides the URL library. Table 8-5 briefly describes the functions built into the WMLScript URL library.

The following sections examine each of the URL library functions in detail.

Function	Example	Purpose
escapeString	result = URL.escapeString(urlAddress);	Returns a string representing the standard URL-escaping characters of the specified URL
getBase	base = URL.getBase("http:// www.WL.com/xyz.wmls#function");	Returns the base information (the information up to the card name) contained in the specified URL
getFragment	frag = URL.getFragment("http:// www.WL.com/xyz.wmls#function");	Returns the fragment information (the card name) contained in the specified URL
getHost	host = URL.getHost("http://www.WL.com/ xyz.wmls#function");	Returns the host information (in this case, www.WL.com) contained in the specified URL

Table 8-5 Functions Provided by the WMLScript URL Library

8

Function	Example	Purpose
getParameters	`params = URL.getParameters ("http://www.WL.com/ xyz.wmls;A;B;C");`	Returns the parameter values (in this case, A; B; C) contained in the specified URL
getPath	`path = URL.getPath("http://www.WL.com/ foldername/xyz.wmls#function");`	Returns the path (folder name) information (in this case, foldername) contained in the specified URL
getPort	`port = URL.getPort("http:// www.WL.com:80/xyz.wmls# function");`	Returns the port number information (in this case, 80) contained in the specified URL
getQuery	`query = URL.getQuery("http:// www.WL.com/xyz.wmls?Name=Phil");`	Returns the query information (in this case, Name=Phil) contained in the specified URL
getReferer	`coming_from = URL.getReferer();`	Returns the URL of the source that called the card
getScheme	`scheme = URL.getScheme("http:// www.WL.com/xyz.wmls");`	Returns the scheme information (in this case, http) contained in the specified URL
isValid	`boolean_value = URL.isValid(urlAdddress);`	Returns "true" if the specified string contains a valid URL syntax (as opposed to a valid URL that corresponds to a site) or "false" otherwise
loadString	`result = URL.loadString(URL, "text/vnd.wap.wml");`	Loads a resource of a specific type into a string variable. Returns the string variable if it successfully loads the document or an integer error status
resolve	`absolute_address = URL.resolve("http://www.WL.com", "game.wml");`	Returns an absolute Web address using a base and relative address
unescapeString	`result = URL.unescapeString (urlAddress);`	Returns a string representing the standard URL-unescaping characters of the specified URL

Table 8-5 Functions Provided by the WMLScript URL Library (*continued*)

Parsing a URL

The following WML application, URLDemo.wml, passes a URL to the
WMLScript ParseURL function that resides in the file BreakupURL.wmls:

```
<?xml version="1.0"?>

<!DOCTYPE wml PUBLIC "-//WAPFORUM//DTD WML 1.2//EN"
    "http://www.wapforum.org/DTD/wml_1.1.xml">

<wml>

<card id="URLDemo">
  <onevent type="onenterforward">
     <go href="BreakupURL.wmls#ParseURL(
'http://www.WirelessLookup.com:80/Developer/test.wml#CardName')"/>
  </onevent>
</card>

</wml>
```

The ParseURL function uses the URL library functions to extract the various
URL attributes:

```
extern function ParseURL(URLString)
 {
   WMLBrowser.setVar("Base", URL.getBase());
   WMLBrowser.setVar("Fragment", URL.getFragment(URLString));
   WMLBrowser.setVar("Host", URL.getHost(URLString));
   WMLBrowser.setVar("Parameters", URL.getParameters(URLString));
   WMLBrowser.setVar("Path", URL.getPath(URLString));
   WMLBrowser.setVar("Port", URL.getPort(URLString));
   WMLBrowser.setVar("Query", URL.getQuery(URLString));
   WMLBrowser.setVar("Referer", URL.getReferer());
   WMLBrowser.setVar("Scheme", URL.getScheme(URLString));
   WMLBrowser.setVar("IsValid", URL.isValid(URLString));

   WMLBrowser.refresh();
   WMLBrowser.go("ShowURLParse.wml");
 }
```

Then, the ParseURL function loads the ShowURLParse.wml card to display
the application's result:

```
<?xml version="1.0"?>
```

```
<!DOCTYPE wml PUBLIC "-//WAPFORUM//DTD WML 1.2//EN"
    "http://www.wapforum.org/DTD/wml_1.1.xml">
<wml>

<card id="ShowURLParse">
 <p>
   Base: $(Base)<br/>
   Fragment: $(Fragment)<br/>
   Host: $(Host)<br/>
   Parameters: $(Parameters)<br/>
   Path: $(Path)<br/>
   Port: $(Port)<br/>
   Query: $(Query)<br/>
   Referer: $(Referer)<br/>
   Scheme: $(Scheme)<br/>
   IsValid: $(IsValid)
 </p>
</card>

</wml>
```

Determining a URL's Base Address

As a WMLScript-based application runs, there may be times when the script must know its own URL. The URL library's getBase function returns an absolute URL to the current script:

```
Base = URL.getBase();
```

Extracting a Fragment from a URL

Within a WML application, a fragment corresponds to an internal link, such as a link to a specific card. The URL library's getFragment function returns the fragment specified in a URL:

```
Fragment = URL.getFragment(
"http://www.WirelessLookup.com/File.wml#CardName");
```

Extracting a Host Name from a URL

When you work with URLs within an application, a common operation you will perform is parsing the URL into various components. To simplify the URL parsing, the URL library provides several functions that return specific parts of the URL. For example, the URL library's getHost function returns the host name from a URL, or an empty string if the URL string does not contain a host. Given the URL www.WirelessLookup.com/pathname/filename, for example, the getHost function would return www.WirelessLookup.com:

```
Host = URL.getHost(
"http://www.WirelessLookup.com/File.wml#CardName");
```

Extracting Parameters from a URL

Depending on the operation the user is performing, there may be times when a URL contains one or more parameters. For example, the URL www.WirelessLookup.com/Card.wml;1;2;3 contains the parameter values 1, 2, and 3. The URL library's getParameters function returns the parameters specified in a URL:

```
Host = URL.getParameters(
"www.WirelessLookup.com/File.wml;1;2;3");
```

Extracting a Directory Path from a URL

Within a URL, the path specifies the relative or absolute set of directories the browser must traverse to locate a specific file. The URL library's getPath function returns the path specified in a URL:

```
Path = URL.getPath(
"www.WirelessLookup.com/Parent/SomeDirectory/File.wml");
```

Extracting a Port Number from a URL

Within TCP/IP (and WAP), software layers assign port numbers to specific applications. For example, an HTTP-based browser uses port 80. When a user specifies a URL that includes a port number, such as www.WirelessLookup.com:80, an application can use the URL library's getPort function to determine the port number. If the URL does not contain a port number, the function returns an empty string:

```
Port = URL.getPort(
"www.WirelessLookup.com:80/Parent/SomeDirectory/File.wml");
```

8

Determining the URL of the Referring Source

There may be times when WMLScript-based applications may need information about the resource that called the script. The application, for example, may want to send a message to the remote system, or may need to validate the system's access to specific data. To determine information about the referring resource, the application can use the URL library's getReferer function:

```
Referer = URL.getReferer();
```

resolveDemo.wml

Project 8-2: Building an Absolute URL

Just as there will be times when an application must break apart a URL, there will also be times when an application must combine a relative URL within a base address to create an absolute address. In such cases, the application can use the URL library's resolve function.

This project creates the WML file, resolveDemo.wml, which passes a base address and a relative address to the function BuildAbsolute, which resides in the WMLScript file Absolute.wml. Within the function, the code assigns the absolute URL to the variable AbsoluteURL and then loads the WML application ShowAbsoluteURL.wml to display the result.

Step-By-Step

1. Using a text editor, create the file ResolveDemo.wml. Within the file, enter the following header information:

```
<?xml version="1.0"?>

<!DOCTYPE wml PUBLIC "-//WAPFORUM//DTD WML 1.2//EN"
    "http://www.wapforum.org/DTD/wml_1.1.xml">

<wml>
```

2. Use a <card> tag to create the card ResolveDemo:

```
<card id="ResolveDemo">
```

3. To pass control and the URL components to the WMLScript BuildAbsolute function, the card will trap the onenterforward event that occurs when the card is first loaded. Within the card, use the following <onevent> statement to trap the event:

```
<onevent type="onenterforward">
   <go href="AbsoluteURL.wmls#BuildAbsolute(
     'http://www.WirelessLookup.com', 'Test.wml')" />
</onevent>
```

4. Use the </card> tag to end the card and the </wml> tag to end the deck. The card's contents should appear as follows:

```
<?xml version="1.0"?>

<!DOCTYPE wml PUBLIC "-//WAPFORUM//DTD WML 1.2//EN"
    "http://www.wapforum.org/DTD/wml_1.1.xml">

<wml>

<card id="ResolveDemo">
  <onevent type="onenterforward">
     <go href="AbsoluteURL.wmls#BuildAbsolute(
        'http://www.WirelessLookup.com', 'Test.wml')" />
  </onevent>
</card>

</wml>
```

5. Using a text editor, create the file AbsoluteURL.wmls. Enter the following statements to create the BuildAbsolute function:

```
extern function BuildAbsolute(Base, Relative)
 {
   WMLBrowser.setVar("Base", Base);
   WMLBrowser.setVar("Relative", Relative);
   WMLBrowser.setVar("Absolute", URL.resolve(Base, Relative));

   WMLBrowser.refresh();
   WMLBrowser.go("ShowAbsoluteURL.wml");
 }
```

8

6. Using a text editor, create the ShowAbsoluteURL.wml file, which displays the contents of the variable Absolute, to which the WMLScript function BuildAbsolute assigned the absolute URL:

```
<?xml version="1.0"?>

<!DOCTYPE wml PUBLIC "-//WAPFORUM//DTD WML 1.2//EN"
    "http://www.wapforum.org/DTD/wml_1.1.xml">

<wml>

<card id="ShowAbsoluteURL">
 <p>
   Base: $(Base)<br/>
   Relative: $(Relative)<br/>
   Absolute: $(Absolute)<br/>
 </p>
</card>

</wml>
```

When you load the resolveDemo.wml application into the phone simulator, the simulator will display the URL information shown in Figure 8-15.

Extracting the Schema from a URL

When a user specifies a URL, the user may include the scheme (method) the program is to use to retrieve the data, such as HTTP or WTAI. The URL

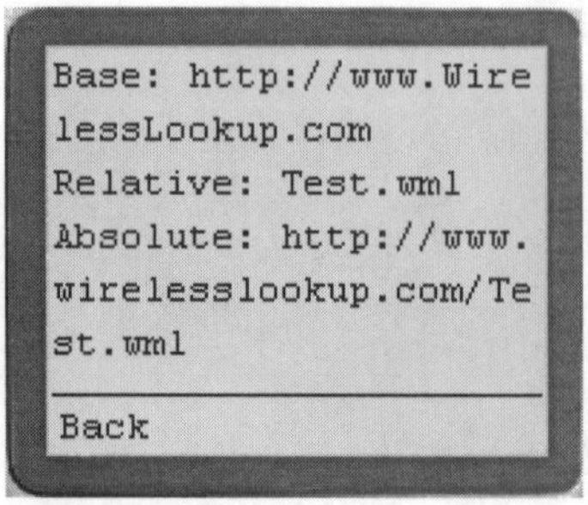

```
Base: http://www.Wire
lessLookup.com
Relative: Test.wml
Absolute: http://www.
wirelesslookup.com/Te
st.wml

Back
```

Figure 8-15 Resolving a URL

library's getScheme function returns the schema specified in a URL, or an empty string if a schema is not present:

```
Schema = URL.getScheme("http://www.WirelessLookup.com");
```

Testing for a Valid URL

Before you perform URL-based operations, you should first check that the URL you want to examine is valid. The URL library's isValid function examines a URL to verify that the URL is syntactically correct. If the URL is valid, the function returns "true". If the URL is invalid, the function returns "false":

```
isValidURL = URL.isValid("http://www.WirelessLookup.com");
```

Loading the Content That Resides at a URL

As your applications become more complex, there will be times when you will need to access information that resides in a file. You might, for example, need to load numbers from a phone-book file, or a list of sites from a bookmark file. In such cases, you can use the loadString function, which lets an application load MIME-based content from a URL into a string variable, which your application can manipulate.

The following statement, for example, loads the file loadStringDemo.wml from the WirelessLookup.com site into the variable Result, using the text/vnd.wap.wml content type:

```
Result =
URL.loadString("http://www.WirelessLookup.com/loadStringDemo.wml",
"text/vnd.wap.wml");
```

Escaping URL Strings

When programmers create Web addresses (URLs), there are times when the programmer (either intentionally or errantly) will use a character within the address that has special meaning within a URL. For example, the pound sign character (#) within a URL identifies a fragment. If a URL contains the pound sign and the character does not correspond to a fragment, you must escape the character by replacing it with its corresponding hexadecimal representation.

Assume, for example, a URL is www.WL.com\Some#File.wml. To escape the pound sign character, you would use www.WL.com\Some%23File.wml. Within ASCII, the hexadecimal value 23 corresponds to the pound sign. The percent sign within the URL indicates to the browser that you are escaping the character. To help you manipulate URLs, the URL library provides the escapeString and unescapeString functions.

Using the WMLScript WMLBrowser Library

Within a WML deck, you can perform operations, such as go, prev, and refresh, to control the browser's processing. To perform similar actions from within WMLScript, you can use the WMLBrowser library. If the current browser does not support the library, each of the functions will return the invalid value. Table 8-6 briefly describes the functions built into the WMLScript WMLBrowser library.

Function	Example	Purpose
GetCurrentCard	`relativeURL = WMLBrowser.getCurrentCard();`	Returns the relative URL of the WML card that is currently executing in the browser
GetVar	`value = WMLBrowser.getVar ("VariableName");`	Returns the value of the specified variable from within the WML context
Go	`WMLBrowser.go ("new_card.wml");`	Loads the specified WML card into the browser for execution
NewContext	`WMLBrowser.newContext();`	Clears the WML history stack and removes the variable context
Prev	`WMLBrowser.prev();`	Returns control to the previous WML card
Refresh	`WMLBrowser.refresh();`	Directs the browser to redisplay the calling card's contents when the WMLScript returns control to the card
SetVar	`boolean_result = WMLBrowser.setVar ("VariableName", Value);`	Assigns a value to the specified variable; returns "true" if the assignment was successful and "false" otherwise

Table 8-6　Functions Provided by the WMLScript WMLBrowser Library

Determining the Current Card

Depending on the script's processing, there may be times when the script must know the current card. In such cases, the application can use the `WMLBrowser.getCurrentCard` function, which returns the relative URL for the current card. The following WML file, getCurrentCardDemo.wml, calls the CurrentCard function, which illustrates the use of getCurrentCard:

```
<?xml version="1.0"?>

<!DOCTYPE wml PUBLIC "-//WAPFORUM//DTD WML 1.2//EN"
    "http://www.wapforum.org/DTD/wml_1.1.xml">

<wml>

<card id="FirstCard">
  <onevent type="onenterforward">
    <go href="CurrentCard.wmls#CurrentCard()" />
  </onevent>
</card>

</wml>
```

Within the CurrentCard function, which resides in the WMLScript CurrentCard.wmls file, the function stores the current card information in the variable CurrentCard. The function then loads the WML application ShowCurrentCard.wml to display the result:

```
extern function CurrentCard()
 {
   WMLBrowser.setVar("CurrentCard", WMLBrowser.getCurrentCard());

   WMLBrowser.refresh();
   WMLBrowser.go("ShowCurrentCard.wml");
 }
```

The following statements implement ShowCurrentCard.wml:

```
<?xml version="1.0"?>

<!DOCTYPE wml PUBLIC "-//WAPFORUM//DTD WML 1.2 //EN"
    "http://www.wapforum.org/DTD/wml_1.1.xml">
```

8

```
<wml>

<card id="ShowCurrentCard">
 <p>
   Current Card: $(CurrentCard)
 </p>
</card>

</wml>
```

When you load the getCurrentCardDemo.wml application into the phone simulator, the simulator will display the output shown in Figure 8-16.

Performing a WML Go Operation to Branch to a URL

The WMLBrowser library's go function directs the browser to jump to a specific URL and then to assign specific parameter values. For example, the following WML file, goDemo.wml, calls the GetName function, which prompts the user to enter his or her first and last name. After the script gets the name, it uses the go function to launch the card SayHello.wml, which displays a hello message:

```
<?xml version="1.0"?>

<!DOCTYPE wml PUBLIC "-//WAPFORUM//DTD WML 1.2//EN"
    "http://www.wapforum.org/DTD/wml_1.1.xml">
```

| **Figure 8-16** | Displaying information about the current card |

```
<wml>

<card id="GoDemo" title="GoDemo">
  <onevent type="onenterforward">
    <go href="GetName.wmls#GetName()" />
  </onevent>
</card>

</wml>
```

The GetName function resides in the GetName.wmls file, as shown here:

```
extern function GetName()
 {
   var Name;

   Name = Dialogs.prompt("Enter your name", "");

   WMLBrowser.setVar("Name", Name);

   WMLBrowser.refresh();
   WMLBrowser.go("SayHello.wml");
 }
```

The following statements implement SayHello.wml:

```
<?xml version="1.0"?>

<!DOCTYPE wml PUBLIC "-//WAPFORUM//DTD WML 1.2//EN"
    "http://www.wapforum.org/DTD/wml_1.1.xml">

<wml>

<card id="SayHello" title="Hello">
 <p>
   Hello, $(Name)
 </p>
</card>

</wml>
```

Performing a WML Prev Operation to Return to the Previous URL

Throughout this module, you have used the `WMLBrowser.go` function to load a specific WML card from within a WMLScript function. There will be times when you will want a script to return to the card that called the current WML card. In such cases, you can use the `WMLBrowser.prev` function, which behaves just like the `<prev/>` tag:

```
WMLBrowser.prev();
```

The `WMLBrowser.prev` function does not return control to the card that called the function, but rather to the card that called the current card.

Performing a WML Refresh Operation

As you have learned, programmers refer to a microbrowser's current variable settings as the browser's context. Depending on the application's processing, there may be times when the application must refresh the current context. In such cases, the application can use the WMLBrowser library's refresh function. As a rule, WMLScript functions should call the refresh function whenever they change the value of a variable within the WML context (a variable used by WML cards as opposed to a variable that resides only within the WMLScript code).

The following statements illustrate the use of the refresh function:

```
extern function CalculateArea(Radius)
{
  WMLBrowser.setVar("Area", (22.0 / 7.0) *
                    Float.pow(Radius, 2));
  WMLBrowser.refresh();
  WMLBrowser.go("ShowArea.wml");
}
```

Setting and Retrieving Variable Values

Throughout this module, you have created WMLScript applications that have used the `WMLBrowser.setVar` function to assign values to variables within the WML context. You have also created WML cards that have passed a variable's value to a WMLScript function as a parameter. Depending on your application's processing, there may be times when a WMLScript function must access a WML variable that it did not receive as a parameter. In such cases, the function can use the `WMLBrowser.getVar` function.

The following WML application, getVarDemo.wml, uses an `<input>` tag to prompt the user for his or her name, which it assigns to the variable Name. The application then calls the WMLScript ShowName function, which resides in the file ShowName.wmls:

```
<?xml version="1.0"?>

<!DOCTYPE wml PUBLIC "-//WAPFORUM//DTD WML 1.2//EN"
    "http://www.wapforum.org/DTD/wml_1.1.xml">

<wml>

<card id="getVarDemo" title="getVar">
 <p>
   Enter Your Name:
   <input name="Name" />

   <do type="accept">
     <go href="ShowName.wmls#ShowName()" />
   </do>
 </p>
</card>

</wml>
```

Within the ShowName function, the code uses the `WMLBrowser.getVar` function to get the value of the variable Name:

```
extern function ShowName()
 {
    var UserName;

    UserName = WMLBrowser.getVar("Name");

    Dialogs.alert("Hello, " + UserName);
 }
```

You should note that the WML application could have (and should have) easily passed the name to the WMLScript function as a parameter. As a rule, WMLScript functions should only view the values of variables they receive as parameters.

8

✓ Mastery Check

1. List the six standard WMLScript libraries.

_____

_____

2. Values an application passes to a function are called:

    a. Manipulators

    b. Delimiters

    c. Parameters

    d. Both A and B

3. How do the Dialogs library's alert and confirm functions differ?

_____

_____

4. What is a delimited string?

_____

_____

5. How can you extract the second element from the string "First/Second/Third"?

_____

_____

6. How can you replace the word "Special" in the string "Special Discount" with the word "Super"?

_____

_____

7. How can you determine whether a browser supports floating-point operations?

_____

_____

☑ *Mastery Check*

8. When should a WMLScript function use the WMLBrowser library's newContext function?

_____

_____

9. How can a WMLScript function determine the WML card that called it?

_____

_____

10. Which statements result in the value 25?

a. `Result = 5 * 5;`

b. `Result = Float.sqrt(625);`

c. `Result = Float.pow(5, 2);`

d. A and C

e. A, B, and C

8

Module 9

Building Real-World WMLScript Applications

The Goals of This Module

- Use the Console library's print and println functions to display messages to the console window

- Learn how to use WMLScript to validate user input

- Understand limitations microbrowsers may place on WMLScript applications

In the previous two modules, you created many small WMLScript applications. As the complexity and size of your WMLScript applications increase, you will face new problems. Many microbrowsers, for example, limit the size of a WMLScript file to less than 4KB. When your scripts become large, you may have to trade size for slower speed or less readability. In this module you will use WMLScript to create a Tic-Tac-Toe game.

The code presented here is actually about one-third the size of my original program. With the seemingly unlimited resources we have when we create Windows-based applications, there are few times when code size is a factor that we must pay considerable attention to. Getting the Tic-Tac-Toe game to fit within 4KB made me appreciate how computing resources have progressed over the past 20 years! Throughout this book you have used the Console window to locate syntax errors, view the value of variables, and troubleshoot various problems. In this module, you will learn to use the Console library from within WMLScript to display messages to the Console window. Using the Console library functions to display messages to the Console window as your programs execute is very convenient for debugging.

Using the Console Window

As the WMLScript applications you create become more complex, you will eventually encounter errors that you must debug. To locate errors within programs, programmers often place "debug-write" statements within their code to display messages the programmers can use to help identify the error. For example, programmers might display a message that shows a variable's value before and after the code performs specific processing.

One way programmers can display such debug messages is to use the Dialogs library's alert function. The following statement, for example, uses the function to display the current value of the Username variable:

```
Dialogs.alert("Username contains " + Username);
```

When the microbrowser encounters the alert function call, it will display the message and then wait for the programmer to respond. By placing similar alert function calls throughout a function, the programmer can track down the source of the error.

In addition to using the alert function to display debug messages, your applications can use the Console library's print and println functions, which display messages to the console window—these messages do not interrupt the application's execution, as does the alert function.

The following statement, for example, uses the Console library's print function to display the value of the Username variable:

```
Console.print("Username contains " + Username);
```

The difference between the Console library's print and println functions is that the println function sends carriage-return and linefeed characters to the console window to advance the cursor to the start of the next line after the printing is done, whereas the print function leaves the cursor on the same line.

The following WMLScript, ConsoleDemo.wmls, provides the ConsoleMessage function, which uses the print and println functions to write messages to the console window:

```
extern function ConsoleMessage()
 {
   Console.print("Hello, ");
   Console.println("Wireless World!");
   Dialogs.alert("View console window for messages");
 }
```

To call the ConsoleMessage function, use the following WML application, ShowConsoleMessage.wml:

```
<?xml version="1.0"?>

<!DOCTYPE wml PUBLIC "-//WAPFORUM//DTD WML 1.2//EN"
    "http://www.wapforum.org/DTD/wml_1.1.xml">

<wml>

<card id="ConsoleMessage">

 <do type="onenterforward">
  <go href="ConsoleDemo.wmls#ConsoleMessage()" />
 </do>

</card>

</wml>
```

9

When you run the application using the phone simulator, the console window displays the message "Hello, Wireless World!", as shown in Figure 9-1.

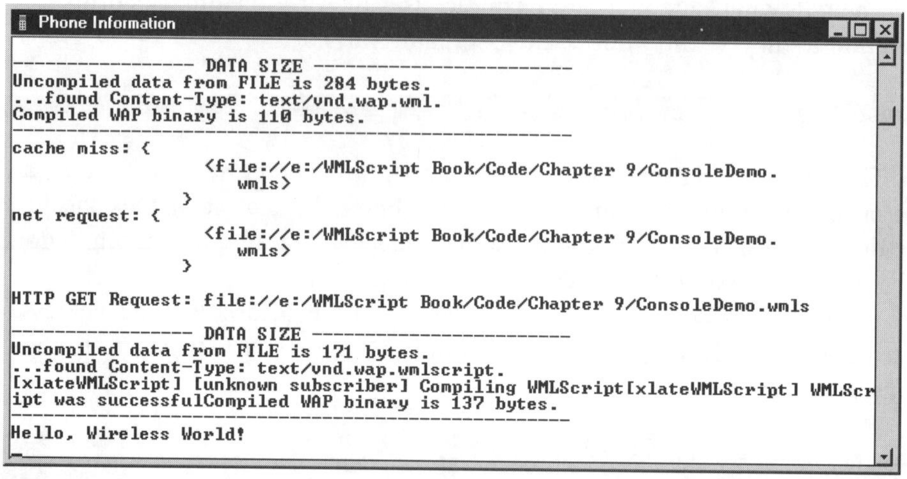

```
    Phone Information                                                _ |□|×|
-------------------- DATA SIZE --------------------
Uncompiled data from FILE is 284 bytes.
...found Content-Type: text/vnd.wap.wml.
Compiled WAP binary is 110 bytes.
-------------------------------------------------
cache miss: {
                    <file://e:/WMLScript Book/Code/Chapter 9/ConsoleDemo.
                        wmls>
            }
net request: {
                    <file://e:/WMLScript Book/Code/Chapter 9/ConsoleDemo.
                        wmls>
            }
HTTP GET Request: file://e:/WMLScript Book/Code/Chapter 9/ConsoleDemo.wmls
-------------------- DATA SIZE --------------------
Uncompiled data from FILE is 171 bytes.
...found Content-Type: text/vnd.wap.wmlscript.
[xlateWMLScript] [unknown subscriber] Compiling WMLScript[xlateWMLScript] WMLScr
ipt was successfulCompiled WAP binary is 137 bytes.
-------------------------------------------------
Hello, Wireless World!
```

Figure 9-1 Displaying messages to the console window

Ask the Expert

Question: How large can my WMLScript applications become?

Answer: Today, the maximum size of a WMLScript application is very dependent on the microbrowser. Some microbrowsers, for example, will not compile a WMLScript file larger than 4KB! That means you must keep your functions compact. If your application is large and complex, you may need to break the application into separate files, creating libraries that you can access using the use url pragma, as discussed in Module 7. As I was creating the Tic-Tac-Toe application that this module presents, I had to rewrite the application several times to reduce its size so the microbrowsers would compile it.

Processing User Input

Depending on the information your application displays, there may be times when you will want the user to enter a password before the user can access the application. Because it can be difficult for the user to type on the cell phone's keypad, your applications should not use the `<input>` tag's `type="password"` attribute, but you may still want the user to enter a password before accessing sensitive data.

To determine if the user's password is valid, your WML applications can call a WMLScript function to validate the password. If the password is valid, the WMLScript function, in turn, can load the next WML card. For example, the following WML application, TopSecret.wml, uses an `<input>` tag to prompt the user for a password. The code then branches to the CheckPassword function that resides in the WMLScript file ValidatePassword.wmls. If the user enters the password "Secret", the function loads the WML card SecretData.wml. If the user's password is invalid, the function displays an error message and returns to the previous card.

The following code implements the WML application TopSecret.wml:

```
<?xml version="1.0"?>

<!DOCTYPE wml PUBLIC "-//WAPFORUM//DTD WML 1.2//EN"
    "http://www.wapforum.org/DTD/wml_1.1.xml">

<wml>

<card id="TopSecret">
  <p>
    Enter password

    <input name="Password" />
  </p>

  <do type="accept">
    <go href="ValidatePassword.wmls#CheckPassword('$Password')" />
  </do>
</card>

</wml>
```

The following code implements the WMLScript function `CheckPassword`. As you can see, the code simply uses an `if` statement to validate the password. If the password is valid, the function uses the WMLBrowser library's go function to load the SecretData.wml card deck. If the password is not valid, the function displays an error message, clears the current context to delete the password the user tried to validate, and then returns to the original application:

```
extern function CheckPassword(Password)
{
   if (Password == "Secret")
     WMLBrowser.go("SecretData.wml");
   else
     {
       Dialogs.alert("Invalid password");
       WMLBrowser.newContext();
       WMLBrowser.go("TopSecret.wml");
     }
}
```

The following code implements the WML application SecretData.wml:

```
<?xml version="1.0"?>

<!DOCTYPE wml PUBLIC "-//WAPFORUM//DTD WML 1.2//EN"
    "http://www.wapforum.org/DTD/wml_1.1.xml">

<wml>

<card id="SecretData">
 <p>
   To call the boss at home, dial 212-555-1212.
 </p>
</card>

</wml>
```

1-Minute Drill

- What is a debug-write message?
- How can you display debug messages within WMLScript?

- A debug-write message is output that a programmer displays to help him or her remove errors from (debug) an application, such as a variable's value at different points in the code.
- Within a WMLScript, programmers use the Dialogs library's alert function, or the Console library's print and println functions to display debug-write messages.

Playing Tic-Tac-Toe

If you search the World Wide Web, you will find that many popular PC-based games are starting to migrate to handheld devices. In this section, you will use WMLScript to create a simple Tic-Tac-Toe game. Although the code is quite simplistic, it illustrates the use of conditional (**if-then**) and iterative processing, as well as the manipulation of a delimited string.

To launch the game, you will use the WML application PlayTicTacToe.wml, whose statements are shown here:

```
<?xml version="1.0"?>

<!DOCTYPE wml PUBLIC "-//WAPFORUM//DTD WML 1.2//EN"
    "http://www.wapforum.org/DTD/wml_1.1.xml">

<wml>

<card id="PlayTicTacToe">
 <p>
   Ready to play?
 </p>

 <do type="accept" label="Play">
   <go href="TicTacToe.wmls#TicTacToe()" />
 </do>
</card>

</wml>
```

When you load the PlayTicTacToe.wml application, the phone will display a prompt asking you if you are ready to play. If you press the accept button, the code will call the WMLScript function TicTacToe, which resides in the file TicTacToe.wmls. The TicTacToe function, in turn, will display the starting board shown in Figure 9-2.

The **TicTacToe** application uses three delimited character strings to represent the three rows of the Tic-Tac-Toe board. Initially, each element within the string contains a period. As the players make their moves, the application replaces the periods with either an X or an O. The string uses a vertical bar to delimit the values.

9

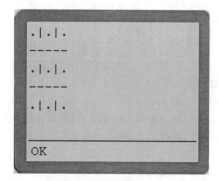

Figure 9-2   Displaying the initial Tic-Tac-Toe board

The following statement, for example, assigns the initial values to row 1 of the board:

```
WMLBrowser.setVar("row1", ".|.|.");
```

The application uses the Dialogs library's prompt function to prompt the user for the row and column in which he or she wants to place an X or an O. The application will first prompt player X for his or her move. Then the application will prompt player O to select a move. The application will continue to prompt the players for their moves until a player wins or a "cat's game" (a draw) occurs. After each move, the application will display the current board, as shown in Figure 9-3.

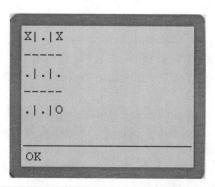

Figure 9-3   Displaying moves in a game of Tic-Tac-Toe

Within the WMLScript file, the TicTacToe function oversees the game. To start, the function uses the WMLBrowser library's setVar function to initialize the board. Then, the function uses a **while** loop to play the game until a player wins or a cat's game occurs. Within the **while** loop, the function calls the GetUserMove function to get the next user move and then the CheckWinner function to see if a player has won. To display the board's contents, the function calls the ShowBoard function.

The following statements implement the TicTacToe function:

```
extern function TicTacToe()
 {
   var Winner = false, CatGame = false;
   var WhoseMove = 1;
   var MoveCount = 0;

   WMLBrowser.setVar("row1", ".|.|.");
   WMLBrowser.setVar("row2", ".|.|.");
   WMLBrowser.setVar("row3", ".|.|.");

   ShowBoard();

   while ((! Winner) && (! CatGame))
     {
       GetUserMove(WhoseMove);

       Winner = CheckWinner();

       if (Winner)
         {
           if (WhoseMove)
             Dialogs.alert("X Wins");
           else
             Dialogs.alert("O Wins");
           ShowBoard();
           WMLBrowser.go("PlayTicTacToe.wml");
         }

       else if (++MoveCount == 9)
         {
           CatGame = true;
           Dialogs.alert("Cat Game");
           ShowBoard();
```

9

```
          WMLBrowser.go("PlayTicTacToe.wml");
        }
     else
        ShowBoard();
     WhoseMove = (WhoseMove) ? 0: 1;
    }
}
```

As you can see, the TicTacToe function uses the WML variables row1, row2, and row3 to store the board's contents. The function uses the variables Winner and CatGame to determine when the game should end. Finally, the function uses the variable MoveCount to track the number of player moves made thus far and the variable WhoseMove to track the current player.

To reduce the size of the TicTacToe.wmls application, you might delete the statements that assign the board's initial values from the TicTacToe function and instead use WML <setvar> tags to assign the values as shown here:

```
<do type="accept" label="Play">
   <go href="TicTacToe.wmls#TicTacToe()">
     <setvar name="row1" value=".|.|."/>
     <setvar name="row2" value=".|.|."/>
     <setvar name="row3" value=".|.|."/>
   </go>
</do>
```

To get each player's move, the TicTacToe function calls the GetUserMove function, which uses a **while** statement to loop until the user specifies a valid location. Row positions from 1 to 3 and column positions from 1 to 3 are valid. The first space on the board, for example, is row 1, column 1. The GetUserMove function uses an **if** statement to verify that the player enters row and column values in the range 1 through 3. Then, GetUserMove uses the String library's elementAt function to determine whether the board position is currently available (if the position is available, it will currently have a period for its value). If the board position is in use, or if the user enters a row or column value outside of the range 1 though 3, the GetUserMove function will display an error message. Otherwise, if the position is valid, the function will use the String library's replaceAt function to replace the period with either an X or an O, depending on the current player.

The following statements implement the GetUserMove function:

```
function GetUserMove(WhoseMove)
 {
   var ValidMove = false;
   var Row, Column;
   var RowData;

   while (! ValidMove)
     {
       Row = Dialogs.prompt("Enter row (1-3)", "");
       Column = Dialogs.prompt("Enter column (1-3)", "");

       if (((Row >= 1) && (Row <= 3)) && ((Column >= 1) &&
           (Column <= 3)))
         {
           RowData = WMLBrowser.getVar("row" + Row);

           if (String.elementAt(RowData, Column-1, "|") == ".")
             {
               ValidMove = true;
               RowData = String.replaceAt(RowData, (WhoseMove) ? "X" :
                   "O", Column-1, "|");
               WMLBrowser.setVar("row"+Row, RowData);
             }
           else
             Dialogs.alert("That position is not available");
         }
       else
         Dialogs.alert("Invalid row or column");
     }
 }
```

Within the GetUserMove function, the code uses the conditional assignment operator to assign either an X or an O to the Tic-Tac-Toe board, based on the current player:

```
RowData = String.replaceAt(RowData, (WhoseMove) ? "X" :
   "O", Column-1, "|");
```

When the WMLScript compiler encounters the conditional assignment operator, it treats the operator like a mini if-else statement. If the expression specified within the parentheses is true, the application will assign the first value specified after the question mark. If, instead, the expression is false, the application will assign the value specified after the colon. In this case, if the variable WhoseMove contains a true value (a nonzero value), the application will assign the value "X". If WhoseMove contains a false value (0), the application will assign the value "O".

After a player makes a valid move, the TicTacToe function calls the CheckWinner function to see if either player has won. The CheckWinner function uses a series of if-else statements to first check the board's rows to see if a player has won. Next, the function checks the board's columns, and finally the two diagonals:

```
function CheckWinner()
 {
   var row1, row2, row3;
   var Winner = false;

   row1 = WMLBrowser.getVar("row1");
   row2 = WMLBrowser.getVar("row2");
   row3 = WMLBrowser.getVar("row3");

   if ((String.elementAt(row1, 0, "|") ==
        String.elementAt(row1, 1, "|")) &&
      (String.elementAt(row1, 1, "|") ==
       String.elementAt(row1, 2, "|")) &&
      (String.elementAt(row1, 0, "|") != "."))
     Winner = true;
   else if ((String.elementAt(row2, 0, "|") ==
             String.elementAt(row2, 1, "|")) &&
      (String.elementAt(row2, 1, "|") ==
       String.elementAt(row2, 2, "|")) &&
      (String.elementAt(row2, 0, "|") != "."))
     Winner = true;
   else if ((String.elementAt(row3, 0, "|") ==
             String.elementAt(row3, 1, "|")) &&
      (String.elementAt(row3, 1, "|") ==
       String.elementAt(row3, 2, "|")) &&
      (String.elementAt(row3, 0, "|") != "."))
     Winner = true;

   else if ((String.elementAt(row1, 0, "|") ==
             String.elementAt(row2, 0, "|")) &&
      (String.elementAt(row2, 0, "|") ==
```

```
        String.elementAt(row3, 0, "|")) &&
      (String.elementAt(row1, 0, "|") != "."))
   Winner = true;
 else if ((String.elementAt(row1, 1, "|") ==
         String.elementAt(row2, 1, "|")) &&
      (String.elementAt(row2, 1, "|") ==
       String.elementAt(row3, 1, "|")) &&
      (String.elementAt(row1, 1, "|") != "."))
   Winner = true;
 else if ((String.elementAt(row1, 2, "|") ==
         String.elementAt(row2, 2, "|")) &&
      (String.elementAt(row2, 2, "|") ==
       String.elementAt(row3, 2, "|")) &&
      (String.elementAt(row1, 2, "|") != "."))
   Winner = true;

 else if ((String.elementAt(row1, 0, "|") ==
         String.elementAt(row2, 1, "|")) &&
      (String.elementAt(row2, 1, "|") ==
       String.elementAt(row3, 2, "|")) &&
      (String.elementAt(row1, 0, "|") != "."))
   Winner = true;
 else if ((String.elementAt(row1, 2, "|") ==
         String.elementAt(row2, 1, "|")) &&
      (String.elementAt(row2, 1, "|") ==
       String.elementAt(row3, 0, "|")) &&
      (String.elementAt(row1, 2, "|") != "."))
   Winner = true;

 return(Winner);
}
```

To display the board's contents, the TicTacToe.wmls script calls the ShowBoard function. Because the script uses a vertical bar (|) to separate elements, the ShowBoard function simply must display each row's contents, separating the second row from the others using a series of dashes, as shown here:

```
function ShowBoard()
 {
   var Board = "";

   Board = WMLBrowser.getVar("row1") +
         "\n-----\n" +
```

```
        WMLBrowser.getVar("row2") +
        "\n-----\n" +
        WMLBrowser.getVar("row3");

    Dialogs.alert(Board);
}
```

ShowWinner.wml

Project 9-1: Reducing the TicTacToe.wmls Script's Size

When the TicTacToe.wmls application detects a winner, the application displays a simple one-line message, shows the board's contents, and then branches control back to the PlayTicTacToe.wml application. In this project, you will create the ShowWinner.wml application that displays the board's contents and a bold message about the winner, as shown in Figure 9-4. The ShowWinner.wml card deck will then return the players to the PlayTicTacToe.wml application. By moving code from the WMLScript application back to WML, you may decrease the size of your WMLScript application, which may be necessary before a microbrowser will compile your code.

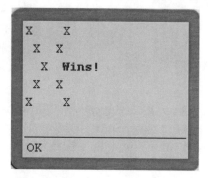
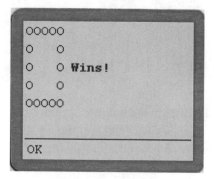

Figure 9-4   Using WML to display a message describing the winner

Step-By-Step

1. Using a text editor, create the file ShowWinner.wml that contains the following statements. The card deck contains a card that displays a message when X wins and a second card for when O wins:

```
<?xml version="1.0"?>

<!DOCTYPE wml PUBLIC "-//WAPFORUM//DTD WML 1.2//EN"
    "http://www.wapforum.org/DTD/wml_1.1.xml">

<wml>

<card id="X">
  <p>
    X    X<br/>
     X  X<br/>
      X  <b>Wins!</b><br/>
     X  X<br/>
    X    X<br/>
  </p>

  <do type="accept">
    <go href="PlayTicTacToe.wml" />
  </do>
</card>

<card id="O">
  <p>
    00000<br/>
    0   0<br/>
    0   0 <b>Wins!</b><br/>
    0   0<br/>
    00000<br/>
  </p>

  <do type="accept">
    <go href="PlayTicTacToe.wml" />
  </do>
</card>

</wml>
```

9

2. Close the ShowWinner.wml file and use the text editor to open the TicTacToe.wmls file.

3. Within TicTacToe.wmls, locate the following code that executes when a player wins the game:

```
if (Winner)
  {
    if (WhoseMove)
      Dialogs.alert("X Wins");
    else
      Dialogs.alert("O Wins");
    ShowBoard();
    WMLBrowser.go("PlayTicTacToe.wml");
  }
```

4. Change the code to use the WMLBrowser library's go function to call your newly created ShowWinner.wml card:

```
if (Winner)
  {
    if (WhoseMove)
      WMLBrowser.go("ShowWinner.wml#X");
    else
      WMLBrowser.go("ShowWinner.wml#O");
  }
```

☑ *Mastery Check*

1. What is the purpose of the Console library?

_____

_____

2. What is the purpose of the Console library's print and println functions?

_____

_____

3. If the variable Age contains the value 18, what value does the following expression assign to the variable Result?

```
Result = (Age >=  21) ? "Legal": "Minor";
```

Module 10

10

Advanced Concepts

The Goals of This Module

- Learn to use the `<go>` tag within a WML application to call a Perl script or active server page
- Use the `<postfield>` tag to pass parameters to a Perl script or active server page
- Understand how to build on-the-fly WML cards from within a Perl script or active server page
- Understand how to let the user view large amounts of information using fixed-size WML cards

As the complexity of your WML applications increase, your applications may eventually need to interact with applications that reside on servers that either store or retrieve information. In this module, you will learn how to use a Perl script or Active Server Page from within a WML application to store or retrieve information. To start, you will create WML applications that store and retrieve an individual's address information using a remote Perl script. Next, you will create an Active Server Page that lets a microbrowser select and display WBMP images that reside in a directory on the remote server. Finally, you will create WML applications that interact with an Active Server Page to manage a "to do" list that resides on a remote server.

Interacting with a Server

As your WML applications become more complex, there will be many times when the application must interact with a remote server. For example, the application may require that the user provide a username and password, or a user may want to look up information that resides in a company database. Many HTML-based Web sites interact with Perl scripts that reside on a server, and as you will learn in this section, WML applications can also provide information to and request information from Perl applications.

To pass information to a Perl script, applications can reference the script using an href attribute within a **<go>** tag. To post (send) information to the script, you must use the **method="post"** attribute. Then, to specify the field values you want to pass to the server, you use the **<postfield>** tag. The following statements, for example, pass the values of several WML variables to a Perl script named AddressListAdd.pl, which resides within the AddressList folder on the server from which the user downloaded the WML application:

```
<go method="post"
  href="../AddressList/AddressListAdd.pl">
  <postfield name="FirstName" value="$FirstName"/>
  <postfield name="LastName" value="$LastName"/>
  <postfield name="Phone" value="$Phone"/>
  <postfield name="Address" value="$Address"/>
  <postfield name="City" value="$City"/>
  <postfield name="State" value="$State"/>
```

```
  <postfield name="Zip" value="$Zip"/>
</go>
```

As you can see, the **<postfield>** tag uses two attributes. The name attribute specifies the field for which you are passing a value. The value attribute specifies the field's value. The Perl script, in turn, can get the values the application passes using the $cgiVars function, as shown here:

```
#Get the CGI variables
%cgiVars = &AppUtils::ParseCGIVars();
$FirstName = $cgiVars{"FirstName"};
$LastName = $cgiVars{"LastName"};
$Phone = $cgiVars{"Phone"};
$Address = $cgiVars{"Address"};
$City = $cgiVars{"City"};
$State = $cgiVars{"State"};
$Zip = $cgiVars{"Zip"};
```

After the Perl script extracts the values, it can store the values to a database or process them as needed.

The following WML application, AddressList.wml, uses a series of **<input>** tags to prompt the user to enter his or her name, phone, and address information. After the user specifies the information, the application asks the user to verify the input, as shown in Figure 10-1. If the user accepts the information, the application then uses a **<go>** tag to pass the information to a Perl script.

10

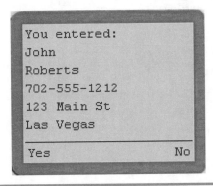

Figure 10-1   Passing name, phone, and address information to a Perl script

Hint

To run Perl scripts on your system, you must be running a Web server and you must have installed Perl. You can download free or shareware versions of Perl from many Web sites. If you are using Windows, you should visit http://aspn.activestate.com/ ASPN/Downloads/ActivePerl/index.

The following statements implement the AddressList.wml application:

```
<?xml version="1.0"?>
<!DOCTYPE wml PUBLIC "-//WAPFORUM//DTD WML 1.1//EN"
                    "http://www.wapforum.org/DTD/wml_1.1.xml">

<wml>

  <head>
    <meta http-equiv="Cache-Control" content="max-age=0"
        forua="true"/>
  </head>

  <card id="AddressList">
    <onevent type="onenterforward">
      <refresh>
        <setvar name="FirstName" value="" />
        <setvar name="LastName" value="" />
        <setvar name="Phone" value="" />
        <setvar name="Address" value="" />
        <setvar name="City" value="" />
        <setvar name="State" value="" />
        <setvar name="Zip" value="" />
      </refresh>
    </onevent>

    <do type="accept">
      <go href="#Confirm" />
    </do>

    <p align="center">
      Address List<br/>
    </p>

    <p align="left">
```

```
    Enter name and address.<br/><br/>
    First Name:
    <input name="FirstName" type="text" format="15M" />
 </p>

 <p align="left">
   Last Name:
   <input name="LastName" type="text" format="15M" />
 </p>

 <p align="left">
   Phone Number:
   <input name="Phone" type="text" format="NNN-NNN-NNNN" />
 </p>

 <p align="left">
   Street Address:
   <input name="Address" type="text" format="25M" />
 </p>

 <p align="left">
   City:
   <input name="City" type="text" format="15M" />
 </p>

 <p align="left">
   State:
   <input name="State" type="text" format="15M" />
 </p>

 <p align="left">
   Zip:
   <input name="Zip" type="text" format="NNNNN" />
 </p>

</card>

<card id="Confirm">
  <do type="accept" label="Yes">
   <go method="post"
     href="../AddressList/AddressListAdd.pl">
      <postfield name="FirstName" value="$FirstName"/>
```

10

```
                <postfield name="LastName" value="$LastName"/>
                <postfield name="Phone" value="$Phone"/>
                <postfield name="Address" value="$Address"/>
                <postfield name="City" value="$City"/>
                <postfield name="State" value="$State"/>
                <postfield name="Zip" value="$Zip"/>
            </go>
        </do>

        <do type="option" label="No">
            <go href="#AddressList" />
        </do>

        <p>
            You entered:<br/>
            $FirstName<br/>
            $LastName<br/>
            $Phone<br/>
            $Address<br/>
            $City<br/>
            $State<br/>
            $Zip<br/>
            Add to the list?
        </p>

    </card>

</wml>
```

As you can see, the application uses a series of `<input>` tags to prompt the user for name, phone, and address information. After the user enters the information, the application loads the Confirm card, which displays the information and then asks the user whether he or she wants to add the information to the database. If the user fails to confirm the information, the application directs the microbrowser to load the AddressList card to prompt the user to re-enter the data.

Within the AddressList card, the application captures the onenterforward event, which reinitializes the variables that will store the user's name, phone, and address information. If instead, the user accepts the data, the card uses a

<go> tag to call a Perl script to store the information within a database, as shown next.

Using a Perl Script to Store Address Information

Unlike other programming languages, WML does not have the ability to perform file operations. To store or retrieve information, a WML application must interact with another application. In the case of the AddressList.wml application, the code interacts with the AddressListAdd.pl Perl script, which simply appends the information a user enters to the end of a file:

```perl
#!/usr/bin/perl

require 'DeckUtils.pl';

#Get the CGI variables
%cgiVars = &AppUtils::ParseCGIVars();
$FirstName = $cgiVars{"FirstName"};
$LastName = $cgiVars{"LastName"};
$Phone = $cgiVars{"Phone"};
$Address = $cgiVars{"Address"};
$City = $cgiVars{"City"};
$State = $cgiVars{"State"};
$Zip = $cgiVars{"Zip"};

#Open the address list file for append access
open(FILE, ">>../AddressList/AddressList.dat");

#Add the new information
$NewLine = $FirstName . "," . $LastName . "," . $Phone .
    "," . $Address . ",";
$NewLine = $NewLine . $City . "," . $State . "," . $Zip;
print FILE $NewLine . "\n";
close(FILE);

#Build a deck to display a success message and
#jump back to add another name
$Deck =
```

10

```
"Content-type: text/vnd.wap.wml

<?xml version=\"1.0\"?>
<!DOCTYPE wml PUBLIC \"-//WAPFORUM//DTD WML 1.1//EN\"
                     \"http://www.wapforum.org/DTD/wml_1.1.xml\">

<wml>

    <head>
        <meta http-equiv=\"Cache-Control\" content=\"max-age=0\"
            forua=\"true\"/>
    </head>

    <card>
        <do type=\"accept\">
            <go href=\"../AddressList/AddressList.wml\" />
        </do>

        <p align=\"center\">
            Address List<br/>
        </p>

        <p align=\"left\" mode=\"nowrap\">
            Added: $FirstName $LastName
        </p>

    </card>

</wml>";

print $Deck;
```

When the Perl script starts, it uses the $cgiVars function to retrieve the information the WML application passes to the script using `<postfield>` tags. Next, the script opens, in append mode, the file AddressList.dat, which resides on the server. The application then uses the `print` statement to append the information to the file and the `close` statement to close the file. Then, the script assigns characters to a variable named $Deck that correspond to the tags that create a WML application. In this case, the tags create a WML application that tells the user that it has added the user information to the file. After the script assigns the WML statements to the variable, the script uses the `print` statement to display the variable's contents.

Normally, the Perl `print` statement will display output to the screen display. In this case, however, the microbrowser intercepts the output. Because the output is in the form of a WML card, the microbrowser executes the tags. In other words, when the application uses the `print` statement to display the contents of the $Deck variable, it essentially loads a WML application with the following tags:

```
<?xml version="1.0"?>
<!DOCTYPE wml PUBLIC "-//WAPFORUM//DTD WML 1.1//EN"
                    "http://www.wapforum.org/DTD/wml_1.1.xml">

<wml>

    <head>
        <meta http-equiv="Cache-Control" content="max-age=0"
            forua="true"/>
    </head>

    <card>
        <do type="accept">
            <go href="../AddressList/AddressList.wml" />
        </do>

        <p align="center">
            Address List<br/>
        </p>

        <p align="left" mode="nowrap">
            Added: $FirstName $LastName
        </p>
```

10

```
    </card>

</wml>
```

As you can see, the WML statements create a card that displays the name of the user that the script added to the database. When the user presses the accept button, the application loads the AddressList.wml application.

Searching the Address List

Just as there will be times when a WML application must store information on a server, there will also be times when an application must retrieve information. In such cases, the application can interact with a Perl script that retrieves information from a file or database.

The following WML application, SearchList.wml, prompts the user for the first and last name of an individual he or she wants the application to search for. The application then uses a <go> tag to pass the name to the Perl script. The script, in turn, will search the database for matching entries and will create a WML card that contains the matching entries, which it will display as shown in Figure 10-2.

| **Figure 10-2** | Retrieving information from a server database |

The following statements implement the SearchList.wml application:

```
<?xml version="1.0"?>
<!DOCTYPE wml PUBLIC "-//WAPFORUM//DTD WML 1.1//EN"
                    "http://www.wapforum.org/DTD/wml_1.1.xml">

<wml>

  <head>
    <meta http-equiv="Cache-Control" content="max-age=0"
       forua="true"/>
  </head>

  <card id="SearchList">
    <onevent type="onenterforward">
      <refresh>
        <setvar name="FirstName" value="" />
        <setvar name="LastName" value="" />
      </refresh>
    </onevent>

    <do type="accept">
      <go href="#Confirm" />
    </do>

    <p align="center">
      Search List<br/>
    </p>

    <p align="left">
      Enter name to search for.<br/><br/>
      First Name:
      <input name="FirstName" type="text" format="15M" />
    </p>

    <p align="left">
      Last Name:
      <input name="LastName" type="text" format="15M" />
    </p>
  </card>
```

10

```
<card id="Confirm">
  <do type="accept" label="Yes">
    <go method="post"
      href="../AddressList/SearchList.pl">
      <postfield name="FirstName" value="$FirstName"/>
      <postfield name="LastName" value="$LastName"/>
      <postfield name="StartDisplay" value="1"/>
    </go>
  </do>

  <do type="option" label="No">
    <go href="#SearchList" />
  </do>

  <p>
    Search for:<br/>
    $FirstName<br/>
    $LastName
  </p>

</card>

</wml>
```

As you can see, the application passes the first and last name to the Perl script using **<postfield>** tags. In addition, the application passes the value 1 for the field StartDisplay, which directs the Perl script to start its display with the first matching name it encounters.

1-Minute Drill

● How does a WML application call a Perl script?

● What is the purpose of the **<postfield>** tag?

● A WML script can call a Perl script by specifying the script's URL within a <go> tag's href attribute.
● The WML <postfield> tag lets an application pass information to a Perl script or other server-based application. Within the <postfield> tag, you specify the name of a variable you are passing to the application, and the variable's value.

Using a Perl Script to Retrieve Information from a Database

In the previous section, you examined the SearchList.wml application, which prompts the user to enter the first and last name of the individual they want to look up. After the user confirms his or her input, the WML application uses a **\<go>** tag to call the Perl script SearchList.pl. The Perl script, in turn, opens the database file AddressList.dat, which resides on the server, and then sequentially searches the file's contents looking for entries that match the first and last name the user has specified. After it finishes searching the file, the script creates a WML card deck, on the fly, that contains matching entries.

The following statements implement SearchList.pl:

```perl
#!/usr/bin/perl

require 'DeckUtils.pl';

#Get the CGI variables
%cgiVars = &AppUtils::ParseCGIVars();
$SearchFirstName = $cgiVars{"FirstName"};
$SearchLastName = $cgiVars{"LastName"};
$StartDisplay = $cgiVars{"StartDisplay"};


#Open the address list file
open(FILE, "../AddressList/AddressList.dat");

#Read the data
@InputLines=<FILE>;
close(FILE);

#Ignore the header line
$Dummy = shift(@InputLines);

#Get the individual data items
$Count=0;
while (defined($NewLine = shift(@InputLines)))
  {
    (@FirstName[$Count], @LastName[$Count], @Phone[$Count],
 @Address[$Count], @City[$Count], @State[$Count],
 @Zip[$Count]) = split(/,/, $NewLine);
    $Count++;
```

10

```
    }

#Build an array with the matching results
$Index = 0;
$CountResult = 0;
while ($Index < $Count)
  {
    if ($SearchFirstName eq "")
      {
        if (($SearchLastName eq "") ||
            ($SearchLastName eq @LastName[$Index]))
          {
            @MatchFirstName[$CountResult] = @FirstName[$Index];
            @MatchLastName[$CountResult] = @LastName[$Index];
            @MatchPhone[$CountResult] = @Phone[$Index];
            $CountResult++;
          }
      }
    elsif ($SearchFirstName eq @FirstName[$Index])
      {
        if (($SearchLastName eq "") ||
            ($SearchLastName eq @LastName[$Index]))
          {
            @MatchFirstName[$CountResult] = @FirstName[$Index];
            @MatchLastName[$CountResult] = @LastName[$Index];
            @MatchPhone[$CountResult] = @Phone[$Index];
            $CountResult++;
          }
      }
    $Index++;
  }

#Build a deck to display the results
$Deck =
"Content-type: text/vnd.wap.wml

<?xml version=\"1.0\"?>
<!DOCTYPE wml PUBLIC \"-//WAPFORUM//DTD WML 1.1//EN\"
                  \"http://www.wapforum.org/DTD/wml_1.1.xml\">

<wml>

    <head>
        <meta http-equiv=\"Cache-Control\" content=\"max-age=0\"
          forua=\"true\"/>
```

```
    </head>

    <card>
      <do type=\"accept\" label=\"Done\">
        <go href=\"../AddressList/SearchList.wml\" />
      </do>

        <p align=\"center\">
           Search List<br/>
        </p>

        <p align=\"left\" mode=\"nowrap\">";
#       Get the names that go on this card
        $Index = $StartDisplay - 1;
        $CardFull = $Index + 10;
        if ($CardFull > $CountResult)
          {
            $CardFull = $CountResult;
          }
        while ($Index < $CardFull)
          {
            $Deck = $Deck . @MatchFirstName[$Index] . " " .
@MatchLastName[$Index] . " " . @MatchPhone[$Index] . "<br/>";
            $Index++;
          }

#       Build a More button if there are more names to display
        if ($CountResult > $StartDisplay + 9)
          {
            $StartDisplay = $StartDisplay + 10;
            $Deck = $Deck . "
            <do type=\"option\" label=\"More\">
              <go method=\"post\"
                href=\"SearchList.pl\">
                <postfield name=\"FirstName\"
                   value=\"$FirstName\"/>
                <postfield name=\"LastName\"
                   value=\"$LastName\"/>
                <postfield name=\"StartDisplay\"
                   value=\"$StartDisplay\"/>
                </go>
            </do>";
          }

#       Add the rest of the deck
```

10

```
        $Deck = $Deck . "

        </p>

    </card>

</wml>";

print $Deck;
```

As the Perl script examines the database, it places records (the first name, last name, and phone number) that match the first and last name specified into three arrays named MatchFirstName, MatchLastName, and MatchPhone. After the script finishes searching the file, it creates a WML deck that will display the results by assigning the deck's contents to a character string variable named $Deck. To place the matching entries within a card, the script uses a `while` loop to index the matching array elements. As the script loops through the array, it keeps track of the number of matching entries it has displayed. After the script has added ten entries to the card, the script stops its processing and places a "More" label on the card that the user can select to view additional entries, as shown in Figure 10-3.

Should the user select the More option, the WML application will again call the SearchList.pl Perl script, passing to the script, the first and last name to match. However, in this case, the card will also pass the index value at which the application should begin its display. Earlier, you saw that the SearchList.wml application passes the value 1 to the script, which directs the script to start its display with the first matching name it encounters. If, for example, 25 names

Figure 10-3   Prompting the user to display more matching names

match, the script would first display the first ten matching names, along with an option letting the user request more. Should the user select the More option, the WML application will pass the value 11 to the script, which causes the script to display the next ten matching names. Should the user again select the More option, the WML application will pass the script the value 21, which causes the script to display the final five names.

Interacting with an Active Server Page

In the previous application, the WML code interacted with a Perl script that resides on a remote server. In addition to interacting with Perl to store or retrieve information, WML applications can interact with Active Server Pages (ASP). The following ASP application, ImageDisplay.asp, searches a directory on the server and displays a list of WBMP images, as shown in Figure 10-4. If you select one

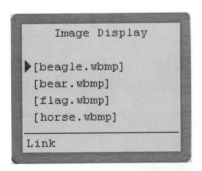

Figure 10-4 Using an ASP page to display images that reside on a server

10

of the images, the application will display the corresponding WBMP file. You can test drive the application at www.WirelessLookup.com/Demo/ImageDisplay/ ImageDisplay.asp.

The following code implements ImageDisplay.asp:

```
<%option explicit%>
<%Dim FSYS, ThisFolder, AllFiles, file

on error resume next

' Output the WML page
Response.ContentType ="text/vnd.wap.wml;"

%>

<!DOCTYPE wml PUBLIC "-//WAPFORUM//DTD WML 1.1//EN"
                     "http://www.wapforum.org/DTD/wml_1.1.xml">

<wml>

  <head>
    <meta http-equiv="Cache-Control" content="max-age=0"
       forua="true"/>
  </head>

  <card id="Start">

    <p align="center">
      Image Display<br/>
    </p>

    <p align="left" mode="nowrap">
<%
'Find all of the WBMP files in the directory
Set FSYS = Server.CreateObject("Scripting.FileSystemObject")
Set ThisFolder = FSYS.GetFolder("e: \ImageDisplay")
Set AllFiles = ThisFolder.Files

'Build the links
For Each file in AllFiles

  If file.Type = "WBMP File" Then
%>
```

```
        <a href="#<%=file.Name%>"><%=file.Name%></a>

<%
End If
Next
%>

    </p>
  </card>


<%
'Build the individual display cards
For Each file in AllFiles
  If file.Type = "WBMP File" Then
%>
    <card id="<%=file.Name%>">

      <do type="accept" label="Back">
        <go href="#Start" />
      </do>

      <p>
        <img src="<%=file.Name%>" alt="<%=file.Name%>" />
      </p>
    </card>
<%
End If
Next
%>

</wml>
```

Normally, ASP creates HTML tags that a browser, such as Microsoft's Internet Explorer, displays. In this case, ASP creates WML cards, which it returns to the microbrowser. ASP first creates a card named Start, within which it uses **<a>** tags to create links to each of the WBMP files that reside in the directory. Next, ASP builds individual cards (whose names correspond to the image's filename) for each image, to which the application will link when the user selects an image. Within an ASP page, the **<%** and **%>** tags group programming statements that the server executes each time a user views the page. The programming statements themselves will not appear on the page, but the output the statements they generate will appear.

Hint

Before you can run ASP from your system, you must be running a server that supports ASP, such as Microsoft's Internet Information Server (IIS).

1-Minute Drill

● How does a WML application call an ASP page?

● Within an ASP page, what is the purpose of the <% and %> tags?

Building a To Do List

In the previous application, you used an ASP page to retrieve information from a server. The following ASP page, ToDo.asp, lets you add events to your To Do list and view the events for a specific date. When the application starts, it will display a menu with both add and view options. If you choose to add an item, the application will prompt you to enter the event's date and time, as well as a description of the event. If you choose to view the events for a day, the application will prompt you to enter the date to be displayed. As shown in Figure 10-5, the application will then display the matching day's events.

```
        To Do List
        05/02/2001


08:30 - Flight home



Back
```

Figure 10-5   Using an ASP page to add and retrieve To Do list events

---

● To call an ASP page, a WML application simply places the URL of the ASP page within the href attribute of a <go> tag.

● Within an ASP page, the <% and %> tags group the programming statements that the server executes each time a user views the page.

The ToDo.wml application begins with the ToDo card, which displays links the user can select to add or view events. If the user chooses to add an event, the code will link to the Add card which uses <input> tags to prompt the user for event information. After the user confirms the information, the code uses a <go> tag to call the Add.asp ASP page, which stores the information within the ToDo.txt database.

If the user chooses to view information, the code links to the View card, which prompts the user for the date he or she wishes to view. The code then uses a <go> tag to branch to the View.asp ASP page, which searches the ToDo.txt file for events matching the date specified. The following code implements the ToDo.asp ASP page:

```
<?xml version="1.0"?>
<!DOCTYPE wml PUBLIC "-//WAPFORUM//DTD WML 1.1//EN"
                    "http://www.wapforum.org/DTD/wml_1.1.xml">

<wml>

<head>
  <meta http-equiv="Cache-Control" content="max-age=0"
     forua="true"/>
</head>

<card id="ToDo">
  <onevent type="onenterforward">
    <refresh>
        <setvar name="ToDoDate" value="" />
        <setvar name="ToDoTime" value="" />
        <setvar name="ToDoEvent" value="" />
    </refresh>
  </onevent>

  <p align="center">
    To Do List<br/>
  </p>

  <p align="left">
    <a href="#Add">Add an entry</a>
    <a href="#View">View</a>
  </p>

</card>
```

10

```
<card id="View">
  <do type="accept" label="View">
    <go href=
"http://www.SomeSite.com/ToDoList/View.asp?Date=$(ToDoDate)" />
  </do>

  <p>
    Enter date to view in the format<br/>
    mm/dd/yyyy:

    <input name="ToDoDate" />
  </p>

</card>

<card id="Add">
  <do type="accept" label="Add">
    <go href="#confirm" />
  </do>

  <p>
    Enter date:
    <input name="ToDoDate" format="NN\/NN\/NNNN" />
    Enter time:
    <input name="ToDoTime" format="NN\:NN" />
    Enter event:
    <input name="ToDoEvent" format="25m" />
  </p>

</card>

<card id="confirm">
  <do type="accept" label="Yes">
    <go href=
"http://www.SomeSite.com/ ToDoList/Add.asp?
Date=$(ToDoDate)&amp;Time=$(ToDoTime)&amp;Event=$(ToDoEvent)" />
  </do>

  <do type="option" label="No">
    <go href="#ToDo" />
  </do>

  <p>
    Enter the following:<br/>
```

```
   $ToDoDate<br/>
   $ToDoTime<br/>
   $ToDoEvent
</p>

</card>

</wml>
```

Adding an Event to the To Do List

As briefly discussed, when the user chooses to add an event, the application prompts the user for the event's date, time, and description, and then passes the information to the Add.asp ASP page. Within the Add.asp page, the code opens the ToDo.txt file and appends the event information. The Add.asp ASP page then builds a WML card, which it returns to the microbrowser, which informs the user that it has successfully added the event:

```
<%option explicit%>
<%Dim strToDoDate, strToDoTime, strToDoEvent
  DIM FSYS, TheFile, NewLine

on error resume next

'Get the input arguments
strToDoDate = Request.QueryString("Date")
strToDoTime = Request.QueryString("Time")
strToDoEvent = Request.QueryString("Event")

'Open the data file and add the new line
Set FSYS = Server.CreateObject("Scripting.FileSystemObject")
Set TheFile = FSYS.OpenTextFile("e:\ ToDoList\ToDo.txt", 8)
NewLine = strToDoDate & ";" & strToDoTime & ";" & strToDoEvent
TheFile.WriteLine NewLine

Set FSYS=Nothing

' Output the WML success page
Response.ContentType ="text/vnd.wap.wml;"

%>

<!DOCTYPE wml PUBLIC "-//WAPFORUM//DTD WML 1.1//EN"
```

10

```
                            "http://www.wapforum.org/DTD/wml_1.1.xml">

<wml>

<head>
  <meta http-equiv="Cache-Control" content="max-age=0"
    forua="true"/>
</head>

<card id="Start">
  <do type="accept">
    <go href="http://www.SomeSite.com/ ToDoList/ToDo.wml" />
  </do>

  <p align="center">
            To Do List
  </p>
  <p align="left">
    Event added:<br/>
    <%=strToDoDate%><br/>
    <%=strToDoTime%><br/>
    <%=strToDoEvent%>
  </p>
</card>

</wml>
```

Ask the Expert

Question: The code the ASP page uses to search for events seems well suited for a true database, such as a SQL database. How can a WML application interface with a SQL database?

Answer: The WML application will quite likely interface with either a Perl script or an ASP page, which, in turn, interacts with the database. In the case of the View.asp ASP page, which you will examine next, the ASP page could use VBScript to open the database and then issue a SQL query to retrieve events for a specific date. The code could then build a WML card, within which it would insert the matching entries.

Viewing a To Do List Entry

When the user chooses to view the To Do list events for a specific date, the View card prompts the user for the date that he or she wishes to view and then passes that date to the View.asp ASP page. Within the ASP page, the code opens the ToDo.txt file and sequentially searches the file's contents for events that match the date specified. The file stores the event information in the form `date;time;event`, as shown here:

```
04/29/2001;08:30;Board Breakfast
04/29/2001;12:30;Conference (Jim)
04/30/2001;09:30;Flight to NY
05/01/2001;04:30;Interview (Times)
05/02/2001;08:30;Flight home
```

To parse the events, the ASP page uses the split function. If an event's date matches the user-specified date, the ASP page places the event information on the WML card it returns to the microbrowser:

```
<%option explicit%>
<%Dim strSearchDate, FSYS, TheFile, InputLine, ToDoArray

on error resume next

strSearchDate = Request.QueryString("Date")

' Output the WML page
Response.ContentType ="text/vnd.wap.wml;"
%>

<!DOCTYPE wml PUBLIC "-//WAPFORUM//DTD WML 1.1//EN"
                     "http://www.wapforum.org/DTD/wml_1.1.xml">

<wml>

<head>
  <meta http-equiv="Cache-Control" content="max-age=0"
     forua="true"/>
</head>

<card id="Start">
  <do type="accept" label="Back">
    <go href="http://www.SomeSite.com/ ToDoList/ToDo.wml" />
```

10

```
</do>

  <p align="center">
    To Do List
  </p>

  <p align="center">
  <%=strSearchDate%><br/>
  </p>

  <p align="left" mode="nowrap">
    <%
    Set FSYS = Server.CreateObject("Scripting.FileSystemObject")
    Set TheFile = FSYS.OpenTextFile("e:\ ToDoList\ToDo.txt")
    While Not TheFile.AtEndOfStream
      InputLine = TheFile.Readline
      ToDoArray = Split(InputLine, ";")
      If ToDoArray(0) = strSearchDate Then
    %>
        <%=ToDoArray(1)%> - <%=ToDoArray(2)%><br/>
      <%
      End If
    Wend

    Set FSYS=Nothing
    %>
  </p>
</card>

</wml>
```

MoreToDo.wml

Project 10-1: Displaying Multiple Events One Page at a Time

In the previous section, you examined the ToDo.wml application that lets you display the events for a specific day. Depending on the number of events you enter for a day, the To Do list may become quite large. In this project, you will modify the application so that it displays only ten events at a time. If the list contains more than ten events for the specified day, the application will display a "More" prompt, which the user can select to display the next set of events.

The application works in much the same way as the address book application presented earlier in this module.

Step-By-Step

1. To start, copy the ToDo.wml file as MoreToDo.wml.

2. Using a text editor, edit the MoreToDo.wml file and change the <go> tag that links to the View.asp file to include the parameter Start=1, which directs the ASP page to begin its display with the first event in the list:

```
<do type="accept" label="View">
  <go href="http://www.SomeSite.com/
ToDoList/View.asp?Date=$(ToDoDate)&amp;Start=1" />
</do>
```

3. Using a text editor, edit the View.asp ASP page to include code that counts the number of events the application has displayed. If the application has displayed ten events, the application will add a More prompt to the current card. If the user selects the More option, the application will link to the View.asp ASP page, passing the Start parameter with the number of the next event the application should display. Your new View.asp file should appear as follows:

```
<%option explicit%>
<%Dim strSearchDate, StartIndex, FSYS, TheFile, InputLine
  DIM ToDoArray, OutputLine(1,50), Index, Count, FullCard

on error resume next

strSearchDate = Request.QueryString("Date")
StartIndex = Request.QueryString("Start")

Set FSYS = Server.CreateObject("Scripting.FileSystemObject")
Set TheFile = FSYS.OpenTextFile("e:\ \ToDoList\ToDo.txt")

'Get the matching items
Index = 0
While Not TheFile.AtEndOfStream
      InputLine = TheFile.Readline
      ToDoArray = Split(InputLine, ";")
      If ToDoArray(0) = strSearchDate Then
            OutputLine(0,Index) = ToDoArray(1)
```

10

```
            OutputLine(1,Index) = ToDoArray(2)
            Index = Index + 1
      End If
Wend
Count = Index

Set FSYS=Nothing

' Build a Deck to display the results
Response.ContentType ="text/vnd.wap.wml;"

%>

<!DOCTYPE wml PUBLIC "-//WAPFORUM//DTD WML 1.1//EN"
                     "http://www.wapforum.org/DTD/wml_1.1.xml">

<wml>

<head>
  <meta http-equiv="Cache-Control" content="max-age=0"
     forua="true"/>
</head>

<card id="Start">

  <do type="accept" label="Back">
    <go href="http://www.SomeSite.com /ToDoList/MoreToDo.wml" />
  </do>

  <p align="center">
    To Do List
  </p>

  <p align="center">
    <%=strSearchDate%><br/>
  </p>
```

```
  <p align="left" mode="nowrap">
<%
    'Get the items that go on this card
    Index = StartIndex - 1
    FullCard = Index + 10
    If FullCard > Count Then
      FullCard = Count
    End If
    While Index < FullCard
%>
    <%=OutputLine(0, Index)%> - <%=OutputLine(1, Index)%><br/>
<%
    Index = Index + 1
    Wend

    'Build a More button if there are more items to display
    If Count > (StartIndex + 9) Then
      StartIndex = StartIndex + 10
%>

    <do type="option" label="More">
      <go href="http://www.SomeSite.com /ToDoList/View.asp?
Date=$(ToDoDate)&amp;Start=<%=StartIndex%>" />
    </do>
<%
    End If
%>
  </p>
</card>

</wml>
```

10

✔ Mastery Check

1. When might a WML application need to interact with a Perl script or ASP page?

_____

_____

2. How does a WML application call a Perl script or ASP page?

_____

_____

3. How does a WML application pass information to a Perl script or ASP page?

_____

_____

4. Provide the WML statements that pass the following values to a Perl script named ShowEm.pl that resides at www.SomeSight.com:

Name	Amanda
Hobbies	Music, Horses
Web Site	www.WirelessLookup.com/Amanda

5. How can a Perl script build a WML card deck on the fly?

_____

_____

6. Create a Perl script named Hello.pl that builds a WML card deck that displays the message "Hello, Wireless World!".

7. Create an ASP page named Hello.asp that builds a WML card that displays the message "Hello, Wireless World!".

Appendix A

Answers to
Mastery Checks

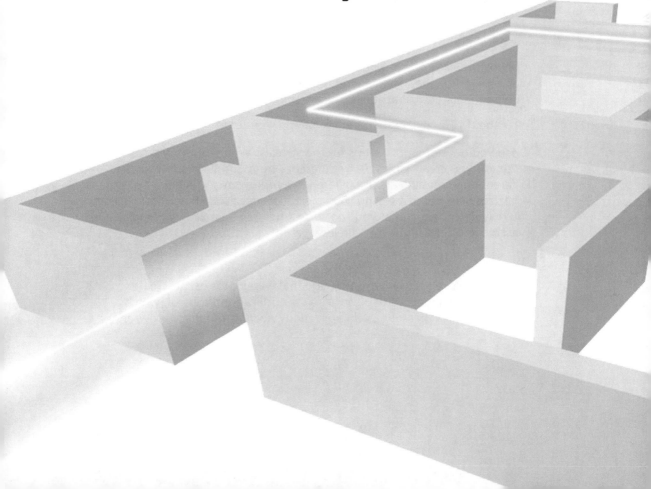

Module 1: Getting Started on the Wireless Web

1. What is a Web-enabled cellular phone?

A Web-enabled phone is a cellular phone containing a built-in microbrowser that you can use to access sites on the Wireless Web. Before you can use a Web-enabled phone, you must direct your cellular provider to enable Wireless Web access for your phone. Most cellular providers do not charge for enabling Wireless Web access. When you connect to the Wireless Web using your phone, your cellular provider will charge you on a per-minute basis, at the same rate you would pay for a standard cellular phone call.

2. How do you specify a site on the Wireless Web?

To specify a site on the Wireless Web, you provide the micro-browser with a URL that corresponds to the site's address, such as http://www.WirelessLookup.com.

3. What is a phone simulator?

A phone simulator is a program that runs on your PC and behaves like a Web-enabled phone. Using a phone simulator, you can surf the Wireless Web from your PC, using your keyboard and mouse.

4. Why should you use more than one phone simulator?

When you develop applications for the Wireless Web, you should run the programs you create on as many different phone simulators as you can. Different phone simulators use different microbrowsers, which may execute WML tags differently. By testing your applications on a wide range of simulators, you may detect errors that you can correct before you make your application available to others across the Wireless Web.

5. How does WML differ from WAP?

WML is the Wireless Markup Language that developers use to create Wireless applications. WAP is the Wireless Application Protocol, which defines the rules that low-level applications, such as the microbrowser, must follow to communicate across the Wireless Web. WML is the Wireless Web's equivalent to HTML, which developers use to create sites on the World Wide Web. WAP is the Wireless Web's equivalent to TCP/IP, the protocol that drives the Internet.

6. What is m-commerce?

M-commerce is short for mobile commerce, the Wireless Web's equivalent to e-commerce on the World Wide Web. You can find a range of sites on the Wireless Web that support m-commerce operations to sell books, flowers, movie tickets, and even airline tickets.

7. What is a fast and easy way to create a Wireless site?

You can find several sites on the World Wide Web, such as WirelessLookup.com, which provide software you can use to create a Wireless Web site without your needing to create a WML application.

8. How do you host a Wireless site?

To host a Wireless Web site, you place the site's WML files on a server (a PC) that is running Web-server software and is connected to the World Wide Web.

Module 2: Creating Your First WML Application

1. What do the letters WML stand for?

WML stands for Wireless Markup Language. Using WML, developers can create sites for use on the Wireless Web.

2. How does WML differ from XML?

XML stands for the Extensible Markup Language. On the traditional World Wide Web, developers use XML to describe data attributes. Using XML, for example, you might describe an e-commerce transaction by specifying the number of items, each item's price, shipping and billing information, and so on. WML is a subset of XML. To create a Wireless

A

application, programmers use WML to specify attributes for one or more cards. Each card, in turn, corresponds to a page within the Wireless application.

3. Create a WML application, named KeyNumbers.wml, that displays the following information:

Name: Amanda
Cell: 281-555-1212
Work: 800-555-1212
Fax: 888-555-1212
E-mail: Amanda@Wireless.com

The following statements implement the KeyNumbers.wml application:

```
<?xml version="1.0"?>

<!DOCTYPE wml PUBLIC "-//WAPFORUM//DTD WML 1.2//EN"
    "http://www.wapforum.org/DTD/wml_1.1.xml">

<wml>

<card id="KeyNumbers">
 <p>
   Name: Amanda<br/>
   Cell: 281-555-1212<br/>
   Work: 800-555-1212<br/>
   Fax: 888-555-1212<br/>
   E-mail: Amanda@Wireless.com
 </p>
</card>

</wml>
```

4. How would you change the application you created in question 3 so that the application will automatically dial the cell and work phone numbers?

To change the KeyNumbers.wml application so that it automatically dials the cell and work phone numbers, you must use the Wireless Telephony Application Interface (WTAI) make call (mc) function, as shown here:

```
<p>
   Name: Amanda<br/>
   <a href="wtai://wp/mc;2815551212" title="Call">
     Cell: 281-555-1212</a>
```

```
    <a href="wtai://wp/mc;18005551212" title="Call">
       Work: 800-555-1212</a>
    Fax: 888-555-1212<br/>
    E-mail: Amanda@Wireless.com
  </p>
```

5. List two ways you can use the phone simulator's console window.

Using the phone simulator's console window, you can view the location and description of syntax errors within your WML code. You can also monitor the WML compilation process to determine the size of your application in bytes. As your applications become more complex, you can use the console window to display the value of variables the application uses to store information as it executes.

6. How can you perform arithmetic operations within WML?

Using WML alone, you cannot perform arithmetic operations. In Module 7, you will learn how to use WMLScript to perform arithmetic operations for a WML application.

7. Create a WML application named BoldItalic.wml that displays the following output:

Amanda Smith
211 Main Street
Houston, Texas 77469

The following statements implement the BoldItalic.wml application:

```
<?xml version="1.0"?>

<!DOCTYPE wml PUBLIC "-//WAPFORUM//DTD WML 1.2//EN"
    "http://www.wapforum.org/DTD/wml_1.1.xml">

<wml>

<card id="BoldItalic">
  <p>
    <b>Amanda Smith</b><br/>
    <i>211 Main Stret</i><br/>
    <i>Houston, Texas 77469</i>
  </p>
</card>

</wml>
```

A

8. What is unique about the WML line-break tag?

The WML line-break tag is unique in that it requires only a single tag <br/>. Most WML tags require an opening and closing tag, such as <b> and </b>, which enable and disable bolding, respectively. Because it is a single-tag element, you must include the ending slash within the tag, meaning the tag is <br/>, not <br>.

9. How do you place an application on the Wireless Web?

To place an application on the Wireless Web, you place the site's WML files on a server (a PC) that is connected to the World Wide Web and is running Web-server software.

Module 3: Formatting Output

1. How would you use WML to center the company's name above their contact information:

Osborne/McGraw-Hill
2600 Tenth Street
Berkeley, CA 94710
www.Osborne.com

The following paragraph <p> tag uses the `align="center"` attribute to center the company information:

```
<p align="center">
Osborne/McGraw-Hill<br/>
2600 Tenth Street<br/>
Berkeley, CA 94710<br/>
www.Osborne.com<br/>
</p>
```

2. If text does not fit on the current line of output, and you have used the `mode=nowrap` attribute, how will the microbrowser display the text?

If text does not fit on the current line of output, and you have used the mode=nowrap attribute, most microbrowsers will flash parts of the text that exceed the margin into view for a few moments. Some microbrowsers may provide a horizontal scroll bar you can use to slide the text into view.

3. Use WML to display the following text with the attributes shown:

Osborne/McGraw-Hill
2600 Tenth Street
Berkeley, CA 94710
www.Osborne.com

The following WML statements will display the text with the attributes shown:

```
<p>
   <b>Osborne/McGraw-Hill</b><br/>
   2600 Tenth Street<br/>
   Berkeley, CA 94710<br/>
   <i>www.Osborne.com</i><br/>
</p>
```

4. How many colors do WBMP images support?

WBMP images are black and white images.

5. What happens when a phone does not support the local-source image you specify within an **<img>** tag?

When a phone does not support a specified localsrc image, the microbrowser will first try to display the WBMP image specified in the src attribute. If the microbrowser cannot display the WBMP image, it will then display the text specified in the alt attribute.

6. Give two reasons why large WBMP images are a problem.

Large WBMP images pose two problems. First, large images can take considerable time to download across slow cellular connections. Second, a large WBMP image may exceed a microbrowser's maximum card size, which is normally 1KB to 2KB.

7. Create a WML table to display the following output:

Name	Office	Phone
Smith	3A	444-1221
Jones	2B	555-1111
Adams	3D	666-1112
Burns	2C	554-3331

A

The following WML statements implement the table to display the output:

```
<table columns="3">
  <tr><td>Name</td><td>Office</td><td>Phone</td></tr>
  <tr><td>Smith</td><td> 3A</td><td>444-1221</td></tr>
  <tr><td>Jones</td><td> 2B</td><td>555-1111</td></tr>
  <tr><td>Adams</td><td> 3D</td><td>666-1112</td></tr>
  <tr><td>Burns</td><td> 2C</td><td>554-3331</td></tr>
</table>
```

8. Modify the WML you used to create the table in question 7 to present the table headings in bold, as shown here:

Name	Office	Phone
Smith	3A	444-1221
Jones	2B	555-1111
Adams	3D	666-1112
Burns	2C	554-3331

The following WML statements bold the table as shown:

```
<table columns="3">
  <tr><td><b>Name</b></td><td><b>Office</b></td>
      <td><b>Phone</b></td></tr>
  <tr><td>Smith</td><td> 3A</td><td>444-1221</td></tr>
  <tr><td>Jones</td><td> 2B</td><td>555-1111</td></tr>
  <tr><td>Adams</td><td> 3D</td><td>666-1112</td></tr>
  <tr><td>Burns</td><td> 2C</td><td>554-3331</td></tr>
</table>
```

9. How would you use WML to display the text "Our Price's"?

With many browsers, to display the text "Our Price's", you simply place the text within your WML deck. However, you should ideally use the text "Our Price's".

10. Write a WML statement to display the output: 4 * 5 < 21.

The following WML statement displays 4 * 5 < 21:

```
<p>
  4 * 5 &lt; 21
</p>
```

Module 4: Working with Multiple Cards and Variables

1. When a WML deck contains two or more cards, which card does the microbrowser load first?

When a WML deck contains multiple cards, the microbrowser loads and executes the card that appears first in the deck (the card nearest the top of the file).

2. What is the purpose of the following `<do>` tag?

```
<do type="accept" label="Go">
  <go href="#PhoneList" />
</do>
```

The `<do>` tag, in this case, specifies the operation the microbrowser will perform when the user presses the phone's accept button. In this case, the microbrowser will load and execute the card named PhoneList, which resides in the current deck. Within the `<do>` tag, the label attribute specifies the text that the microbrowser will display above the accept button.

3. What is the purpose of the `<prev />` tag?

The `<prev/>` tag directs the microbrowser to reload and execute the previous card. In other words, the `<prev/>` tag lets the user back up to the previous card.

4. Create a WML application named GoThere.wml that uses the `<a>` tag to create links to the following sites:

http://www.WirelessLookup.com
http://mobile.sports.com
http://wap.goshop.com

The following statements implement the WML application GoThere.wml:

```
<?xml version="1.0"?>

<!DOCTYPE wml PUBLIC "-//WAPFORUM//DTD WML 1.2//EN"
```

A

```
         "http://www.wapforum.org/DTD/wml_1.1.xml">

  <wml>

  <card id="GoThere">
   <p>
     <a
  href="http://www.WirelessLookup.com">WirelessLookup.com</a>
     <a href="http://mobile.sports.com">mobile.sports.com</a>
     <a href="http://wap.goshop.com">wap.goshop.com</a>
   </p>
  </card>

  </wml>
```

5. What is a variable?

A variable provides a named memory location within which the microbrowser can store information as it executes a WML application. Using a variable, for example, you might store a user's name, phone number, e-mail address, and so on.

6. What two WML tags assign values to variables?

The WML <setvar> and <input> tags assign values to variables.

7. How do you display a WML variable's value?

To display a WML variable's value, you simply precede the variable's name with a dollar sign. For example, the following statement will display the contents of the variable Name:

```
<p>
  $Name
</p>
```

8. Create a WML application that assigns the current day, month, and year to the variables Day, Month, and Year, and then uses the ShowDate card to display the current date.

The following application assigns the current day, month, and year to variables and then uses the ShowDate card to display the variable's contents:

```
<?xml version="1.0"?>

<!DOCTYPE wml PUBLIC "-//WAPFORUM//DTD WML 1.2//EN"
    "http://www.wapforum.org/DTD/wml_1.1.xml">

<wml>

<card id="DateVar">
 <p>
   Assume today is 12-31-01
 </p>

 <do type="accept" label="Go">
   <go href="#ShowDate">
      <setvar name="Month" value="December"/>
      <setvar name="Day" value="31"/>
      <setvar name="Year" value="2001"/>
   </go>
 </do>
</card>

<card id="ShowDate">
 <p>
   Date: $Month $Day, $Year
 </p>
</card>

</wml>
```

9. Why should you place comments in your code?

Within a WML application, you should place comments that explain the processing your code performs. That way, should you or another programmer later need to make changes to the application, you (or the other programmer) can read the comments to understand the code's processing.

A

Module 5: Performing User Input Operations

1. How do the following `<input>` tag format specifiers differ: 5N, NNNNN, *N?

The format specifier 5N directs the microbrowser to accept up to five numeric digits. The format specifier NNNNN directs the microbrowser to accept exactly five numeric digits. The format specifier *N directs the microbrowser to accept any number of numeric digits.

2. What is the purpose of the `<input>` tag's value attribute?

The `<input>` tag's value attribute specifies a default value for the input operation.

3. Use an `<input>` tag's format specifier to prompt the user to enter a currency amount in the form $NN.NN.

```
<input name="Amount"  form="/$NN/.NN"  />
```

4. What is the purpose of noesc in `$(Variable:noesc)`?

The purpose of the noesc in `$(Variable:noesc)` is to direct the microbrowser not to escape the contents of the variable. If, for example, you are using `$(Variable:noesc)` within the href attribute of a <go> tag, the microbrowser may try to replace characters not suited for a URL. The noesc setting directs the microbrowser not to change the variable's contents.

5. How do the `<input>` tag's size and maxlength attributes differ?

The `<input>` tag's size attribute tells the microbrowser the width of an input field. Most microbrowsers ignore the size attribute. The `<input>` tag's maxlength attribute specifies the maximum number of characters the user can input.

6. Use a <select> element to create the following menu:

```
Wireless Sites

Nokia
Ericsson
Openwave
WAPForum
```

The following `<select>` element creates the menu:

```
<p>
  Wireless Sites<br/>

  <select name="Site">
     <option value="Nokia">Nokia</option>
     <option value="Ericsson">Ericsson</option>
     <option value="Openwave">Openwave</option>
     <option value="WAPForum">WAPForum</option>
  </select>
</p>
```

7. Specify the `<onevent>` element that is functionally equivalent to the following `<card>` tag onenterforward attribute:

```
<card id="Test" onenterforward="#ShowDateTime">
```

The following <onevent> tag is equivalent:

```
<onevent  type="onenterforward">
  <go href="#ShowDateTime"/>
</onevent>
```

8. Create a WML application that uses a `<timer>` element to toggle the display between three different cards, every 15 seconds.

The following statements implement the ToggleCard15.wml application:

```
<?xml version="1.0"?>

<!DOCTYPE wml PUBLIC "-//WAPFORUM//DTD WML 1.2//EN"
    "http://www.wapforum.org/DTD/wml_1.1.xml">
```

A

```wml
<wml>

<card id="One" ontimer="#Two">
  <timer value="150" />

  <p>
     111111<br/>
     111111<br/>
     111111<br/>
     111111<br/>
  </p>

  <do type="accept" label="Done">
    <go href="#Done" />
  </do>
</card>

<card id="Two" ontimer="#Three">
  <timer value="150" />

  <p>
     222222<br/>
     222222<br/>
     222222<br/>
     222222<br/>
  </p>

  <do type="accept" label="Done">
    <go href="#Done" />
  </do>
</card>

<card id="Three" ontimer="#One">
  <timer value="150" />

  <p>
     333333<br/>
     333333<br/>
     333333<br/>
     333333<br/>
  </p>
```

```
    <do type="accept" label="Done">
      <go href="#Done" />
    </do>
  </card>

  <card id="Done">
    <p>
      Done
    </p>
  </card>

</wml>
```

9. Use a **<template>** tag to specify generic code that directs each card in a deck to return to the application's first page after 30 seconds of inactivity. Assume that the first card is named StartDeck.

The following application, TemplateDemo.wml, uses a **<template>** tag to create the generic code:

```
<?xml version="1.0"?>

<!DOCTYPE wml PUBLIC "-//WAPFORUM//DTD WML 1.2//EN"
    "http://www.wapforum.org/DTD/wml_1.1.xml">

<wml>

<template>
  <onevent type="ontimer">
    <go href="#Start" />
  </onevent>
</template>

<card id="Start">
  <p>
      111111<br/>
      111111<br/>
      111111<br/>
      111111<br/>
  </p>
```

A

```
        <do type="accept" label="Next">
          <go href="#Two" />
        </do>
    </card>

    <card id="Two">
      <timer value="300" />

      <p>
         222222<br/>
         222222<br/>
         222222<br/>
         222222<br/>
      </p>

      <do type="accept" label="Next">
        <go href="#Three" />
      </do>
    </card>

    <card id="Three">
      <timer value="300" />

      <p>
         333333<br/>
         333333<br/>
         333333<br/>
         333333<br/>
      </p>

      <do type="accept" label="Back">
        <go href="#Two" />
      </do>
    </card>

    </wml>
```

10. What is the purpose of the WML `<meta>` tag?

The `<meta>` tag lets you specify information about the WML deck. Normally, programmers use the `<meta>` tag to control how the microbrowser caches the application's cards.

Module 6: Building Real-World WML Applications

1. To align text on a page, there may be times when you will use the ` ` special character. Why can't you simply use a space character to align the text?

Most microbrowsers will ignore multiple successive whitespace characters (such as several spaces or tabs). To align text using spaces, you must use the special non-breaking space character ` `.

2. How would you modify the Locator.wml application to display information about the following restaurant franchise locations?

> Super Burger
> Chicago
> > 1133 Michigan Avenue, 800-555-1212
> > 4441 Delaware, 888-555-1212
> New York
> > 13 Broadway, 212-555-1212
> > 4544 Park Avenue, 888-555-1212
> > 33 Lincoln, 800-555-1212
> Houston
> > 121 Rodeo Way, 713-555-1212

The following statements implement the WML application Locator.wml:

```
<?xml version="1.0"?>

<!DOCTYPE wml PUBLIC "-//WAPFORUM//DTD WML 1.2//EN"
    "http://www.wapforum.org/DTD/wml_1.1.xml">

<wml>

<card id="Locator">
  <p align="center">Welcome</p>
  <p align="center">Super Burger</p>
```

```
    <p>
      <br/>
      <a href="#Chicago">Chicago</a>
      <a href="#NewYork">New York</a>
      <a href="#Houston">Houston</a>
    </p>
  </card>

  <card id="Chicago">
    <p>
      1133 Michigan Avenue, 800-555-1212<br/><br/>
      4441 Delaware, 888-555-1212<br/>

      <do type="prev" label="Back"><prev/></do>
    </p>
  </card>

  <card id="NewYork">
    <p>
      13 Broadway, 212-555-1212<br/><br/>
      4544 Park Avenue, 888-555-1212<br/><br/>
      33 Lincoln, 800-555-1212<br/>

      <do type="prev" label="Back"><prev/></do>
    </p>
  </card>

  <card id="Houston">
    <p>
      121 Rodeo Way, 713-555-1212<br/>

      <do type="prev" label="Back"><prev/></do>
    </p>
  </card>

</wml>
```

3. When should you consider using the **\<meta\>** tag to disable caching within a microbrowser?

When a multi-card application updates variables, you may want to use the **\<meta\>** tag to direct the microbrowser not to cache the deck's contents. By preventing caching, you can ensure that the microbrowser always displays the most recent card contents, which may reflect changes to a variable's value.

Module 7: Automating WML Applications Using WMLScript

1. How does a WML application call a WMLScript function?

A WML application calls a WMLScript function by referencing the name of the WMLScript file within which the function resides, followed by a pound sign (#) and the function name and parameters within an href entry, like this:

```
<go href="SomeFile.wmls#FunctionName(Parameter1, Parameter2)" />
```

2. How do WMLScript variables differ from variables used in other programming languages?

WMLScript variables are "weakly typed" variables, which means when you declare a WMLScript variable, you do not specify the variable's type (such as integer, floating point, Boolean, or character string).

3. How do you declare a variable within WMLScript?

To declare a variable in WMLScript, you simply place the variable's name after the var keyword:

```
var  VariableName;
```

4. What is the output of the following expression:

```
Result = 3 + 2 * 5 - 3;
```

The result of the expression is 10:

```
Result = 3 + 2 * 5 - 3;
Result = 3 + 10 - 3;
Result = 13 - 3;
Result = 10;
```

5. What is a parameter?

A parameter is a value passed to a function.

A

6. Create a WMLScript function named Cube that returns the cube of the value passed to the function as a parameter.

```
extern function cube(A)
  {
      return(A*A*A);
  }
```

7. What is a pragma?

A pragma is a compiler directive. Programmers often use the use access pragma to restrict who can access a WMLScript file's contents. Programmers use the use url pragma to specify the name of a WMLScript library file.

8. Create an if statement to test whether the variable Salary contains a value in the range 35,000 to 75,000.

```
if ((salary >= 35000) && (salary < 75000))
```

9. Create a for loop that displays the numbers 0.25, 0.50, 0.75, and 1.0.

```
for (value = 0.25; value <= 1.0; value += 0.25)
    Dialogs.alert(value);
```

10. When should you use a for loop as opposed to a while loop?

WMLScript applications should use a for loop to repeat an operation a specific number of times. WMLScript applications should use a while loop to repeat statements until a specific condition is met, such as the user selecting the Quit option from a menu.

Module 8: Using the WMLScript Libraries

1. List the six standard WMLScript libraries.

The standard WMLScript libraries are Dialogs, Float, Lang, String, URL, and WMLBrowser.

2. Values an application passes to a function are called:

    a. Manipulators

    b. Delimiters

    c. Parameters

    d. Both a and b

    C. Values an application passes to a function are called parameters.

3. How do the Dialogs library's alert and confirm functions differ?

The Dialogs library's alert function displays a message and waits for the user to press the accept button. The Dialogs library's confirm function displays a message and gives the user a choice of two responses.

4. What is a delimited string?

A delimited string is a string that contains elements separated by a specific character, such as a semicolon, comma, or slash. The following string uses a semicolon to delimit the name, age, and phone number elements: "Jones;33;212-555-1212".

5. How can you extract the second element from the string "First/Second/Third"?

The following statement uses the String library's elementAt function to extract the element "Second":

```
Result = String.elementAt("First/Second/Third", 1, "/");
```

6. How can you replace the word "Special" in the string "Special Discount" with the word "Super"?

The following statement uses the String library's replace function to replace the substring "Special" with "Super":

```
Result = String.replace("Special Discount", "Special", "Super");
```

A

7. How can you determine whether a browser supports floating-point operations?

To determine whether a microbrowser supports floating-point operations, you use the Lang library's float function, as shown here:

```
if (Lang.float())
```

8. When should a WMLScript function use the WMLBrowser library's newContext function?

A function should use the WMLBrowser library's newContext function when the application wants to delete the history stack and all WML variables.

9. How can a WMLScript function determine the WML card that called it?

To determine the card that called it, a WMLScript function can use the WMLBrowser library's getCurrentCard function.

10. Which statements result in the value 25?

a. Result = 5 * 5;

b. Result = Float.sqrt(625);

c. Result = Float.pow(5, 2);

d. a and c

e. a, b, and c

E. All of the above statements (a, b, and c) result in the value 25.

Module 9: Building Real-World WMLScript Applications

1. What is the purpose of the Console library?

The Console library provides functions you can use to send messages to the console window. Programmers often use Console library functions to debug applications by writing the value of variables and other messages to the console as the application executes.

2. What is the purpose of the Console library's print and println functions?

The Console library's print and println functions display information to the console window. The difference between the two functions is that println writes carriage-return and linefeed characters to the console following its output in order to advance the cursor to the start of the next line.

3. If the variable Age contains the value 18, what value does the following expression assign to the variable Result?

```
Result = (Age >=  21) ? "Legal": "Minor";
```

The expression will assign the value "Minor" to the variable Result. The conditional assignment operator evaluates the expression within the parentheses. If the expression is true, it will assign the first value that follows the question mark. If the expression is false, it will assign the value that follows the colon.

Module 10: Advanced Concepts

1. When might a WML application need to interact with a Perl script or ASP page?

When an application must store information or retrieve information from a file that resides on a server, the application may interact with a Perl script or ASP page.

2. How does a WML application call a Perl script or ASP page?

To call a Perl script or active server page, the application specifies the script's or page's URL within the href attribute of a <go> tag.

3. How does a WML application pass information to a Perl script or ASP page?

To pass information to a Perl script or active server page, a WML application uses the <postfield> tag.

A

4. Provide the WML statements that pass the following values to a Perl script named ShowEm.pl that resides at www.SomeSight.com:

Name	Amanda
Hobbies	Music, Horses
Web Site	www.WirelessLookup.com/Amanda

```
<go method="post" href= "http://www.SomeSight.com/ShowEm.pl">
  <postfield name="Name" value="Amanda"/>
  <postfield name="Hobbies" value="Music, Horses"/>
  <postfield name="WebSite"
    value="www.WirelessLookup.com/Amanda"/>
</go>
```

5. How can a Perl script build a WML card deck on the fly?

When a WML application calls a Perl script, any output the script displays is sent back to the microbrowser. To create a WML card deck on the fly, a Perl script simply must output the tags that correspond to the deck using the print statement.

6. Create a Perl script named Hello.pl that builds a WML card deck that displays the message "Hello, Wireless World!".

```
#!/usr/bin/perl

require 'DeckUtils.pl';

#Build a deck to display the message
$Deck =
"Content-type: text/vnd.wap.wml

<?xml version=\"1.0\"?>
<!DOCTYPE wml PUBLIC \"-//WAPFORUM//DTD WML 1.1//EN\"
                     \"http://www.wapforum.org/DTD/wml_1.1.xml\">

<wml>
<card id=\"Message\">
  <p>
```

```
      Hello, Wireless World!
   </p>
</card>

</wml>";

print $Deck;
```

7. Create an ASP page named Hello.asp that builds a WML card that displays the message "Hello, Wireless World!".

```
<%
on error resume next

' Output the WML page
Response.ContentType ="text/vnd.wap.wml;"

%>

<!DOCTYPE wml PUBLIC "-//WAPFORUM//DTD WML 1.1//EN"
                     "http://www.wapforum.org/DTD/wml_1.1.xml">

<wml>
<card id="Hello">
  <p>
     Hello, Wireless World!
  </p>
</card>

</wml>
```

Appendix B

WML Language
Reference

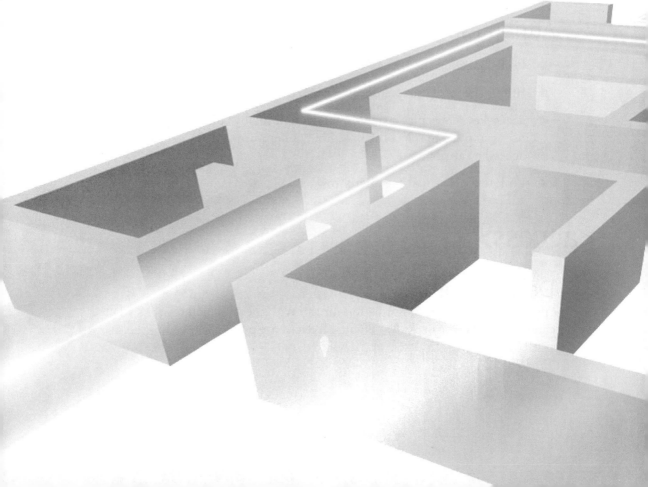

\<a\>

Description:

A short form of the \<anchor\> tag. Directs the microbrowser to create a link using the specified text. When the user selects the link by highlighting the text and pressing the accept button, the microbrowser will load the card or deck that corresponds to the URL specified in the href attribute.

Format:

```
<a href="url" title="label" accesskey="key">
    Link text
</a>
```

Attributes:

- **href**   Specifies the URL of the card or deck that corresponds to the link.

- **title**   The label the microbrowser will display for the accept key.

- **accesskey**   Specifies a single character, normally "0" through "9", the user can press to select the link. Many microbrowsers do not support the accesskey attribute.

- **Link text**   The text the microbrowser will associate with the link.

\<access\>

Description:

Specifies access-control information for the WML deck, which restricts what cards can access the deck. By default, all decks are public.

Format:

```
<head>
    <access domain="domain" path="path" />
</head>
```

Attributes:

- **domain**   Specifies the URL domain of other decks that can access cards in the deck. The default is the domain of the current deck.

- **path**   The URL root of other decks that can access the cards in the deck.

<anchor>

Description:

Creates a link using the text or image that appears between the **<anchor>** and **</anchor>** tags. When the user selects the link text and presses the accept button, the device will execute the specified task.

Format:

```
<anchor title="label" accesskey="key">
    task
    text
</anchor>
```

Attributes:

- **title**   Specifies the label for the link. If you do not specify a title, the microbrowser will display the word "Link". The microbrowser may use

B

the title as a label for the accept key, so you should restrict your title to no more than five characters.

- **accesskey**   Specifies a single character, normally "0" through "9" that the user can press to select the link. Many microbrowsers do not support the accesskey attribute.

- **task**   The task the microbrowser will perform when the user selects the link. The task must be **\<go>**, **\<prev>**, or **\<refresh>**.

- **text**   The text the microbrowser will associate with the link. The microbrowser normally highlights the link in some way, such as by enclosing the link text in brackets.

\<b>

Description:
Displays text using a bold font.

Format:

```
<b>text</b>
```

Attributes:

- **text**   The text the microbrowser will display using a bold font.

\<big>

Description:
Displays text using a large font.

Format:

```
<big>text</big>
```

Attributes:

- **text**   The text the microbrowser will display using a large font.

Description:

Directs the microbrowser to perform a line break, which causes subsequent text to appear on a new line.

Format:

```
<br/>
```

<card>

Description:

Groups related WML statements into a named card. A WML application, which developers refer to as a deck, may consist of multiple cards.

Format:

```
<card id="name" title="label" newcontext="Boolean"
ordered="Boolean" onenterforward="url"
onenterbackward="url" ontimer="url">
    content
</card>
```

Attributes:

- **id**   Specifies the card's unique name. Using the card name within a tag such as <go>, <a>, or <anchor>, an application can direct the microbrowser to load and execute a card's contents.

- **title**   Specifies a label for the card. A microbrowser may or may not display the title. The browser will use the label as the default bookmark name if the user bookmarks the card.

- **newcontext**   When set to true, directs the microbrowser to initialize the device context when the user navigates to the card. Initializing the device context removes all context-specific variables, clears the history stack, and resets the device to a known state. The default value is false.

- **ordered**   Specifies the organization of the card. When set to true, the default value, it directs the microbrowser to display the content of the card in a fixed sequence. When set to false, the microbrowser may display the card's content based on fields and fieldsets.

- **onenterforward**   Specifies the URL of a card or deck the microbrowser will load and execute if the user navigates to the card using a <go> task.

- **onenterbackward**   Specifies the URL of a card or deck the microbrowser will load and execute if the user navigates to the card using a <prev> task.

- **ontimer**   Specifies the URL of the card or deck the microbrowser will load and execute if a <timer> expires.

- **content**   Specifies the card's statements, which can include any of the following tags: <a>, <anchor>, <do>, <fieldset>, <img>, <input>, <onevent>, <p>, <select>, <timer>.

\<do\>

Description:

Associates a task with a function key or other user-interface element. When the user presses the corresponding button, the microbrowser will perform the specified task.

Format:

```
<do type="type" label="label" name="name" optional="Boolean">
    task
</do>
```

Attributes:

- **type**   Specifies the user action that triggers the task. The type must be "accept", "delete", "help", "options", "prev", or "reset".

- **label**   Specifies the text the microbrowser will display for the function key label. To increase the number of devices that will display the label, you should use no more than five characters. Only the accept and options types support a label.

- **name**   Specifies the element's name.

- **optional**   When set to true, specifies that the microbrowser can ignore the element. The default value is false.

- **task**   The action the microbrowser will perform when the user initiates the specific action. The task must be **\<go\>**, **\<prev\>**, **\<noop\>**, or **\<refresh\>**.

B

<em>

Description:

Displays text using an emphasized font.

Format:

```
<em>text</em>
```

Attributes:

● **text**   The text the microbrowser is to display using an emphasized font.

<fieldset>

Description:

Groups multiple text or input items within a card. A microbrowser may choose
to display related elements in a meaningful way.

Format:

```
<fieldset title="label">
    content
</fieldset>
```

Attributes:

● **title**   Specifies a label for the fieldset group. A microbrowser may display
the title when it executes the statement the fieldset contains.

● **content**   Specifies the related items the microbrowser is to group.

<go>

Description:

Directs the microbrowser to load and execute the card or deck at the specified URL. If the URL includes a card name, the microbrowser will display that card. If the URL contains only a deck name, the microbrowser will display the first card in the deck.

Format:

```
<go href="url" sendreferer="Boolean" method="method"
accept-charset="charset" enctype="contenttype"
cache-control="setting">
<postfield name="data" value="value" />
   content
</go>
```

Attributes:

- **href**   The URL of the card or deck.

- **sendreferer**   Specifies whether the microbrowser should include the deck URL in the request. When set to true, the microbrowser will set the HTTP_REFERER header to the deck's relative URL. The default value is false.

- **method**   Specifies the HTTP submission method. The default method is "get". If you specify "post" or include a **<postfield>** element, the microbrowser will perform a post method.

- **accept-charset**   Specifies the character encodings that the application supports.

- **enctype**   Specifies the type of content used to submit a parameter to a server via a post operation. Most systems support only "application/ x-www-form-urlencoded" or "multipart/form-data". Many microbrowsers do not yet support the enctype attribute.

B

- **cache-control**   Controls whether the client can use a cached copy of the card or whether the client must download the card from the server. The value "no-cache" directs the client to download the card from the server. Many microbrowsers do not yet support the cache-control attribute.

<head>

Description:
Specifies information about the deck, such as access-control information and metadata.

Format:

```
<head>
    content
</head>
```

Attributes:

- **content**   The header information, which can be an **<access>** tag or one or more **<meta>** elements.

<i>

Description:
Displays text using an italic font.

Format:

```
<i>text</i>
```

Attributes:

● **text**   The text the microbrowser will display using an italic font.

<img>

Description:
Displays an image.

Format:

```
<img alt="text" src="url" localsrc="icon"
align="alignment" height="n" width="n" hspace="n"
vspace="n"/>
```

Attributes:

● **alt**   Specifies text the microbrowser will display if it does not support images or if it cannot locate the specified image.

● **src**   Specifies the URL of the image. The microbrowser will ignore the src attribute if the **<img>** tag contains a valid localsrc icon.

● **localsrc**   Specifies the name of an icon built into the phone device. The microbrowser will try to load the local-source image from the phone's read-only memory (ROM). If the local-source name is valid, the microbrowser will ignore the alt and src attributes. You must, however, still provide values for the alt and src attributes.

● **align**   Specifies how the microbrowser will align the image relative to the current text line. The value must be "top", "middle", or "bottom". Bottom is the default value.

● **height**   Provides the microbrowser with an estimate of the image height so the browser can continue to lay out the screen while it renders the

B

image. If you specify a percentage, the microbrowser will use the remaining vertical space.

- **width**   Provides the microbrowser with an estimate of the image width so the browser can continue to lay out the screen while it renders the image. If you specify a percentage, the microbrowser will use the remaining horizontal space.

- **hspace**   Specifies the amount of space the microbrowser will place to the left and right of the image.

- **vspace**   Specifies the amount of space the microbrowser will place above and below the image.

\<input>

Description:

Gets input from the user, which the microbrowser will assign to the specified variable.

Format:

```
<input name="variable" title="label" type="type"
value="value" format="format" emptyok="Boolean"
maxlength="n" size="n"/>
```

Attributes:

- **name**   Specifies the name of the variable to which the microbrowser will assign the user input.

- **title**   Specifies a label for the item. The microbrowser may or may not display the title when the \<input> tag is active.

● **type**   Specifies how the microbrowser will display the text the user types. The value "text" directs the microbrowser to display the typed text. The value "password" directs the microbrowser to replace the typed text with an asterisk (*) character to hide the input.

● **value**   Specifies a default value for the variable. The microbrowser will normally display the default value on the screen. To use the default value, the user can simply press the accept button. To change the value, the user must delete the default characters.

● **format**   Specifies the format that the user input must follow. The format specification can have the following values:

Value	Description
A	Any symbol or uppercase character
a	Any symbol or lowercase character
N	Any numeric character
X	Any symbol, number, or uppercase character
x	Any symbol, number, or lowercase character
M	Any symbol, number, or uppercase character (may be changed to lowercase)
m	Any symbol, number, or lowercase character (may be changed to uppercase)
/c	Directs the microbrowser to display the specified character

● **emptyok**   If true, directs the microbrowser to proceed if the user does not enter a value. If false, the microbrowser will force the user to enter a value.

● **maxlength**   Specifies the maximum number of characters the user can enter.

● **size**   Specifies the width of the input field in characters. Most microbrowsers will ignore the size attribute.

To limit the number of characters the user can enter, you can specify a number before the format specification, such as 3N or NNN. In the first case, the user can enter from one to three numeric characters. In the second case, the user must enter exactly three numeric characters. If you specify an asterisk, the user can enter any number of characters.

B

<meta>

Description:

Provides information to the microbrowser about the deck itself. Meta-information is essentially data about the deck's data. The meta-information typically tells the microbrowser to treat the data (the cards) in a specific way, such as caching or not caching the card's contents.

Format:

```
<meta name="value" http-equiv="property" content="value"
forua="Boolean" scheme="form">
```

Attributes:

- **name**   Specifies the name of the property that corresponds to the meta-information.

- **property**   May be used in place of the name property to specify information the microbrowser should interpret as an HTTP header, such as `http-equiv="Cache-Control"` which tells the WAP browser that this piece of meta-information applies to the memory-caching system.

- **content**   Specifies the value to assign to the property, such as `content=max-age=10`, which specifies the maximum time the microbrowser should keep the contents of this deck in its cache.

- **forua**   When set to true, specifies that the property must reach the microbrowser (as opposed to a proxy server or some other program that may intercept the WML statements). When set to false, a program other than the microbrowser can process and extract the meta command.

- **scheme**   Specifies the form the microbrowser should use to interpret the property value.

\<noop\>

Description:

Instructs the microbrowser to perform no operation; in other words, to do nothing.

Format:

```
<noop />
```

\<onevent\>

Description:

Associates an event with a task. When the event occurs, the microbrowser will perform the associated task.

Format:

```
<onevent type="type">task</onevent>
```

Attributes:

- **type**   Specifies the action that causes the event. The action must be `onpick`, `onenterforward`, `onenterbackward`, or `ontimer`.

- **task**   Specifies the task the microbrowser will perform when the event occurs. The task must be `<go>`, `<prev>`, `<noop>`, or `<refresh>`.

B

<optgroup>

Description:

Groups multiple **<option>** elements within a **<select>** tag. The microbrowser may display grouped elements in a meaningful way.

Format:

```
<optgroup title="label">content</optgroup>
```

Attributes:

- **title**   Specifies a label for the group. The microbrowser may display the label when the grouped elements are active.

- **content**   Specifies the elements to group. The content may be an **<option>** element or another **<optgroup>** element.

<option>

Description:

Specifies a choice within a **<select>** statement.

Format:

```
<option title="label" value="value" onpick="url">
    content
</option>
```

Attributes:

- **title**   Specifies a label that identifies the option. The microbrowser may display the title as a label for the accept key when the user selects the option. To increase the number of devices that can display the label, you should restrict the label's length to six characters or less.

- **value**   Specifies the value WML will assign to the variable specified in the `<select>` statement if the user selects the option.

- **onpick**   Specifies the URL of a card or deck that the microbrowser will load and execute if the user selects the option.

- **content**   Specifies the text the microbrowser will display for the option, and optionally an action the microbrowser will perform if the user selects the option.

<p>

Description:
Specifies the start of a new paragraph. Each paragraph can control text alignment and wrapping options.

Format:

```
<p align="alignment" mode="wrapmode">
    content
</p>
```

Attributes:

- **align**   Specifies text alignment within the paragraph. The alignment must be "left", "right", or "center". The default alignment is left.

- **mode**   Specifies the text-wrapping mode. The wrapping option must be "wrap" or "nowrap". When set to nowrap, the microbrowser may use horizontal scrolling to display long lines, or the microbrowser may toggle the display of the line's contents, letting the user view parts of the line at one time. In contrast, when set to wrap, the microbrowser will wrap text that does not fit on the current line to the start of the next line. The default mode is wrap.

- **content**   Specifies the paragraph text and formatting elements.

<postfield>

Description:

Defines a name/value pair containing information the application will pass to a server via a <go> operation.

Format:

```
<postfield name="name" value="value" />
```

Attributes:

- **name**   The name of the variable.
- **value**   A string giving the value of the named variable.

<pre>

Description:

Informs the microbrowser that the content that follows is preformatted. The microbrowser should do its best to display the information as formatted (such as leaving whitespace unchanged). Many microbrowsers do not yet support the <pre> tag.

Format:

```
<pre>content</pre>
```

Attributes:

- **content**   Specifies the preformatted content.

<prev>

Description:

Directs the microbrowser to reload and execute the previous card. If there is no previous card on the history stack, the operation has no effect.

Format:

```
<prev>content</prev>
```

Attributes:

- **content**   Specifies one or more **\<setvar\>** statements that assign values to variables before the microbrowser reloads and executes the previous card. The content is optional. If you do not specify any content, you must use the **\<prev/\>** syntax.

<refresh>

B

Description:

Directs the microbrowser to refresh the variables specified in the content. The microbrowser will also refresh the display, meaning that it will show the most recent values for variables whose values are currently displayed.

Format:

```
<refresh>content</refresh>
```

Attributes:

- **content** Specifies one or more **<setvar>** statements.

<select>

Description:

Specifies a list of menu options from which the user can select.

Format:

```
<select title="label" multiple="Boolean"
name="variable" value="default" iname="index"
ivalue="default">
    content
</select>
```

Attributes:

- **title** Specifies a label for the select list. The microbrowser may display the title when the **<select>** tag is active.

- **multiple** When set to true, specifies that the user can select multiple items from the list. The default value is false. If the user selects multiple options, WML will assign each option's value to the variable, separated by a semicolon.

- **name** Specifies the name of the variable to which WML will assign the value associated with the option the user selects.

- **value**   Specifies the default value for the variable specified by the name parameter.

- **iname**   Specifies the name of the variable to which WML will assign the index associated with the option selected by the user. The index value for each option is that option's position in the select list. The first position has an index value of 1.

- **ivalue**   Specifies the default index value for the variable specified by iname.

- **content**   Specifies the list of menu items. The list must contain one or more **<option>** elements.

<setvar>

Description:

Sets a variable to a specific value before a device executes a **<go>**, **<prev>**, or **<refresh>** operation.

Format:

```
<setvar name="name" value="value" />
```

Attributes:

- **name**   The name of the variable to which WML will assign the value.

- **value**   The value to assign to the variable.

B

<small>

Description:

Displays text using a small font.

Format:

```
<small>text</small>
```

Attributes:

- **text** The text the microbrowser will display using a small font.

<strong>

Description:

Displays text using an emphasized font.

Format:

```
<strong>text</strong>
```

Attributes:

- **text** The text the microbrowser is to display using the emphasized font.

<table>

Description:

Displays information organized in a table format.

Format:

```
<table title="name" align="alignment" columns="n">
    table data
</table>
```

Attributes:

- **title** Specifies an optional label for the table. The microbrowser may display the table's label when it displays the table elements.

- **align** Specifies text alignment within columns. The alignment must be "left", "center", or "right". The default alignment is left.

- **columns** Specifies the number of columns in the table. You must specify a value for this setting, and the value cannot be 0.

- **table data** The **<tr>** and **<td>** elements that define the table rows and data within each row.

<td>

Description:
Specifies the data for a single table cell.

Format:

```
<td>content</td>
```

B

Attributes:

- **content** Specifies the text **img** or **<anchor>** elements that provide the table cell's content.

<template>

Description:

Specifies deck-level actions that apply to all cards in the deck. The application can overwrite these actions for a particular card by specifying the same event within the **<card>** definition.

Format:

```
<template onenterforward="url" onenterbackward="url"
ontimer="url">
    content
</template>
```

Attributes:

- **onenterforward**   Specifies the URL of a deck or card the microbrowser will open when the user enters the card through a **<go>** task.

- **onenterbackward**   Specifies the URL of a deck or card the microbrowser will open when the user enters the card through a **<prev>** task.

- **ontimer**   Specifies the URL of a deck or card the microbrowser will open when a **<timer>** element expires.

- **content**   Specifies an action the microbrowser will take when an event occurs. The content can include **<do>** and **<onevent>** elements.

<timer>

Description:

Provides a way to start a task automatically after a period of user inactivity. The timer starts when the card is entered and stops when any task executes. You can only define one task per timer and one timer per card.

Format:

```
<timer name="variable" value="value" />
```

Attributes:

- **name**   Specifies the name of the variable that stores the value of the timer. When the user exits the card, the variable is set to the current value of the timer (which is counting down from its initial value to 0) or 0 if the timer has expired.

- **value**   A string that specifies the timer's initial value. The value is specified in tenths of a second. A value of 0 disables the timer.

\<tr>

Description:
Specifies the data for a single table row.

Format:

```
<tr>
    <td>content</td>
</tr>
```

Attributes:

- **content**   Specifies the **\<td>** elements that define the content of the table row.

B

<u>

Description:
Displays text with an underline.

Format:

```
<u>text</u>
```

Attributes:

- **text**   The text the microbrowser will display using an underline.

<wml>

Description:
Specifies the start and end of a WML deck.

Format:

```
<wml>
    content
</wml>
```

Attributes:

- **content**   All the elements that specify the actions performed by the deck.

Appendix C

Wireless References on the World Wide Web

Y ou can find many very good references regarding WML, WMLScript, and Wireless Access Protocol (WAP) on the World Wide Web. As you search for information on Wireless topics, you may want to start with the sites listed here.

Site	Content
www.allwapped.com	Links and resources
www.anywhereyougo.com	News and information
www.ericsson.com	Software development kit with a phone simulator
www.gingco.de/wap/	Software for converting WBMP mages
www.gixom.com	Directory of Wireless sites
www.inetis.com	Tools for developing WAP sites
www.mobilewap.com	News and information
www.mopilot.com	Directory of Wireless sites
www.nokia.com	Software development kit with a phone simulator
www.openwave.com	Software development kit with a phone simulator
www.tagtag.com	Build a Wireless Web site without WML
www.w3schools.com	Online tutorials for WML
www.wap.net	Extensive information and resources
www.wapdesign.org.uk	Information, links, and resources
www.wap-dev.net	WAP mailing lists
www.wapforum.org	Standards, specifications, and protocols
www.wapjump.com	Directory of Wireless sites
www.waply.com	Directory of Wireless sites
www.wapology.com	Directory of Wireless sites and tutorials
www.wap-shareware.com	Wide range of tools and information
www.wapsight.com	News and information
www.waptiger.de	Software to convert WBMP images
www.wapwarp.com	Directory of Wireless sites
www.winwap.org	WAP directory and WML browser for Windows
www.wirelessdevnet.com	Wireless Developer Network
www.WirelessGames.com	Games for handhelds and phones
www.Wirelessinanutshell.net	Resources, links, and more
www.WirelessLookup.com	Build a free Wireless Web site
www.wmlxtras.com	Wide range of information, including books, events, and more
www.yospace.com	Wide range of tools, games, and information

Index

INTERNATIONAL CONTACT INFORMATION

AUSTRALIA
McGraw-Hill Book Company Australia Pty. Ltd.
TEL +61-2-9417-9899
FAX +61-2-9417-5687
http://www.mcgraw-hill.com.au
books-it_sydney@mcgraw-hill.com

CANADA
McGraw-Hill Ryerson Ltd.
TEL +905-430-5000
FAX +905-430-5020
http://www.mcgrawhill.ca

GREECE, MIDDLE EAST,
NORTHERN AFRICA
McGraw-Hill Hellas
TEL +30-1-656-0990-3-4
FAX +30-1-654-5525

MEXICO (Also serving Latin America)
McGraw-Hill Interamericana Editores S.A. de C.V.
TEL +525-117-1583
FAX +525-117-1589
http://www.mcgraw-hill.com.mx
fernando_castellanos@mcgraw-hill.com

SINGAPORE (Serving Asia)
McGraw-Hill Book Company
TEL +65-863-1580
FAX +65-862-3354
http://www.mcgraw-hill.com.sg
mghasia@mcgraw-hill.com

SOUTH AFRICA
McGraw-Hill South Africa
TEL +27-11-622-7512
FAX +27-11-622-9045
robyn_swanepoel@mcgraw-hill.com

UNITED KINGDOM & EUROPE
(Excluding Southern Europe)
McGraw-Hill Education Europe
TEL +44-1-628-502500
FAX +44-1-628-770224
http://www.mcgraw-hill.co.uk
computing_neurope@mcgraw-hill.com

ALL OTHER INQUIRIES Contact:
Osborne/McGraw-Hill
TEL +1-510-549-6600
FAX +1-510-883-7600
http://www.osborne.com
omg_international@mcgraw-hill.com